"There is a lot of confusion about Islam ~~~~~~~~~~~~~~ arent similarities between the Qur'an and the b~~~~, ~~~~ ~~~~ neous conclusions and devised unbiblical approaches to Muslims. If you have ever been confused, read this book; it will clear your mind. What I love about the book is that while it is compassionate and loving toward Muslims, and acknowledges the similarities, it does not obscure the reality of fundamental differences. Dr. Bennett will challenge you to engage Muslims effectively by sharing with them the truth in love."

—Georges Houssney,
president, Horizons International;
author of *Engaging Islam*

"In *The Qur'an and the Christian,* Matthew Bennett invites and equips Christians to read the Qur'an with an informed understanding, in order to better understand and share the gospel with their Muslim neighbors. Warning readers about the dangers of focusing on similarities between the Bible and the Qur'an without comprehending real and profound differences, Bennett argues—with great erudition—that knowing how the Qur'an bends the worldview of its followers away from biblical truth is an 'essential first step' to introducing Muslims to the Jesus of the Bible. This book is an outstanding tool to help Christians understand the spiritual worldview of Muslims and share the love of Christ with them."

—Mark Durie,
senior research fellow, Arthur Jeffery Centre for the Study of Islam,
Melbourne School of Theology;
director, Institute for Spiritual Awareness

"Written with a comfortable mastery of the subject, Matthew Bennett's *The Qur'an and the Christian* is a well-articulated, charitable work of solid scholarship. Designed to enhance meaningful discussions with one's Muslim neighbors, it also serves as an excellent introduction to Islam. Bennett leaves no doubt about the important differences between the Qur'an and biblical revelation, but helpfully opens the door to understand how Muslims think, especially about Christians and the Bible."

—Ant Greenham,
retired professor of missions and Islamic studies, Southeastern Seminary;
coauthor of *Muslim Conversions to Christ:
A Critique of Insider Movements in Islamic Contexts*

"Matthew Bennett's newest study is one more example of his deep understanding of Islam, rigorous scholarship, and sincere passion for Christ. What a wonderful guide for Christians who seek to reflect the image of Christ to their Muslim neighbors!"

—Ayman S. Ibrahim, PhD,
Bill and Connie Jenkins Professor of Islamic Studies,
and director, Jenkins Center for the Christian Understanding of Islam

"This book is an excellent extension of some of the things Muslim practitioners have been telling us at the Heart for Muslims conference in New York City. However, it is more academic while still accessible to a layperson. Definitely, a must-read for pastors in urban areas. It portrays a realistic perspective of Muslims/Islam: it doesn't try to cover up differences but to understand, making it a good book for Muslim scholarship. It provides a good emphasis on why and how Christians should read the Quran, along with helpful commentary on how to understand the Quran, which makes it a valuable resource for missions, evangelism, and academics."

—Dr. Alfonse Javed,
executive director of Heart for Muslim Conference, NYC;
author of *The Muslim Next Door*

"In *the Qur'an and the Christian*, Matthew Bennett takes a deep dive into Islam's holy book. In this helpful work, the author skillfully enters into the Muslim worldview through the prism of the Qur'an. Simultaneously fascinating and frightening, the Qur'an provides the clearest window into the Muslim mind. Most Christians, even missiologists, avoid actually studying Islam's holy book in detail. The author shows that Christians omit such analysis at their peril. Thankfully, Matthew Bennett provides a trustworthy guide for the church to understand the Qur'an which is the key to evangelizing Muslims for Christ. I wholeheartedly recommend that each missionary, pastor, and layman interested in understanding and reaching Muslims for Jesus read this outstanding book."

—Robin Dale Hadaway,
senior professor of missions,
Midwestern Baptist Theological Seminary, Kansas City, MO

"The Qur'an is one of the world's most important books since it is the fundamental source of rituals, creeds, ethics, and laws for Muslims worldwide. Yet the Qur'an is also an extremely foreign and confusing scripture to most Christians. Matthew Bennett's *The Qur'an and the Christian* is a valuable guide, providing readers with easy access to this most challenging scripture. Bennett especially helps us recognize how differently words and concepts vital to a true understanding of the gospel—such as sin, atonement, and salvation—function within the Qur'an. He also shows us how very differently God is presented in the Qur'an from the Bible. His basic concern is to enable Christians to present the gospel with clarity, and he provides many helpful suggestions along that line. Bennett effectively demonstrates some of the more significant ways the Qur'an subverts biblical truth and, to his credit, he does so without rancor or acrimony, out of a sincere desire to see Muslims receive God's grace. Bennett's guide will prove very useful to anyone serious about understanding Muslims and communicating the gospel effectively to them."

—Mark Robert Anderson,
author of *The Qur'an in Context: A Christian Exploration*

The Qur'an and the Christian

AN IN-DEPTH LOOK INTO THE BOOK OF ISLAM FOR FOLLOWERS OF JESUS

MATTHEW AARON
BENNETT

The Qur'an and the Christian: An In-Depth Look into the Book of Islam for Followers of Jesus

© 2022 by Matthew Aaron Bennett

Published by Kregel Academic, an imprint of Kregel Publications, 2450 Oak Industrial Dr. NE, Grand Rapids, MI 49505-6020.

ISBN 978-0-8254-4708-2

Printed in the United States of America

22 23 24 25 26 / 5 4 3 2 1

To Anabelle, Elliot, and Oliver.
May you grow up in the gospel and be used by the Lord to bring it to the ends of the earth.

CONTENTS

Preface 9

Introduction 11

PART 1: THE QUR'AN AS REVELATION

1. The Event of the Qur'an...21
2. The Revelation of the Qur'an 45
3. The Instruction of the Qur'an 69

PART 2: THE QUR'AN AS A TEXT

4. The Qur'an and Previous Texts...95
5. The Qur'an and the People of the Book 115
6. The Qur'an as Mosaic...133

PART 3: THE QUR'AN AND THE CHRISTIAN

7. Should Christians Read the Qur'an? 159
8. Should Christians Use the Qur'an? 197
9. The Gospel and the Problem of the Qur'an 229

Conclusion 251

PREFACE

A s a Christian attempting to discuss the sacred text and religious faith of my Muslim friends, I approach this task from a posture of caution and with a desire to exhibit charity. I recognize within myself the human desire to validate my own faith and, if unchecked, this desire could incline me toward a biased presentation of my conversation partners.

At the same time, I also am committed to the Christian message of salvation in Jesus Christ alone. Any alternative message and worldview that distorts or denies that good news is something that is incompatible with the biblical worldview that I believe to be objectively true. Therefore, in this book I intend to walk the line between presenting my understanding of my Muslim friends and their beliefs in ways that they would recognize as accurate while also being clear to demonstrate where their claims and beliefs diverge from biblical teaching.

While some might contend that exposing areas of presumed common ground as superficial is detrimental to the cause of loving our Muslim neighbors, I beg to differ. I believe that an accurate presentation of the differences between these two faiths is the best way to cultivate an honest understanding of Islam and to maintain a Christian commitment to the gospel of Jesus. If we take the time and invest the labor required to understand the formative influences shaping our neighbor's worldview, we prove ourselves to be concerned to understand their convictions rather than settling for shallow agreement over assumed similarities.

This book is my humble attempt to help Christians avoid the tendency to hastily agree with superficially similar beliefs that we have not taken the time to understand. I have benefitted from the work and insight of many scholars, global Christians, and friends who have helped me to deepen in my love for my Muslim neighbors while seeing increasingly divergent worldviews. While there are too many to list exhaustively, I would specifically like to extend my gratitude to Ayman Ibrahim, Gabriel Said Reynolds, Mark Anderson, Mark Durie, and Gordon Nickel for their insightful, charitable, and scholarly contributions that have shaped my thinking and approach to many of these matters through their writings and, for some, through personal interactions. I am grateful for you, brothers. I am also grateful for the work of the late Evelyne Reisacher, whose dedication to ministry among Muslims is characterized by the title of one of her final volumes before she passed into glory: *Joyful Witness in the Muslim World*.

I hope that this investigation of the Qur'an will consolidate some of the valuable insights I have gleaned from these and many others. I recognize that I am standing on the shoulders of those who have gone before me and have been supported by those beside me, so I credit any beneficial aspects of this project to that host of contributors to my thinking while also taking responsibility for any deficiencies or infelicities herein as my own shortcomings.

If you are reading this book as a Christian, I want to say thank you for your engagement with this material. I also want you to know that I am praying for you, that this book would be helpful in your thinking and fruitfully formative in your engagement with your Muslim friends. I am praying that you would deepen in your love for Muslims and also in your conviction that the Qur'an obscures and undermines the gospel of Jesus. And would it be that God would use you to speak meaningfully and beautifully to your Muslim friends of the hope that there is in the biblical Jesus, as a result of your investment in working through this book.

INTRODUCTION

This is indeed [a Book] sent down by the Lord of all the worlds, brought down by the Trustworthy Spirit upon your heart (so that you may be one of the warners), in a clear Arabic language. It is indeed [foretold] in the scriptures of the ancients.

Qur'an 26:192–196

Traditional Islamic theology teaches that the Qur'an is a book like no other. Though it is only considered to be authentic in its original Arabic form, it commends itself to all of humankind as guidance and as a reminder of the ways of God. Muslims contend that the Qur'an exhibits its truth and power through its scientific insight, its ethical teaching, and its incomparable beauty. In fact, stories of non-Muslims converting to Islam as a result of simply hearing the beauty of the Qur'an recited proliferate throughout the Muslim world.

Believing it to be the heavenly and incorruptible record of God's revealed will, Muslims view the Qur'an as a merciful gift to humanity from God. Indeed, to the believing Muslim, the Qur'an is a truly unique book. Different audiences, however, respond to the purported uniqueness of the Qur'an in a variety of ways.

A VARIETY OF APPROACHES: BELIEVERS, SCHOLARS, AND MISSIONARIES

For believing Muslims, the Qur'an's uniqueness proves its message persuasive. For secular scholars, on the other hand, this claim proves historically questionable. For Christian witnesses among Muslim populations, it proves problematic. Though this book will consider all three audiences and their approaches to the Qur'an, it is this final category of readers—Christian witnesses—who are likely to benefit most from a broad consideration of Islam's sacred text.

The present book is an attempt to listen to the insights gleaned by various readers of the Qur'an—believing adherents, skeptical scholars, and Christian communicators. In a way, it might be seen to offer *introductions* to the Qur'an in the plural rather than presenting a singular, monolithic approach. Yet the purpose of this multi-perspectival introduction is not simply to provide a survey of the field. Rather, by including each of these perspectives, this book intends to equip Christian readers with a better understanding of what the Qur'an is, how to read it, and what influence the Qur'an has had on their Muslims neighbors. By taking all of these perspectives together, a Christian will be better equipped to communicate the biblical Gospel to their Muslim friends.

In an effort to encourage this understanding, the following chapters attempt to approach the Qur'an from a posture of charity, seeking to hear it speak its own message in its own voice. Such an approach should not be understood as an endorsement of the Qur'an's message. Rather, this posture encourages a Christian to listen to the Qur'an closely in order to understand how and where it employs language, concepts, and narratives that appear to be shared with the Bible, yet which function within the Qur'an to promote its own distinct message and concerns. Such awareness will help a Christian witness to discern and distinguish common ground from that which leads down a theologically divergent path.

TO THE CHRISTIAN READER OF THE QUR'AN

Though this book urges Christians to familiarize themselves with the Qur'an, a few issues must be made clear from the outset. First of all, the teaching of the Qur'an cannot be reconciled with the biblical Gospel without doing violence to both. Though the pluralistic character of our day bristles at such a suggestion, attempts to make the message of Islam and Christianity commensurate fail to account for the actual beliefs held by members of each faith. Consider the words of Islamic scholar, Muhammad Mustafa al-Azami:

> Let us recall two of the major doctrines of Christianity: Original Sin and Atonement. The former is the automatic inheritance of every human, being the progeny of Adam, whilst the latter embodies the belief that God sacrificed His only begotten Son as the sole means of absolving this Sin. The Qur'an categorically rejects both.[1]

In other words, Muslims themselves recognize that although the Qur'an claims to continue the true biblical message, it is diametrically opposed to central doctrines taught therein. Thus, we do a better job of both respecting our Muslim neighbor's beliefs and maintaining the integrity of the biblical message when we are willing to acknowledge that Islam and Christianity diverge.

Second, the Arabic language as it is spoken today is indelibly shaped by qur'anic theology. Since the writing of the Qur'an appears to be the first occasion that the Arabic language was used to record a substantial text, the implicit and explicit definitions given to words as they appear in the Qur'an have born influence on the subsequent use of the language.[2] Therefore, in order to communicate biblical concepts such as God, sin, humanity, and eschatology to

---

1   Muhammad Mustafa al-Azami, *The History of the Qur'anic Text: From Revelation to Compilation* (Lahore, Pakistan: Suhail Academy, 2005), 307.
2   For a fascinating discussion on these issues, see Sidney Griffith, *The Bible in Arabic: The Scriptures of the "People of the Book" in the Language of Islam* (Princeton, NJ: Princeton University Press, 2013).

Muslims, one must be conscious of the effect that the Qur'an bears on such language, whether one is speaking in Arabic or expressing these ideas in English.

Third, if you pick up the Qur'an expecting it to read like the texts with which you are familiar, you will likely encounter frustration. The Qur'an is not simply a Muslim version of the Bible. It does not contain much narrative or history. Rather, it is primarily didactic material, instructing believers through repetition concerning the importance of remembering God, submitting to his will, and striving toward upright living.

As you read the Qur'an, let me encourage you to actively fight the temptation to skip over seemingly repeated phrases and ideas. Semitic literature often uses repetition to highlight those things that are of central importance to the text. Try to discover why the Qur'an is concerned to highlight this particular material and whether or not it presents these concepts in a way that conflicts with biblical teaching.

Finally, though Western readers have been notorious for their less-than-charitable descriptions of the Qur'an as a text, I would encourage a Christian reader of the Qur'an to undertake this task as an act of neighborly love. The concepts, words, and phrases contained in this book have likely impressed themselves on your Muslim neighbor from the day they were born through to the present. By studying this book, you not only learn about how your Muslim neighbor views the world, you also show him or her that you care.

Reading the Qur'an will allow you to have increasingly engaged, meaningful conversations in which your questions and disagreements come not from a secondhand account of what the Qur'an teaches but from your own encounter of its message. Your Muslim neighbor will likely appreciate your efforts, and you will have more credibility in their eyes when you say that you have compared the Qur'an and the Bible and remain convinced of the beauty of the Gospel. Likewise, as you read the Qur'an, it may provide you opportunities to naturally invite your Muslim neighbor to consider reading the Bible.

TO THE CHRISTIAN COMMUNICATOR

As mentioned above, the uniqueness of the Qur'an can prove problematic for Christian communicators. As you read the Qur'an, some of the problems that arise may present themselves to you in the form of questions: How should a Christian view this book that lays claim to biblical characters who are barely recognizable in its accounts? Where does shared vocabulary indicate shared concepts? More troublingly, where does it obscure differences? And what role does the Qur'an play in shaping our evangelism and discipleship?

The final question above might raise some eyebrows among readers familiar with some of the intramural missiological discussions regarding various contextualization strategies from the CAMEL Method to Insider Movements. We will address questions regarding the legitimacy of such strategies in due course. For the moment, however, I want to simply contend that the Qur'an and its language must inform the manner by which we discuss the Gospel with our Arabic-speaking friends. If we are ignorant of the Qur'an and its message, we will likely struggle to understand why our Muslim neighbors misunderstand us when we speak of the atonement offered through the Gospel of Jesus the Messiah.

In order to illustrate this claim, consider the fact that the previous sentence alone employs four instances of biblical language that are in conflict with qur'anic concepts yet are expressed by the same vocabulary. The words *atonement, Gospel, Jesus,* and *Messiah* all appear in the Qur'an, with irreconcilably different meanings associated with them. In order to make disciples, we must ensure that what we intend to communicate is actually understood. Thus, one of the primary purposes for writing this book is to begin to acquaint Christian witnesses with the ways that the Qur'an has influenced the theological language necessary for communicating the Gospel among Muslim peoples.

METHODOLOGY: TRADITION, SCHOLARSHIP, AND MISSION

In order to provide a broad a treatment of the Qur'an and its influence, this book will approach the sacred text of Islam from the three perspectives mentioned above. More specifically, part one approaches the Qur'an from the perspective of a confessional audience in order to provide a summary of a traditional Islamic view of the role of the Qur'an in Islam, its origins, and its content. Such a presentation will help to provide a glimpse of the worldview framework that the Qur'an constructs for Muslims.

Though perhaps an obvious statement, it should be noted that this traditional perspective will not characterize the understanding of every Muslim community. With a global population of nearly two billion adherents, Islam is certainly not monolithic, and a variety of confessional Muslim approaches to the Qur'an might be taken.[3] By restricting myself to the most common traditions, I admit my inability to adequately represent many of the interesting approaches to the Qur'an taken by minority Muslim communities. Yet for the purposes intended herein, my priority is to offer as broad a representation of Islamic understanding as possible.

In order to provide the most common understanding, I will predominantly draw on the accounts from the Sunni traditions (*Sunnah*) and those recorded the biography of Muhammad's life (*Sirat Rasul Allah*, hereafter *Sira*). Unless otherwise noted, the material will be drawn from Sunni accounts, due to the fact that Sunni expressions of Islam account for approximately 90 percent of the world's population of Muslims. Where appropriate, I will use footnotes to direct the reader to additional resources that are concerned to explore issues in greater depth than is permitted by the scope of this current project.

Following the traditional treatment, part two approaches the Qur'an from the perspective of contemporary critical scholarship. This section aims to provide some context for how the last hundred years of secular scholarship have questioned the veracity of the traditional narratives surrounding the origins of the Qur'an. Through such an investigation, the reader will become acquainted with some of the

---

3   See the helpful chapter by Evelyne Reisacher, "Defining Islam and Muslim Societies in Missiological Discourse," in *Dynamics of Muslim Worlds*, 219–41 (Downers Grove, IL: IVP Academic, 2017).

most pressing textual issues that appear to suggest a different audience than is presumed by traditional Islamic history.

Though these chapters will present information that is sometimes used to construct a polemic against Islam, this book is not interested in such an endeavor. Instead of utilizing the findings of critical scholarship to discredit the Qur'an, they will be used to encourage a reader to hear its message more clearly. By hearing its message clearly, we will begin to identify the places that our Gospel presentations must labor more rigorously to ensure communication occurs.

Finally, in light of parts one and two, the third part of this book will offer some missiological reasons that a Christian should be familiar with the Qur'an. These chapters will address both why and how a Christian witness should read the Qur'an. Ultimately, this book argues that it is crucial for a Christian disciple-maker to understand the Qur'an in order to effectively communicate biblical truths and the gospel to their Muslim friends and neighbors.

PURPOSE: INSPECTING BRIDGES WITHOUT BURNING THEM

As I write this, Western nations all around the world are struggling with how to view Muslim refugees who are streaming across their borders. Western churches within those nations are also embroiled in their own debates regarding how to interact with their newly arrived Muslim neighbors. Unfortunately, the many political issues that attend immigration and diversity discussions can often overshadow some of the Great Commission opportunities presented by these people movements.

In the midst of such discussions, many who view the influx of Muslim peoples as an opportunity for the church to both embody and proclaim the Gospel through hospitality and compassion have urged Christians to find common ground with Muslims. In so doing, some have used the language of crossing bridges of commonality to Islam. Using such language, Christians are urged to view apparently common ethical and theological common ground as a bridge to understanding the similarities between themselves and their Muslim friends.

My prayer is that through this book I might add my voice to those who are encouraging a compassionate and intentional engagement with Muslims—not only with these communities of newly arrived displaced people but also with the Muslims who have long lived as our neighbors, coworkers, and friends. At the same time, I also pray that this book might help to clarify where exactly our common ground exists and where some of the apparently shared theological concepts actually set us on divergent trajectories.

While myriad bridges to friendships with Muslims exist, Christians should be quick to inspect bridges constructed of apparent theological similarity before crossing them. If this book achieves its goal, the reader will gain an ability to ask helpfully informed, conversation-deepening questions of their Muslim neighbors. Most of these questions must be asked at the very places that appear to be points of commonality.

Highlighting the underlying differences between Islam and Christianity may seem discourteous to Western readers raised in politely pluralistic societies. It may even seem counterintuitive to a Christian seeking to establish friendly relations with Muslim communities—all the more so when encouraged to probe beyond apparent agreement to discover dissimilarity. Yet by uncritically embracing superficial similarity, one actually inhibits the process of mutual understanding.

In the end, this book does not intend to encourage boorish Christians who stubbornly refuse to admit that there is any commonality between Christianity and Islam. Nor do I hope it promotes nitpicking every word our Muslim friends say. Instead, I hope that we begin to ask good questions, listen well to the answers, and learn how to clearly define and communicate the way the Bible uses the words that also appear in the Qur'an. Might it be that we learn, not to burn nor to uncritically cross bridges of apparently shared theological concepts, but to inspect them with missiological wisdom and with biblical precision. Ultimately, the purpose of this book is to help Christians deepen friendships, promote understanding, and clarify the biblical Gospel for our Muslim friends and neighbors.

PART ONE
THE QUR'AN
AS REVELATION

1

THE EVENT OF THE QUR'AN

In the Name of God, the Merciful, the Compassionate. Recite in the Name of your Lord who creates; creates the human from a clot. Recite, for your Lord is the Most Generous, who teaches by the pen, teaches the human what he does not know.

Qur'an 96:1–5

According to Islamic tradition, the first verses of the Qur'an that the angel Jibril revealed to Muhammad are found in Qur'an 96:1–5.[1] In many ways, these five verses prepare the reader for the major themes with which the rest of the Qur'an concerns itself. These verses introduce the creator as a beneficent and merciful sovereign. They depict humanity as the result of God's creative act. And they demonstrate that a life rightly lived consists of learning God's teaching.

---

1   A. Guillaume, trans., *The Life of Muhammad: A Translation of Ibn Ishaq's Sirat Rasul Allah* (Karachi, Pakistan: Oxford University Press, 1982), 106.

On the other end of the spectrum, many commentators believe that the final words of the Qur'an that Muhammad received are found in Qur'an 5:3: "Today I have perfected your religion for you, and I have completed my blessing on you, and I have approved Islam for you as a religion."[2] Thus, the Qur'an concludes its teachings with a transcendent affirmation of Islam as the perfection of human religion. What lies between these two passages suffices to instruct all of humanity on how to live a life that is in keeping with God's revealed will.

As you may have already noticed, the first verses and the final verse are not where one expects to find them. Most readers are accustomed to finding the first events of a book on the first page, and the final events on the last page. That this is not the case with the Qur'an provides an important initial observation about how different the Qur'an is from other works.

In order to draw out these differences, we must consider the Qur'an from a variety of angles. The first part of this book will primarily lean on traditional Islamic accounts of the reception, function, and miracle of the Qur'an. As a component of this approach, the current chapter looks at the event of the Qur'an as God's final and incorruptible communication of the divine will to humanity.

Understanding the traditional perspective requires investigation into the body of material known as the *Sunnah*. These extra-qur'anic records consist of Muhammad's biography (known as the *Sira*), traditional accounts of Muhammad's explanation and exhibition of qur'anic living (*hadith*), and some of the earliest qur'anic commentators (*tafsir*). This material is the only available means of reconstructing the historical context surrounding the Qur'an, because the Qur'an itself contains very little historical narrative and admits only the slightest hints of its chronology.[3]

---

2   See also, Michel Cuypers, *The Banquet: A Reading of the Fifth Sura of the Qur'an* (Miami: Convivium, 2009), 85.

3   Gabriel Said Reynolds, *The Qur'an and Its Biblical Subtext* (New York: Routledge, 2009), 9. While noting the tendency of scholars and believers to trust the *Sunnah* as historically reliable, Reynolds argues that the biography of Muhammad should not be understood as history. Rather, it should be viewed as a product of qur'anic exegesis, and should not be used to interpret the Qur'an since such an approach is simply a circular argument. Part 2 of this book will revisit this idea in more detail.

As such, the Qur'an proves unique in a variety of ways. Recognition of these distinctions is vital for a Christian as they engage their Muslim friends and neighbors lest they make the mistake of assuming the Qur'an to be the Muslim equivalent of the Bible. In fact, the Qur'an is a thoroughly different book that plays a different role in Islam than the Bible plays in Christianity.

Perhaps the best place to begin our investigation, then, is with the traditional backstory of the one who received God's final dispensation of revelation. Though Muhammad is not considered to be the author of the Qur'an, as its chosen recipient, his biography plays an important role in validating the message of the Qur'an. This chapter will highlight a few aspects of his life that help to illuminate why Muslims believe the Qur'an itself to be a miracle.

MUHAMMAD: A BRIEF BIOGRAPHY

Most evangelical Christians view the Bible as having sixty-six books written by around forty human authors. These human authors express their thoughts using vocabulary, grammar, and phrases that bear the marks of their context. At the same time, 2 Timothy 3:16 clearly states that the Scriptures have been inspired (lit. "breathed out") by the divine author who superintended the writing of Scripture. Thus, while we can speak truly of the human authors of the Bible, the Holy Spirit stands behind and over the text of the biblical canon.

In contrast to a Christian understanding of human-divine authorship of the Bible, the Qur'an exists apart from Muhammad's reception, recitation, and transmission. In fact, as we will see later on in this chapter, many Muslims believe that the Qur'an is an eternal book that has always existed with God in the heavenly realm. Muhammad is merely the human conduit by whom God has made the content of this eternal book known to his creatures. In several ways Muhammad's life story reinforces the divine origins of the text he transmitted.

A TRAGIC BEGINNING

According to Islamic tradition, Muhammad was born in 570 CE into the Quraysh tribe in the region of Mecca on the Arabian Peninsula.

His childhood was marked by tragedy and loss. Muhammad's father died before he was born, and his mother died when he was six. As an orphan of such a tender age, he was admitted into the care of his grandfather. However, his grandfather also died before Muhammad had turned eight years old.

Thus, from the age of eight through adolescence, Muhammad's uncle, Abu Talib, took responsibility for raising him. The home of Abu Talib provided a loving and caring environment, and one rich with opportunity for experience beyond his immediate surroundings. Including Muhammad on his trading journeys, Abu Talib exposed his nephew to the people and places stretching from the Arabian Peninsula to Syria. Despite the instability of living in three different households and being part of a trading caravan during the first decade of his life, Muhammad grew up and gained the reputation of being a well-rounded, respectful, and pious young man.

AN UNLETTERED MAN

Not only was Muhammad known for his character, but even from his youth he was reported to have exhibited natural intelligence and wisdom. In a recent biography, Safiur-Rahman al-Mubarakpuri refers to Muhammad as "an exemplary man of weighty mind and faultless insight. He was favored with intelligence, originality of thought and accurate choice of the means leading to accurate goals."[4] Such lauding of Muhammad's intellect is not surprising considering that he is viewed in Islam as the only proper and perfect interpreter of the Qur'an.

What is surprising, however, is the fact that most Muslims believe that he was not afforded the opportunity of formal education. This belief derives from places in the Qur'an such as Qur'an 7:157–58, where Muhammad is twice identified as the 'ummi prophet. Muslims have long understood the Arabic word 'ummi to mean that Muhammad was unlettered or illiterate.

---

4   Safiur-Rahman Al Mubarakpuri, *The Sealed Nectar: Biography of the Noble Prophet*, rev. ed. (Riyadh, KSA: Darussalam, 2002), 64.

Further support for the idea that Muhammad was illiterate comes from Qur'an 29:48, which addresses Muhammad, saying, "You were not accustomed to read from any book before it, or to write it with your right (hand), (for) then the perpetrators of falsehood would indeed have had (reason to) doubt (you)." Thus, many early Muslim commentators contend that Muhammad was neither able to read nor write.[5] Though some contemporary scholars have argued that *'ummi* should not be understood to refer to Muhammad's education, the idea of Muhammad's illiteracy is still employed as evidence of the miraculous nature of his reception of the Qur'an.[6] Regardless of how one understands the word *'ummi*, Muhammad's educational background is not the only aspect of his biography that supports his role as a prophet.

PROPHETIC MARKERS

According to the *Sira*, several signs identified Muhammad as a prophet long before he received his call. First, when Muhammad's mother, Amina, was pregnant, she reported hearing a voice that told her, "You are pregnant with the lord of this people and when he is born say, 'I put him in the care of the One from the evil of every envier; then call him Muhammad.'"[7] When Amina told this story to Abd Muttalib, Muhammad's grandfather, he brought the infant Muhammad into the Ka'ba where he thanked God for the child. Thus, Muhammad's life began with prophetic premonition and with a pilgrimage to the Ka'ba.

---

5   Muhammad Mustafa al-Azami, *The History of the Qur'anic Text: From Revelation to Compilation* (Lahore, Oakistan: Suhail Academy, 2005), 55.

6   A. J. Droge, *The Qur'an: A New Annotated Translation* (Bristol, CT: Equinox, 2015), 102n152. Droge writes, "Traditional scholars interpret *ummi* as 'illiterate,' and claim that Muhammad could not read or write (further emphasizing the miraculous character of the Qur'an)." See also Guillaume, *The Life of Muhammad*, 252n1. Guillaume states, "Practically all Arab writers claim that he means that he could not read or write." Guillaume, however, contends that "gentile" is a better translation and a more appropriate interpretation of *'ummi*. Perhaps the clearest reason that Muslims might consider abandoning this claim to Muhammad's illiteracy is that the *Sira* records Muhammad writing the constitution of Medina (Guillaume, *The Life of Muhammad*, 231–33).

7   Guillaume, *The Life of Muhammad*, 69. In addition to this prophetic premonition, Amina claimed to have emitted a mysterious light in which she was able to see a projection of the castles of Busra in Syria.

Second, as per custom of the people, a Bedouin wet nurse named Halima took Muhammad into her care. At this time, Halima and her husband had a camel that would not yield milk, and she herself struggled to produce sufficient milk. As soon as she brought Muhammad to her bosom, however, her supply of milk rushed in, and she was able to feed not only Muhammad but also her own infant son. When her husband went out to check on their livestock, he found that the camel, too, had resumed milk production and was able to provide sustenance for the family amid the famine that surrounded them.[8]

In addition to these events, the *Sira* records various occasions when Christians recognized the bright future that stood before Muhammad. For example, just before Halima returned the weaned Muhammad to Amina, a group of Abyssinian Christians attempted to take Muhammad, declaring, "Let us take this boy, and bring him to our king and our country; for he will have a great future. We know all about him."[9]

Likewise, on a trip to Syria, Muhammad's caravan was stopped by a Christian monk named Bahira. This monk possessed a book that spoke of a child who would bear the mark of a great prophet on his body. After speaking with Muhammad and finding him to be devoted to God, Bahira eventually asked to see the child's back. The *Sira* reports that Bahira discovered between Muhammad's shoulder blades the seal of prophethood in the very place described in his book.[10] Before the caravan left, Bahira is reported to have told Muhammad's uncle, "Take your nephew back to his country and guard him carefully against the Jews, for by Allah! if they see him and know about him what I know, they will do him evil. A great future lies before this nephew of yours so take him home quickly."[11]

These events—along with many other similar accounts—provide the prescript to Muhammad's prophetic call. However, evidence of Muhammad's prophetic future is not exhausted by such passive and

---

8   Guillaume, *The Life of Muhammad*, 70–71.
9   Guillaume, *The Life of Muhammad*, 73.
10 Guillaume, *The Life of Muhammad*, 80.
11 Guillaume, *The Life of Muhammad*, 81.

external support. Reports of his reputation as a pious and prayerful youth along with his impeccable record of honesty in his adult life endorse him as a summarily suitable prophet.

RELIGIOUS REPUTATION

According to the traditional narrative, Muhammad was born into a polytheistic pagan society. His hometown of Mecca reportedly served both as a bustling hub of trade and as a place of religious pilgrimage due to the temple housed in the city. Muslims believe that this temple—the Ka'ba—was originally built by Ibrahim and Ismail as a place of worship dedicated to the one true God. However, by the time Muhammad was born, it had been desecrated by the polytheists, having come to serve as a house of worship for some 360 idols.

Despite the surrounding milieu of pagan worship and the often dishonest business practices to which Muhammad would have been privy, he was known as "an honest man of unusual moral sensitivity."[12] Such was his reputation within his community that "his fellow citizens, by common consent, gave him the title of *Al-Ameen* (the trustworthy)."[13] Not only was Muhammad known for his integrity and character, but he also was known to be pious and dutiful in his pursuit of religious truth.

Perhaps the central manifestation of Muhammad's piety was his fervent opposition of polytheism from a young age. For instance, in his dialogue with the Syrian monk Bahira, he refused to swear by two pagan gods, saying, "Do not ask me by al-Lat and al-Uzza, for by Allah nothing is more hateful to me than these two."[14] As a result of his rejection of polytheism, Muhammad often sought spiritual truth and guidance by retiring to the desert for long periods of prayer, meditation, and fasting. In his fortieth year, during one such visit to a small cave named Hiraa', Muhammad had an encounter that would change history.

---

12   Fazlur Rahman, *Islam* (New York: Holt, Rinehart, and Winston, 1966), 11.
13   Mubarakpuri, *The Sealed Nectar*, 65.
14   Guillaume, *The Life of Muhammad*, 80.

THE CAVE OF HIRAA' AND THE ANGEL JIBRIL

Located about four miles outside of Mecca, one can find a small, nondescript cave just big enough for an adult to take shelter in. This cave is called Hiraa', and it is where Islamic tradition reports that Muhammad encountered the angel Jibril. Though he did not understand it immediately, Muhammad's biography cites this event as the moment that "God sent [Muhammad] in compassion to mankind, 'as an evangelist to all men.'"[15] This night, as Muhammad met Jibril in the cave, he received his prophetic call.

It should be noted that neither the Qur'an nor the *Sunnah* explicitly record the exact date on which Muhammad began to receive revelations. However, by drawing inferences from various hints throughout the literature, Islamic scholars generally believe that the events of the cave of Hiraa' occurred sometime in August of the year 610 CE.[16] What is clear according to Qur'an 2:185 is that the Qur'an was sent down during the month of Ramadan.

ASCETIC TENDENCIES

As mentioned above, Muhammad's pursuit of religious truth pushed him away from the city of Mecca and into the seclusion of the desert, hills, and valleys in the surrounding area. This devotional impulse was not necessarily unique to Muhammad but had apparently been a part of prior Qurayshi custom.[17]

Each year during the month of Ramadan, Muhammad retreated to the cave of Hiraa' to pray and seek spiritual understanding. Though there was nothing ostensibly different about the month of Ramadan in 610 CE, it was this year that God chose to commission Muhammad as a messenger of God's will and as the Seal of the Prophets. He did so by sending the angel Jibril, who transmitted the message of the Qur'an to Muhammad.

---

15 Guillaume, *The Life of Muhammad*, 104.
16 Mubarakpuri, *The Sealed Nectar*, 68n2.
17 Guillaume, *The Life of Muhammad*, 105. The *Sira* records, "The apostle [Muhammad] would pray in seclusion on Hiraa' every year for a month to practice *tahannuth* as was the custom of the Quraysh in heathen days. *Tahannuth* is religious devotion."

"RECITE!"

Throughout the Qur'an one finds various references to Jibril as the conduit of divine revelation to Muhammad. For instance, Qur'an 2:97 reports Jibril as the one who brings down the Qur'an as guidance and good news. Likewise, some commentators understand the phrase "holy spirit" in Qur'an 26:192–200 to refer to Jibril and his role as the transmitter of the Qur'an.[18]

This qur'anic allusion to Jibril as the angelic messenger who taught Muhammad the Qur'an is reinforced and made explicit in the *Sira*. According to the traditional narrative, Muhammad was sleeping in the cave of Hiraa' when Jibril appeared to him suddenly. The angel pressed upon Muhammad to the point that Muhammad thought he was going to die, and he repeated the instruction to "Recite!" three times.[19]

After each command, Muhammad responded by asking, "What shall I recite?" Finally, Jibril said, "Recite: In the Name of God, the Merciful, the Compassionate. Recite in the Name of your Lord who creates; creates the human from a clot. Recite, for your Lord is the Most Generous, who teaches by the pen, teaches the human what he does not know."[20] Thus, the *Sira* provides the source of the tradition that the first verses revealed are found in Qur'an 96:1–5.

Muhammad awoke and emerged from the cave after this encounter in a state of confusion and despair. The *Sira* even records that Muhammad considered killing himself as he was unsure as to whether he had been possessed by a demon or had an ecstatic experience like the ones described by the pagan poets he so despised. As he was descending the mountain, Jibril again appeared to him, saying, "O

---

18 Droge, *The Qur'an*, 244n70.
19 It should be noted that there is disagreement over how to understand Jibril's instruction to Muhammad. The Arabic word *iqra'* could be understood as a command to recite or to read. Most traditional scholars, believing Muhammad to be illiterate, render this as a command to recite. Al-Azami, *The History of the Qur'anic Text*, 47, retains the more natural translation, "Read!" However, he takes some liberties in translating Muhammad's response as indicating that he could not read. Others, however, find it more appropriate and natural to translate it as a command to read, eschewing the idea that Muhammad was illiterate. See Guillaume, *The Life of Muhammad*, 106.
20 Qur'an 96:1–5.

Muhammad! Thou are the apostle of God and I am Jibril!"[21] Once Muhammad regained his faculties from this encounter, he returned to his wife Khadija and told her what he had just experienced.

AFFIRMATIONS

Even after the second encounter with Jibril on the mountain, Muhammad was unconvinced that he was not being oppressed by a demon. Upon recounting the tale to Khadija, however, his wife assured him that he was neither ecstatic nor possessed. Rather, she exclaimed, "Rejoice, O son of my uncle, and be of good heart. Verily, by Him in whose hand is Khadija's soul, I have hope that thou wilt be the prophet of this people."[22] By recognizing Muhammad as a prophet, Khadija is known in Islamic history as the first person Muhammad converted to Islam.

Not only did Khadija accept her husband's prophethood, but she also related the events to her cousin, Waraqa, who also affirmed Muhammad as a messenger of God. Waraqa was known as a Christian learned in the Scriptures. Upon hearing Khadija's report of Muhammad's experience, he exclaimed, "Holy! Holy! Verily by Him in whose hand is Waraqa's soul, if thou hast spoken the truth, O Khadija, there hath come unto him [Gabriel] who came to Moses aforetime, and lo, he is the prophet of this people. Bid him be of good heart."[23]

In the course of time, Muhammad gathered additional followers from among a variety of peoples. The *Sira* records the testimony of one group of polytheists who became Muslims because of the prophecy about Muhammad that came from the Jews. The Jews had been threatening these idolaters by saying that a prophet would arise who would help them in destroying polytheism. When Muhammad arrived, however, the polytheists recognized Muhammad's authority as the prophet, while the Jews rejected him.[24]

The *Sira* and the compilations of traditions known as the Hadith are littered with such stories of conversion. Some from among the

---

21 Guillaume, *The Life of Muhammad*, 106.
22 Guillaume, *The Life of Muhammad*, 107.
23 Guillaume, *The Life of Muhammad*, 107.
24 Guillaume, *The Life of Muhammad*, 93.

Jews, Christians, pagans, and foreigners recognize Muhammad as a prophet of God with a sacred message. These stories of diverse recognition of Muhammad as a prophet are told and retold to demonstrate broad affirmation that he truly heard from heaven on what has come to be known as the Night of Power (*Laylat al-Qadr*).

THE NIGHT OF POWER

Though the Qur'an itself is not forthcoming with a lot of details regarding the circumstances of its transmission, it does refer to the time of year that Muhammad began receiving revelations. As we have already seen, Qur'an 2:185 affirms that God sent the Qur'an down to Muhammad in the month of Ramadan. Furthermore, Qur'an 44:3 and Qur'an 97 single out the day on which Muhammad encountered Jibril as a night of blessing.

This night is hallowed by Qur'an 97:3–5, which declares, "The Night of [Power] is better than a thousand months. The angels and the spirit come down during it, by the permission of their Lord, on account of every command. It is (a night of) peace, until the rising of the dawn."[25] Subsequently, it has come to be a tenet of Islamic practice to consider prayers offered during the last ten days of Ramadan to be especially meritorious. Though the specific day is unknown, one of the last ten days of the annual fast is thought to correspond with the Night of Power and is marked by the angels drawing near and God being more inclined to bless the faithful.

Along with the question of which night of Ramadan is the Night of Power, scholars debate whether or not Muhammad was given the entire Qur'an on this night. Multiple places throughout the Qur'an appear to indicate that God sent down the entire Qur'an to Muhammad in the cave of Hiraa'. However, traditional understanding of the process of reception favors occasional revelations corresponding to the developing needs of the community. Some interpreters resolve

---

25   The Arabic should be translated, as Droge does, "The night of destiny" or "The night of decree." However, in common Islamic parlance, this night is referred to as the Night of Power; thus, I have glossed Droge's translation to make the connection with contemporary practice more apparent for the reader.

this apparent discrepancy by saying that God sent the Qur'an down from the highest heaven to the lowest heaven on the Night of Power, and that it was from there that Muhammad received its message on the appropriate occasions.[26]

Regardless of how one understands how much of the Qur'an Muhammad was privy to on the Night of Power, most all Muslims contend that various verses, passages, and chapters of the Qur'an were given to address specific moments in Muhammad's life and in the circumstances of the community of believers. In order to begin to understand how the Qur'an functions to inform Islamic faith and practice, we must consider how this process of revelation affects the interpretation and application of each passage.

OCCASIONS OF REVELATION (*ASBAB AN-NAZUL*)
The introduction to this chapter highlights a peculiarity about the Qur'an that often confuses new readers: what are thought to be its first verses (Qur'an 96:1–5) are recorded long after one reads its final verse (Qur'an 5:3). Furthermore, the chapters of the Qur'an appear disconnected from one another, and narrative sections that would suggest a chronological order are few and far between. In light of this, Gabriel Said Reynolds concludes, "Without the library of [qur'anic commentaries], scholars might feel themselves in a sort of intellectual wilderness, with no orienting landmarks to guide their thoughts."[27]

In order to assign a chronology to various parts, and to set the Qur'an's verses in a historical context, one must refer to the *Sunnah* to decipher the occasions of revelation. The following section, then, will provide a glimpse of some of the salient features of the Qur'an that one must understand in order to make sense of the traditional approach to distilling Islamic theology and practice from its pages.

---

26 Droge, *The Qur'an*, 442n1. Droge writes, "The references to the descent of the Qur'an on a single night reflect a different understanding that the traditional one, according to which the Qur'an was 'sent down' or revealed at intervals over a period of some twenty years. Some interpreters understand this verse as referring to the descent of the Qur'an from the highest to the lowest of the seven heavens, whence it was revealed to Muhammad as occasion required."

27 Reynolds, *The Qur'an and Its Biblical Subtext*, 18.

THE PROCESS OF REVELATION
AND COMPILATION

Since the Qur'an admits of very little historical context, most Islamic scholars lean on Muhammad's biography and reports contained in the traditions to discern likely occasions when various verses were revealed. Later chapters will address some of the historical-critical difficulties this presents.[28] For the present, however, we will consider the traditional approach to the material, which typically understands its historical claims to be reliable.

According to the *Sira*, after Muhammad encountered Jibril in the cave of Hiraa', he received verses of the Qur'an over the next twenty-three years. From 610 CE through his death in 632 CE, Muhammad experienced moments of revelation (*wahy*) wherein he would often appear to others to be in a catatonic state, sweating despite cold weather, and exhibiting other physiological changes.[29]

Muhammad claimed that he could not control when *wahy* occurred. Though it would come upon him spontaneously, when he was relieved of the experience, he would recite what he received to nearby companions, who wrote it down. According to Muhammad Mustafa al-Azami, approximately sixty-five different companions served as scribes at one time or another.[30] The process of compiling the Qur'an, then, required collection of all of the records of revelation as written by various scribes on a wide variety of materials.

Though such a process appears to be unwieldy, tradition records that Muhammad was involved not only in the reception of the Qur'an but also with its arrangement. Al-Azami reports several traditions that describe how Muhammad directed his companions as to how each verse or section was to be inserted in the larger context of the Qur'an. In fact, some accounts even include Jibril instructing Muhammad as to how he was to order his scribes to arrange the revelation.[31]

---

28   Reynolds, *The Qur'an and Its Biblical Subtext*, 9.
29   Al-Azami, *The History of the Qur'anic Text*, 46.
30   Al-Azami, *The History of the Qur'anic Text*, 68.
31   Al-Azami, *The History of the Qur'anic Text*, 71.

As one can imagine, weaving new revelation into the fabric of older revelation further complicates the process of reconstructing the historical context in which each section was received. This task has prompted Muslim scholars to scour the *Sunnah* for any and all information that might suggest a contextual background for each chapter and verse of the Qur'an. Such scholars have produced volumes of material that speculate about and explain the situations and settings behind the verses of the Qur'an.

THE SUPPLIED NARRATIVE OF THE *SUNNAH*

The most important document for reconstructing the occasions of revelation is the biography of Muhammad known as the *Sirat Rasul Allah* (commonly shortened to *Sira*). Through this biography, the Muslim community has access to the earliest written account of Muhammad's life available. Though Islamic tradition attributes the content of the *Sira* to a man named Ibn Ishaq (d. 768 CE), the only extant account of this biography comes through the reports of Ibn Hisham (d. 833), who reportedly memorized and edited Ibn Ishaq's original work.[32]

This biography, coupled with the extensive volumes of hadith literature, serve the Islamic community by supplying the narrative backdrop for much of the Qur'an. For instance, many contemporary copies of the Qur'an will supply a note at the beginning of each chapter indicating approximately when it is believed to have been written. More specifically, through commentaries and works known as *Asbab an-Nazul* (Reasons for Revelation), scholars sifted through the Qur'an and the *Sunnah* in order to purportedly assign various revelations to specific events in Muhammad's life and ministry.

While not all early schools of thought appreciated these efforts, many from the ninth century CE onward considered these traditions

---

32   Guillaume, *The Life of Muhammad*, 691. Ibn Hisham notes that he is intentionally omitting some of the original material that seemed extraneous to the purpose if introducing Muhammad and also screening out some of the material that would distress certain people and that which is disgraceful to discuss.

to be vital to the process of rightly understanding the Qur'an.[33] These narrative explanations are often included as supplementary data, printed alongside of the qur'anic text in contemporary editions of the Qur'an.[34] In addition to the obvious desire to locate the teachings of the Qur'an in Muhammad's historical setting, Muslims must have a sense of the Qur'an's chronology in order to know how they are to live out their faith.

THE DOCTRINE OF ABROGATION

In part, Islamic scholars have dedicated themselves to reconstructing the narrative development of the Qur'an because of a doctrine known as abrogation. Abrogation (*nasikh*) is the teaching that maintains God's ultimate freedom to command anything that he wills—including that which apparently contradicts what he had previously commanded. Such teaching derives from verses such as Qur'an 2:106, which states, "Whatever verse We cancel or cause to be forgotten, We bring a better (one) than it, or (one) similar to it. Do you not know that God is powerful over everything?" Thus, it appears that the Qur'an intends to reserve for God the freedom to alter his instructions over time.

If this doctrine of abrogation is to be applied internally to the Qur'an, then it would seem most natural that the most recent revelations would be those which are binding on the contemporary community. Hence, the desire to ascertain the chronological order of the Qur'an derives from more than mere narrative appeal. It has vital implications for which instructions the community is to regard as having contemporary authority.

In his recent book, *The Qur'an in Context*, Mark Anderson cites common examples of this doctrine in action. Anderson demonstrates that Qur'an 2:219 implies that alcohol is to be treated with care. Likewise, Qur'an 4:43 prohibits believers from coming to prayer intoxicated,

---

33   See the discussion on the various schools of interpretation provided by Binyan Abra-hamov, "Scripturalist and Traditionalist Theology," in *Oxford Handbook of Islamic Theology*, 263–79 (Oxford, UK: Oxford University Press, 2016).

34   "Asbab al-Nuzul," *The Oxford Dictionary of Islam*, ed. John L. Esposito (Oxford Islam-ic Studies Online), http://www.oxfordislamicstudies.com/article/opr/t125/e205.

but implies that consumption of alcohol at other times might be acceptable.[35] However, in Qur'an 5:93, alcohol is prohibited altogether.[36] Though this progression from permission to prohibition might appear to be obvious, since this particular example appears to follow a natural sequence of numerical progression, there is nothing in the context to indicate when each verse was revealed. Thus, there is little internal reason to claim that Qur'an 5:93 was revealed after Qur'an 2:219.

The example above regarding the Qur'an's perspective on alcohol is rather benign. Regardless of one's understanding of which verses are most recent, the overall effect on the practice of Islam is minimal. However, there are far more vital issues that arise when various communities of Muslims attempt to discern which verses are binding and which were only authoritative for the time in which they were given.

In contemporary society, perhaps the most poignant example of the importance of chronology for application is the so-called "Sword verse." In Qur'an 9:5 one reads, "Then, when the sacred months have passed, kill the idolaters wherever you find them, and seize them, and besiege them, and sit (in wait) for them at every place of ambush. If they turn (in repentance), and observe the prayer and give the alms, let them go their way. Surely God is forgiving, compassionate." Most Muslims believe that this was a verse revealed for a specific and limited time, while the verses that commend peaceful coexistence with non-Muslims are more universally applicable. Yet various radical Islamist groups contend that this verse is late and not restricted to its time. Thus, for these interpreters, violent aggression against non-Muslims is obligatory for contemporary Islamic practice.[37]

As is evident from this brief account, the process of interpreting the Qur'an is not as straightforward as one might think. Despite the

---

35   Droge, *The Qur'an*, 50n46, draws the same permissive conclusion regarding Qur'an 4:43.

36   Mark Anderson, *The Qur'an in Context: A Christian Exploration* (Downers Grove, IL: IVP Academic, 2016), 160n58.

37   For a helpful discussion of these issues as they pertain to the textual foundation for violence as described by the leaders of ISIS/DAESH, see *Open Letter to Dr. Ibrahim Awwad al-Badri, Alias 'Abu Bakr al-Baghdadi and to the Fighters and Followers of the Self-Declared Islamic State* (2014), www.LetterToBaghdadi.com.

fact that the Qur'an boasts that its contents have been given as clear guidance for all mankind, following this guidance fourteen centuries after its transmission is anything but clear. In fact, even in the days of its initial reception, many of Muhammad's opponents challenged his teaching and role as a prophet of God.

CHALLENGES TO MUHAMMAD'S CLAIMS

Within the pages of the Qur'an itself, Muhammad was already dealing with members of his audience who thought his claims preposterous. One hears the echoes of the voices of these opponents in Qur'an 16:101, which states, "When we exchange a verse in place of (another) verse—and God knows what He sends down—they say, 'You are only a forger!' No! But most of them do not know (anything)." The same chapter goes on to indicate that Muhammad was accused of having a foreigner—tradition suggests a Jewish or Christian helper—who instructed him regarding what he should write.

Similarly, tradition teaches that the polytheists opposed Muhammad as a troublemaker whose smooth, poetic words were either the result of sorcery or demon possession. In fact, they tried to silence Muhammad's recitations of the Qur'an because "among other things, women and children were known to eavesdrop on his recitations, and were naturally more susceptible to such an influence."[38] The pagans, then, rejected Muhammad as a prophet, yet they feared the influence his sublime eloquence would have on their community.

Finally, when Muhammad relocated from Mecca to Medina in 622 CE, he encountered a Jewish community. Since Muhammad understood himself to be a messenger of the same kind as the Old Testament prophets, he expected a warm reception from the Jewish leaders. Courting their approval, tradition records that Muhammad instructed his followers to pray facing Jerusalem and to keep the ten-day fast that the Jews were observing upon his arrival.[39]

---

38   Al-Azami, *The History of the Qur'anic Text*, 50.
39   Bernard Lewis, *The Arabs in History*, 6th ed. (Oxford, UK: Oxford University Press, 2002), 39.

The Jews, however, rejected Muhammad as a prophet. Following this incident, tradition teaches that Muhammad received Qur'an 2:142–52. This passage explains that the Muslim community is to change the direction of prayer to be oriented toward the Ka'ba—the Sacred Temple in Mecca. Later in the chapter, in Qur'an 2:185, one reads that the month of Ramadan—as the holy month in which Muhammad received the Qur'an—is to be a holy month of fasting for the Islamic community. Thus, after Muhammad was rejected by the Jews, he received qur'anic revelation that his community was to observe a fast of thirty days and that they were no longer to pray towards Jerusalem.

The Qur'an and the *Sunnah* do not attempt to obscure the fact that Muhammad's message was not universally accepted. However, even the depictions of Muhammad's opponents serve to promote the overarching message that the Qur'an is a book like no other. Those who despise it—such as the polytheists—yet recognize its persuasive beauty. Those who reject it—as with the Jews of Medina—are cut off by its message. And those who would argue that Muhammad is a forger are confronted with the claim that the Qur'an is written in pure Arabic of a quality that could not be but divinely inspired.

THE MIRACLE OF THE QUR'AN

All that has been seen up to this point regarding Muhammad's background is considered to be evidence in support of the miraculous nature of the Qur'an. As a child of tragic origins, Muhammad was not trained formally and could not be expected to produce the marvelous prose exhibited within the Qur'an. Yet, even from a young age, Muhammad was identified as one who would become a prophet of his people. And finally, despite Muhammad's humble origins, he was known as a man of the highest integrity, whose sterling reputation was fitting for a prophet.

All of this biographical information is leveraged by Muslim apologists to reinforce the idea that Muhammad was the ideal candidate to receive the Qur'an. Furthermore, Muhammad's personal history integrates supportively into the narrative of events that exalt the Qur'an as a miracle. In addition to Muhammad's role as an unlikely-yet-perfect transmitter, several internal aspects of the Qur'an provide proof for the Muslim community of its divine origins.

INIMITABLE BEAUTY

On the first page of his book *The History of the Qur'anic Text*, Muhammad Mustafa al-Azami summarizes the confessional view of the Qur'an's contents as being, "Guidance, comfort, and beauty. For the believing Muslim, the Holy Qur'an is all this and much more: the heartbeat of faith, a remembrance in times of joy and anguish, a fountain of precise scientific reality and the most exquisite lyricism, a treasury of wisdom and supplications."[40] Al-Azami's reference to exquisite lyricism picks up on a claim repeated throughout the Qur'an and the *Sunnah* regarding the inimitability of the Qur'an's beauty as proof of its veracity.

The Qur'an makes this argument for itself in verses such as Qur'an 17:88, which states, "If indeed humankind and the jinn joined together to produce something like this Qur'an, they would not produce anything like it, even if they were supporters of each other." In other places, the Qur'an records the same idea phrased as a challenge to the audience to produce a verse or a chapter like it.[41] Likewise, the *Sira* records multiple occasions of those who converted to Islam simply as a result of appreciating the beauty of the Qur'an.[42]

Tradition makes much of the idea that the pagans of Mecca were well-known for their admiration of poetry. Thus, when the pagans themselves recognize something wholly unique in Muhammad's recitation of the Qur'an, it serves as proof that even those who were antagonists of Muhammad knew that his words were otherworldly. In one such account, three men stole away at night to eavesdrop on

---

40   Al-Azami, *The History of the Qur'anic Text*, 3.
41   See similar challenges in Qur'an 2:23, 10:38, and 11:13.
42   See especially the account of 'Umar who was prepared to attack several of his relatives who had converted to Islam and then read a portion of the Qur'an and immediately asked to be brought to Muhammad so as to become a Muslim himself. Guillaume, *The Life of Muhammad*, 156–157.

Muhammad as he recited the Qur'an. Night after night the men listened to Muhammad and, though they continued to reject and envy him, they exclaimed to one another that surely this man received his revelations from the heavens.[43]

The beauty of the Qur'an, along with the apparent fact that none can replicate it, has come to provide the Islamic community with confidence that it derives from a heavenly source. Al-Azami concludes, "As an Arab [Muhammad] was familiar with all sorts of Arabic expressions, with poetry and prose, but nothing bore the resemblance to these verses. . . . These ineffable Words, this Qur'an, became the first and greatest miracle bestowed upon him."[44] Despite the repeated objection that such a subjective and indefinite criteria as beauty cannot be proven to be objectively true, many Muslims remain convinced that the apparently inimitable quality of the Qur'an supports its claims as divine revelation. As revelation from the one true God, Muslims also believe that it has been perfectly preserved by God.

INCORRUPTIBLE TEXT

In addition to the beauty of the qur'anic language, Muslims also support its heavenly origin by claiming that God has protected the Qur'an from alteration and corruption. Such protection begins with the belief that Muhammad was involved in both receiving and arranging the Qur'an. While his companions committed his revelations to writing, Muhammad continued to be actively involved in ordering various verses within each chapter. This ongoing activity is reported by the third caliph, 'Uthman, who said that when Muhammad received new revelation, he would call a scribe and instruct them, "Place this verse [or these verses] in the [chapter] where such-and-such is mentioned."[45]

Some Shiite Muslims believe that the Qur'an was fixed in its written form prior to Muhammad's death. Most Sunni Muslims,

---

43   See this account in al-Azami, *The History of the Qur'anic Text*, 49.
44   Al-Azami, *The History of the Qur'anic Text*, 48.
45   Al-Azami, *The History of the Qur'anic Text*, 70.

on the other hand, tend to view the process of compiling the written Qur'an as a task completed by Muhammad's successors after his death. Both branches of Islam, however, understand that the content of the Qur'an—including the verse order of each chapter—was established prior to Muhammad's death. According to al-Azami, there are some reports that suggest different ordering for the chapters throughout the Qur'an, though each chapter is a self-contained entity, so varied arrangement of the chapters does not affect the overall meaning of the text.

This confidence in a fixed Qur'an prior to Muhammad's death is vitally important to the Muslim community. This is because the *Sira* acknowledges that by the time the third caliph 'Uthman began leading the community of Muslims, multiple readings of the Qur'an proliferated throughout the empire. 'Uthman's greatest contribution to subsequent generations of Muslims is that he determined the true Qur'an from among the various readings and ordered the competing copies to be destroyed. Since Muslims believe that the Qur'an had been established in its final form prior to 'Uthman's caliphate, they can contend that 'Uthman *recognized* the correct reading of the Qur'an rather than simply *selecting* one based on personal preference.

Following his identification of the proper reading, 'Uthman commissioned the replication and dissemination of a single, authoritative copy of the Qur'an throughout the expanding Islamic empire. To this day, Muslim communities around the world contend that they are reading exact replicas of this authorized copy.[46] All of this is important because Islamic theology teaches that the Qur'an did not originate with Muhammad's interpretation of Gabriel's message but is the exact transcription of the heavenly record, known as the Mother of the Book (*'Umm al-Kitab*).

---

46 More will be discussed on the veracity of this claim in subsequent chapters, but it is worth noting at this point that the claim that the Qur'an has never undergone any alteration or corruption has been challenged on multiple occasions. For example, see Fred Leemhuis, "From Palm Leaves to the Internet," in *Cambridge Companion to the Qur'an*, ed. Jane McAuliffe (New York: Cambridge University Press, 2006), 149–51.

THE MOTHER OF THE BOOK ('*UMM AL-KITAB*)

The Qur'an bears evidence of its miraculous origin by its apparently inimitable beauty and its unaltered preservation. Both of these features are tied to the understanding that neither Jibril nor Muhammad produced the Qur'an. Rather, both were involved in transmitting what is contained in '*Umm al-Kitab*, which is the record of the divine will, kept in heaven with God.

Thus, Muslims believe that by reading the Qur'an, they are accessing heavenly language, ideas, and communication as directly as possible. The Qur'an reinforces this account of its own heavenly origins when it refers to a guarded tablet (*al-Loh al-Mahfouz*) in Qur'an 85:21–22, where it states, "Yes! It is a glorious Qur'an, in a guarded tablet." Not only does the content of the Qur'an exist in the heavenly record, but it also continues along and completes the same trajectory that previous revelation began.

CONTINUITY WITH PRIOR REVELATION

The Qur'an claims in multiple places that its message is congruent with that which was revealed to previous generations of monotheists. For example, Qur'an 3:64 addresses Jews and Christians as those who share a common understanding about who God is and who have also received revelation from him. Thus, throughout the Qur'an one finds Christians and Jews considered to be among the People of the Book, or people who have received divine revelation.

We have already said that the Qur'an contains very little sustained narrative. Yet it appears to assume its audience is familiar with some of the stories of prior prophets and biblical characters. Evidence for this assumption can be found in the regular references to apparently biblical figures such as Adam, Noah, Abraham, David, and Jesus. The Qur'an teaches that God is the creator of the universe, that he made special agreements with the Jews and Christians, and that there will one day be a reckoning whereby humans will be judged according to how they lived their lives.

Thus, it appears that the Qur'an views itself as a final dispensation of heavenly revelation, derived from the same source as the Torah, the Psalms, and the Gospels.[47] This continuity is further reinforced in Qur'an 10:37, which states, "The Qur'an is not the kind (of Book) that it could have been forged apart from God. (It is) a confirmation of what was before it, and a distinct setting forth of the Book—there is no doubt about it—from the Lord of the worlds." Thus, while the Qur'an is the final dispensation of divine revelation, it is confirmation of that which remains unsullied in the biblical text.

CONCLUSION

The Qur'an is, in many ways, a unique book. Its uniqueness is not expressly due to its distinctive content, but more to the Islamic account of the events surrounding its arrival. For many Muslims, the reception of the Qur'an, its apparent beauty, and its unadulterated preservation suffice to prove its divine origins. In other words, before the Qur'an is a text containing supernatural content, it is understood as a text that exists because of a supernatural event. Thus, it is prudent to begin an investigation of the Qur'an by highlighting the relevant traditional understandings of its arrival prior to investigating its content.

As noted above, most Muslims believe that the Bible as it exists today has been corrupted by Jews and Christians. Yet there are still sufficient glimmers of truth within the Bible in its contemporary form that are corroborated by the Qur'an, allowing Muslims to claim continuity with—and perfection of—the biblical story. By claiming continuity with biblical concepts and characters the Qur'an situates itself in the context of biblical ideas and narrative. However, a Christian seeking to understand and communicate with a Muslim friend does well to probe beyond the veneer of claimed continuity in order to assess whether or not common language and character references truly admit of shared concepts and narrative arc.

Therefore, as the rest of this book will demonstrate, there is much more to be said about the manner in which the content of the Qur'an

---

47   Much remains to be discussed as to whether or not such a claim can be substantiated—or should be accepted by Christians in evangelistic conversations. However, for the purposes of this chapter, it suffices to report the traditional Muslim perspective on the Qur'an as continuity.

claims to overlap with the Bible. However, it suffices for the purposes of the present chapter to simply note that the Qur'an intends itself as a sequel to the Bible while not endorsing all that is currently recorded in its pages. The event of its revelation marks the final dispensation of God's communication of his will to humankind. What is contained in that revelation is the subject of the following chapter.

2

THE REVELATION OF THE QUR'AN

In the Name of God, the Merciful, the Compassionate.
Praise (be) to God, Lord of the worlds, the Merciful,
the Compassionate, Master of the Day of Judgment.
You we serve and You we seek for help. Guide us to
the straight path: the path of those whom You have
blessed, not (the path) of those on whom (Your) anger
falls, nor of those who go astray.
Qur'an 1, "al-Fatiha"

Having surveyed the traditional reports regarding the supernatural events surrounding the Qur'an's reception, this chapter will explore the question, "What does the Qur'an reveal?" Islam teaches that the Qur'an reveals God's will and guidance. Yet, in some streams of Islamic thought and theology, the God of Islam himself remains transcendent and inscrutable.[1]

---

1   In the history of Islamic theology there has been much discussion about what can be known of God in his essence. See the complicated history of philosophical reflection

Other streams of Islamic thought contend that one can speak truly of knowing about God provided that any such knowledge of God is restricted to how the Qur'an has described him.[2] Yet, even those Muslims who contend that the Qur'an reveals something about God that can be known stop short of the intimate, interpersonal knowledge of God as Father—much less as God who takes on flesh and walks among us—of which the Bible speaks.[3]

---

on the relationship of God to creation as articulated by Peter Adamson, "Philosophical Theology," in *The Oxford Handbook of Islamic Theology*, ed. Sabine Schmidtke, 296–312 (New York: Oxford University Press, 2016). Some strains of thought have followed the highly philosophical reflections of a group known as the Mu'tazilites, allowing reason to have pride of place in determining what can be known of God. For a helpful explanation of this discussion, see David Bennett, "The Mu'tazilite Movement (II)," in *The Oxford Handbook of Islamic Theology*, ed. Sabine Schmidtke, 142–58 (New York: Oxford University Press, 2016). Bennett explains that in the early Mu'tazilite understanding of God's oneness (*tawhid*), any positive statement made concerning God's attributes—particularly those that suggest anthropomorphism—involved the implicit danger of *shirk*, or associating coeternal "partners" with God by asserting a variety of eternal attributes of God. Thus, for Mu'tazilites, what can be said about God consists of saying that he is "Always knowing, powerful, and living" (152). The priority the Mu'tazilite approach gave to philosophical reflection resulted in a concept of God that remains even more unknowable than how the Qur'an presents him. In the eleventh century, the influential Muslim thinker Al-Ghazali dealt a devastating blow to the philosophical school of thought by writing his treatise "On the Incoherence of the Philosophers." See Michael Marmura, trans., *On the Incoherence of the Philosophers*, 2nd ed. (Provo, UT: Brigham Young University Press, 2000).

2   In reaction against the rationalism of the Mu'tazilites, a group that came to be more popular within the development of Islamic thought is known as the Ash'arites. See Mashhad Al-Allaf, "Islamic Theology," in *The Bloomsbury Companion to Islamic Studies*, ed. Clinton Bennett, 119–34 (New York: Bloomsbury Academic, 2015), 127. The Ash'arites allow for the idea that the Qur'an reveals knowledge about God and also that human reason can discern some theological truths in so far as they do not contradict the Qur'an. This school advocates for the idea that one can know God through what has been revealed in his actions and attributes, and from the position of a servant knowing his master. The founder of the Ahs'arites, al-Ash'ari, believed that one could say that whatever the Qur'an said of God's attributes could be understood as being true of God eternally (i.e., one can know that God has knowledge and power from eternity past) while also not holding these attributes to be identical with God. In other words, Ash'arites believe that "God's eternal attributes are neither identical to, nor other than Him." (Jan Thiele, "Between Cordoba and Nisabur: The Emergence and Consolidation of Ash'arism," in *The Oxford Handbook of Islamic Theology*, ed. Sabine Schmidtke, 225–41 [New York: Oxford University Press, 2016], 228.)

3   Isma'il al-Furuqi, *At-Tawhid: Its Implications on Thought and Life* (Herndon, VA: The International Institute of Islamic Thought, 2000), 24, states, "This is the first assertion

Former Muslim Nabeel Qureshi highlights this qur'anic distinction from biblical revelation clear as he writes, "As a part of our understanding of *tawhid*, we need to include a balanced understanding of Allah's self-revelation. Allah intends man to pursue the relationship of a servant to his master, but not the relationship of a child with his father. Nothing in the Qur'an suggests that Allah desires intimacy with humanity."[4] It is the doctrine of *tawhid*—God's monadic unity and undivided singularity—that prohibits God from engaging humanity relationally because it establishes God himself as one in whom there exists no interpersonal relationship from eternity past.[5]

Though the Qur'an is full of statements about God, it is not primarily concerned with introducing the reader to God himself. Renowned Islamic scholar Fazlur Rahman makes this clear as he writes, "The Qur'an is no treatise about God and His nature: His existence, for the Qur'an, is strictly functional—He is Creator and Sustainer of the universe and of man, and particularly the giver of guidance for man and He who judges man, individually and collectively, and metes out to him merciful justice."[6] Some Muslim theologians even go so far as to deny that God reveals himself at all.

For instance, Isma'il al-Furuqi distinguishes Christian conceptions of revelation from Islamic teaching, saying, "God does *not* reveal

---

of the Islamic creed that 'There is no god but God,' which the Muslim understands as denial of any associates to God in His rulership and judgeship of the universe, as well as a denial of the possibility for any creature to represent, personify or in any way express the divine Being." See also Muhammad Abdel Haleem, *Understanding the Qur'an: Themes and Style* (London: I. B. Tauris, 2010), 25. Haleem investigates the supposed parallels between *al-Fatiha* and the Lord's Prayer and concludes that they are incomparable from the beginning because, "Muslims would not speak of God as a 'father' or a 'son.'"

4   Nabeel Qureshi, *No God but One* (Grand Rapids: Zondervan, 2016), 62.

5   Qureshi, *No God but One*, 62. Qureshi writes, "There is an intrinsic reason why Allah does not desire a relationship with humans, whereas Yahweh does. On account of *tawhid*, Allah is a monad; he is not inherently relational."

6   Fazlur Rahman, *Major Themes of the Qur'an* (Chicago: University of Chicago Press, 2009), 1. See the similar conclusion reached by Gabriel Said Reynolds, *Allah: God in the Qur'an* (New Haven, CT: Yale University Press, 2020), 234: "The Qur'an means intentionally to keep God's nature a mystery. The Qur'an is not a theological guidebook that describes God in a precise and coherent manner. It is closer to a sermon, an exhortation, or an argument meant to persuade humans to believe."

Himself. He does not reveal Himself to anyone in any way. God reveals only His will. . . . God is transcendent, and once you talk about self-revelation you have hierophancy and immanence, and then the transcendence of God is compromised."[7] While perhaps an extreme example of Islamic thought, al-Furuqi's conclusion clearly demonstrates the tendency for Muslims to elevate God's total transcendence. In other words, while God is the proper object of worship and the sovereign power over creation, the Qur'an does not primarily concern itself with the task of calling its readers to know God. Rather, the Qur'an calls its audience to know God's will, his law, and his guidance.

For a Christian, such an answer should immediately expose a foundational difference between the Islamic and Christian understandings of divine revelation. The Christian concept of God certainly includes a recognition of the partial the hiddenness of God due to the impossibility of comprehending his infinite nature. Yet, the Bible teaches that God has made himself known and knowable—most centrally in Christ.[8] Thus, the primary content of revelation within Christian theology is God himself. The beauty—and perhaps audacity—of the biblical invitation to know God emerges from the fact that he has made himself imminent in part that he might relate personally and even intimately with his creation.

Since the object of revelation is of a different nature, discussion about a book of revelation must take into account these differences. A Christian who is either inspecting the Qur'an or conversing with someone under its influence must understand that what is revealed in the Qur'an is a will not a person. This fact can often be obscured by what superficially appears to be shared concepts about God, hu-

---

7   The Islamic Foundation, *Christian Mission and Islamic Da'wah: Proceedings of the Chambesy Dialogue Consultation* (Leicester, UK: The Islamic Foundation, 1982), 47–48. During the proceedings of the Chambesy Dialogue Consultation, Isma'il al-Furuqi interjected the quote above in response to the Christian claim that God reveals himself.

8   Consider Hebrews 1:1–2, which demonstrates that God has spoken through prophets and through the Son. Likewise, John's prologue includes a clear reference to the incarnate Word as the one who has communicated God's glory to humanity. Colossians 1:15–20 also references Christ as the image of the invisible God, making the knowledge of God available to creation.

manity's role as his subjects, and how to please him. Yet upon closer inspection, significant differences emerge beginning with the first chapter of the Qur'an.

AL-FATIHA AS OVERVIEW

If you pick up the Qur'an and begin reading on the first page, you will encounter the short seven-verse sura known as *Al-Fatiha*: "The Opening." This sura is recorded in its entirety at the beginning of this chapter. Despite its brevity, *Al-Fatiha* provides a fitting and formative introduction to the rest of the Qur'an.[9] It is fitting in that the content of *Al-Fatiha* is repeated, expanded upon, and explained throughout the rest of the Qur'an. It is formative in that these verses are recited by the Muslim community multiple times per day as a component of their ritual prayers. As such, investigation of the contents of *Al-Fatiha* provides insight into what the Qur'an intends to discuss and what the Qur'an claims to reveal.

The Bismillah *— In the Name of God*

The first verse of this chapter is so commonly used within Islamic practice that it has its own shorthand reference: the Bismillah. The invocation of God's name appears at the beginning of each of the Qur'an's 114 chapters with chapter 9 being the sole exception. It is common practice among Muslims to recite the Bismillah at the beginning of any undertaking as a plea for God's help.[10] Even such a seemingly mundane task as turning on the ignition in one's car is often accompanied by an appeal to God's name. Yet it is interesting to consider the fact that despite the regularity of invoking the name of

---

9   Muhammad Abdel Haleem, *Understanding the Qur'an: Themes and Style* (New York: I. B. Tauris, 2019), 15. Having established that *al-Fatiha* is recited multiple times throughout the daily ritual prayers of a faithful Muslim, Haleem goes on to state the importance of this sura for its content, writing, "[*al-Fatiha*] embodies the essence of Islam, which is *tawhid* (oneness of God)."

10   Abdullah Yusuf Ali, *The Qur'an: Text, Translation, and Commentary* (Elmhurst, NY: Tahrike Tarsile Qur'an, 2005), 14n19, writes, "the formula [of the Bismillah] . . . is repeated at the beginning of every act by the Muslim who dedicates his life to God, and whose hope is in His Mercy."

God, the Qur'an nowhere provides the reader with a personal name by which God might be known.

To those unfamiliar with the Arabic language, it is common to mistake the word Allah as the personal name of the Islamic deity. Yet formally, Allah is merely a word formed by attaching the definite article (*al*) to the generic Arabic word for god (*ilaha*).[11] Thus, Allah is typically not understood as a personal name.[12] It is simply a way of referring to the one and only God.

The idea of God's names has at times been a contentious issue within Islamic theology. For instance, Qur'an 17:110 instructs the reader to "call on God or call on the merciful—whichever you call on, to Him (belong) the best names." Prompted by this verse, many early Muslims began to collect and compile all the qur'anic and traditional names used to refer to God. The result was a list of ninety-nine names used in reference to or description of God. Such a collection, however, caused early Islamic scholars to fear introducing divisions and distinctions into the concept of God, thus compromising the divine unity of God's essence.[13]

Though it is common today to see Muslims thumbing through a chain of prayer beads which bear the ninety-nine divine "names," the names are more properly understood as "characteristics" or "attributes" of God. Taken as "characteristics" of God, then, the plurality of "names" does no violence to the Islamic doctrine of God's undivided singularity (*tawhid*). Through the repetition of *al-Fatiha*, Muslims begin their prayers, the act of reading the Qur'an, and engaging in daily tasks with an appeal to the name of God for help. At the same

---

11   Daniel Madigan, "Themes and Topics," in *The Cambridge Companion to the Qur'an*, ed. Jane McAuliffe, 79–95 (New York: Cambridge University Press, 2006), 80.

12   There are, of course, exceptions to this statement. For instance, Muhammad Abdel Haleem, *Understanding the Qur'an: Themes and Style* (New York: I. B. Tauris, 2011), 16, writes, "In Islam, 'Allah' is the name of God in the absolute sense, the only 'personal' name. All other 'beautiful' names are adjectives and attributes." Even with this cautious recognition of the absolute nature of Allah, however, there is no indication that Allah functions as intimately as the name YHWH does in the Bible.

13   John Kaltner and Younus Mirza, *The Bible and the Qur'an* (New York: Bloomsbury, 2018), 51.

time, the very recognition that God's personal name is unknown reinforces God's total transcendence and maintains the separation between God and humanity.

The Compassionate and the Merciful

Moving on to the second phrase of *al-Fatiha,* the reader encounters two references to God repeatedly used throughout the Qur'an: the compassionate (*ar-Rahman*) and merciful (*ar-Rahim*). The Qur'an applies the first of these two references—*ar-Rahman*—only to God. In light of the unique application of this word to God, Islamic scholar David Burrell notes that most Muslims take *ar-Rahman* "to be the most expressive name of Allah."[14] The phrase, *ar-Rahman ar-Rahim,* appears twice in *al-Fatiha,* foreshadowing its centrality as a reference to God throughout the rest of the Qur'an.

God's compassion and mercy are exhibited and exemplified throughout the rest of the Qur'an. Most centrally, this compassion is expressed by providing specific instructions on how to obey his will. For example, when Satan (*Shaytan*) causes Adam and his wife to slip from paradise, they are sent down to the earth as a result. Yet the Qur'an records God's compassionate act of communicating instructions to Adam regarding how to repent and find forgiveness. Such compassionate instruction displayed in Qur'an 2:37: "Then Adam received certain words from his Lord, and He turned to him (in forgiveness). Surely He—He is the One who turns (in forgiveness), the Compassionate [*ar-Rahim*]."[15] In other words, in response to the human need for direction following their fall from paradise, God provides words of guidance as evidence of his compassion. Therefore,

---

14   David Burrell, "Naming the Names of God: Muslims, Jews, and Christians," *Theology Today* 47, no. 1 (1990): 24.

15   It is worth noting that the two words we've encountered, *ar-Rahman* and *ar-Rahim,* are built from the same root, causing translations to differ over what the most appropriate English translation should be. A. J. Droge, *The Qur'an: A New Annotated Translation* (Bristol, CT: Equinox, 2013), 1n1, notes that, "There is no great difference in meaning between 'merciful' (Ar. *Rahman*) and 'compassionate' (Ar. *Rahim*)." Thus, though the reader may encounter translations that prefer to use alternative words, the lexical difference is more or less negligible.

even as these first names of God—*ar-Rahman* and *ar-Rahim*—exhibit his compassion, they reinforce the Qur'an's central concern to reveal the will of God and the instructions on how to submit to it. In the Qur'an, God is compassionate and merciful as he reveals guidance and reminders of his will.

Praise (Be) to the Lord, Creator of the Worlds

As noted by Fazlur Rahman's comments in the introduction to this chapter, the Qur'an is satisfied in assuming Allah to be the God who sovereignly stands behind and above all things in creation. Allah is the creator and sustainer. He is worthy of the worship and submission of his creatures by virtue of these qualities. Thus, the relationship between God the creator and humankind as his creation is that of a sovereign and his subjects. Humanity is obligated to submit to God and to render unto him praise and worship in light of his creative power and work.

Reinforcing and reminding the reader that God is the creator, the Qur'an includes several accounts of God's act of creation. As is characteristic of other narrative sections of the Qur'an, details of the account are rather sparse. This paucity of detail emphasizes the fact that, for the Qur'an, God's power exhibited in creating is the foundation for his exercise of supreme authority over the universe. For instance, Qur'an 7:54 states,

> Surely your Lord is God, who created the heavens and the earth in six days. Then He mounted the throne. The night covers the day, which it pursues urgently, and the sun, and the moon, and the starts are subjected, (all) by his command. Is it not (a fact) that to Him (belong) the creation and the command? Blessed (be) God, Lord of the worlds.

This particular verse not only reinforces God's total authority over his creation, it refers to God as the "Lord of the worlds," thus repeating the same phrase found in *al-Fatiha*.

Other accounts of creation likewise establish God as the sovereign over his creation by depicting him mounting his throne and reigning over the universe,[16] establishing the night and day and hanging the sun and the moon,[17] and creating humanity from various materials.[18] The most important aspect of each of the Qur'an's creation accounts, however, is God's dominion and authority over all created things. Islamic scholar Mark Anderson includes the qur'anic attention to God as creator as one of six most central images that the Qur'an employs to describe God. These images are distinct from the "names" the Qur'an gives to God in that the images establish God's role in relation to creation. According to Anderson, the Qur'an presents God as master, judge, creator, king, guide, and deliverer.[19] Each of these images—creator included—reinforces the role of sovereign authority that the Qur'an invests in God alone by its use of the phrase, "Creator of the worlds."

Master of the Day of Judgment

A fourth aspect of the qur'anic content of revelation is the reality of impending eschatological judgment. Again, the first verses of *al-Fatiha* introduce the idea, though the coming Day of Judgment will prove to be a recurring theme throughout the rest of the Qur'an. Connected to the Qur'an's conception of God, this phrase here in *al-Fatiha* establishes God himself as the final arbiter who will mete out judgment on the last day. Indeed, God in the Qur'an is the master over the eschatological fate of all those who will pass under his judgment.

Though the Qur'an consistently references God's role as the final arbiter of judgment, the event of judgment itself is a central aspect of what the Qur'an intends to reveal. Throughout the Qur'an readers are warned to consider their lives in light of the coming Day of Judgment. In the words of Daniel Madigan, "The Qur'an is replete with cataclysmic details of the end of the world."[20] Madigan continues, "No one, we are assured repeatedly, will escape death, and so it is

---

16   Qur'an 57:4.
17   Qur'an 21:33.
18   Qur'an 3:49 (dust); 21:30 (water); 15:26–34 (clay/mud); 16:3 (semen).
19   Mark Anderson, *The Qur'an in Context* (Downers Grove, IL: IVP Academic, 2016), 57.
20   Madigan, "Text and Topics," 90.

understood that at a certain point everything will perish. . . . Then all will be brought to life once more and gathered for judgment before the throne of God."[21]

Moreover, as the Qur'an warns of the coming Day of Judgment, it does so in terms that are both future-looking and unpredictably immanent. Mark Anderson lists Qur'an 74, 82, 96, 102, and 111 as being particularly acute examples of qur'anic warning that, "the eschaton may at any point break through into the here and now to obliterate the heedless."[22] Thus, as *al-Fatiha* introduces the reader to judgment in the first few verses of the Qur'an, it presents the reader with another aspect of qur'anic revelation. From this first sura onward, eschatological judgment will become a regular reminder that all people will be resurrected prior to facing divine judgment regarding how they lived their lives.

You We Serve, and You We Seek for Help
A fifth aspect of the Qur'an's revelation that emerges within *al-Fatiha* is the responsibility of human beings to serve/worship Allah and to depend upon his help. Since *al-Fatiha* has first recognized God as the creator of the worlds, it naturally progresses to hold human beings accountable for taking an appropriate posture of worship, service, and submission to this God.

One noteworthy aspect of this particular section of *al-Fatiha* is the Arabic word that is translated "serve" above. The root of this word occurs some 275 times throughout the Qur'an.[23] Depending upon context, this word group can refer to either worship or service/slavery.[24] As it occurs here in *al-Fatiha*, translators are justified to

---

21 Madigan, "Text and Topics," 90.
22 Anderson, *The Qur'an in Context*, 57.
23 See the helpful qur'anic research website, *The Qur'anic Arabic Corpus*, http://corpus.quran.com/search.jsp?q=root%3Aعبد. This website provides a searchable database of every occurrence of words, roots, and stems throughout the Qur'an.
24 For example, in Qur'an 4:118, Satan threatens that, "I shall indeed take an obligatory portion of your servants." Here it is perhaps more natural to read the word as a reference to servants or slaves due to the presence of the possessive pronoun. Both Droge, *The Qur'an*, and Ali, *The Qur'an*, translate this word as "servants/slaves" rather than worshippers.

render this verb in English either as "we serve" or as "we worship."[25] Such linguistic flexibility reinforces the conceptual proximity of the Qur'an's teaching on servitude and worship: a servant of Allah is at one and the same time a worshipper of Allah.

Throughout its pages, the Qur'an reveals humans as those who are created by God for the purposes of serving and worshipping him. As those under God's sovereign authority, the proper posture for a human to take within God's world is submission. The concept of submission is intimately ingrained within Islam, to the extent that it provides the etymological root from which one forms the related Arabic words Islam and Muslim.[26]

Therefore, one of the central aspects of the Islamic doctrine of revelation is the recognition that humans are servants of God who are to worship him by submitting to his will. The content of his will is disclosed to the reader of the Qur'an as divine guidance. This leads us to *al-Fatiha's* sixth contribution to the doctrine of revelation: guidance to the straight path.

Guide Us to the Straight Path

The Qur'an regularly refers to itself as guidance from God. One clear example of the Qur'an's self-description as guidance can be seen in Qur'an 16:89, which states, "We have sent down on you the Book as an explanation for everything, and as a guidance and mercy, and as good news for those who submit." This guidance is understood as the disclosure of God's will, a register of ethical expectations for

---

25 For consistency throughout this book, I have chosen to default to the clear and readable translation provided by Droge, *The Qur'an*. However, upon consulting other English translations, such as the well-known Ali, *The Qur'an*, 14, chooses to translate Qur'an 1:5 as, "Thee do we worship, and Thine aid we seek."

26 The Arabic root from which both Islam and Muslim derive is *slm*. Though it certainly carries a more formal, religious meaning when it is used to refer to the religion of Islam, as a noun, Islam can be translated as "submission." Similarly, the word Muslim carries religious freight beyond its mere etymology, but it can be translated as "a submitted one." For example, see Naqi Elmi, *Does the Qur'an (Koran) Really Say That? Truths and Misconceptions about Islam* (Bloomington, IN: Archway, 2019), 5, who states, "The word *Islam* does not refer to any person, nation, or time, just to *submission* and *surrender*" (italics original).

those who seeking to live according to God's will, and as a reminder of the things that humans are quick to forget.

In chapter 3 we will concern ourselves with tracing some of the specific ethical teachings contained in the Qur'an. However, for the current purpose of exploring a more general doctrine of revelation, it suffices to note that the Qur'an intends to be received as the means by which God guides believers to "the straight path."[27] In his commentary on this verse, A. J. Droge describes the straight path as "the revealed 'path' of religious truth and right conduct."[28] In other words, this path provides ethical and spiritual guidance to the reader as the instructions for how to live according to God's revealed will.

Finally, al-Fatiha describes the straight path as the path that God has blessed. Similar promises of blessing for the devout Muslim are pervasive throughout the Qur'an, connecting ethical living to divine favor. While the Qur'an beckons Muslims to dutifully live out their roles as servants of God, it also holds out promise of reward and blessing for the faithful. Furthermore, this straight path stands in contrast to paths which lead people astray and paths upon which God pours out his anger. In this way, al-Fatiha concludes by petitioning God to guide those who are submitted to his will and to pour out blessings upon those who follow the straight path.

SUMMARY OF THE QUR'ANIC DOCTRINE OF REVELATION

The first chapter of the Qur'an, al-Fatiha, not only opens the Qur'an, but it establishes the Qur'an itself as the vehicle of God's guidance and the mechanism by which God's will is revealed. When a person receives such revelation from God, submission to it is the expected response and posture. And the proper result of such submission is attentive living according to the Qur'an's teaching, following it as a guide leading down the straight path.

---

27   The straight path is a reference to a way of life that is characterized as being submitted to God's will and walking in accordance with it. In Arabic, the phrase "the straight path" is *as-sirat al-mustaqim,* and it features regularly in discussions surrounding Islamic ethics.

28   Droge, *The Qur'an,* 1n7.

The essence of the Islamic doctrine of revelation, then, is that the Qur'an reveals the will of God to creatures who are obligated to follow it. In so doing, the Qur'an refers to itself as serving two primary roles: offering guidance and providing reminders. As seen above, guidance is requested from God in *al-Fatiha*, and the Qur'an presents itself as God's merciful answer to this request. Additionally, it is important to note that elsewhere the Qur'an identifies itself as a book of reminder.[29]

In his commentary on one such instance, Qur'an scholar A. J. Droge notes that the word "reminder" as it appears in the Qur'an refers specifically to the Qur'an as God's mechanism for helping humans "[keep] something before the mind by repeatedly calling it to attention, with the sense of 'admonition,' 'exhortation,' and even 'warning.'"[30] In other words, the Qur'an records the reminders of God's commands that humans are wont to forget.

Furthermore, the presentation of the Qur'an as a reminder of God's ways reinforces the basic Islamic conception of humanity as being inherently forgetful and negligent of the ways of God. As Islamic scholar Seyyed Hossein Nasr states, "Without the aid of God man cannot discover by himself the way of salvation, the 'Straight Path.' Man needs revelation because . . . he is by nature negligent and forgetful; he is by nature imperfect. Therefore he needs to be reminded."[31] As a result of this Islamic understanding of human weakness, the Qur'an presents itself as the answer by providing divine guidance toward the straight path and also by prompting remembrance of teachings that humans tend to forget or set aside.

While the Bible certainly makes similar claims and provides guidance and insight into God's will, it also points beyond these secondary aspects of revelation. In other words, the Bible does not merely reveal the will of God. Instead, a Christian understanding of

---

29 For instance, in the midst of a call to belief and righteous deeds, Qur'an 3:58 says, "We recite it to you from the signs and the wise reminder." See also 7:63; 69; 16:43–44.

30 Droge, *The Qur'an*, 36n85. In this note, Droge is commenting on Qur'an 3:58—the verse cited in the previous footnote.

31 Seyyed Hossein Nasr, *Ideals and Realities of Islam* (San Francisco: Aquarian, 1994), 22.

revelation contends that what is revealed—through the prophets, the Bible, and ultimately through the incarnation—is God himself.[32] Before concluding this chapter, then, we must consider some of the ramifications of this essential distinction.

BIBLICAL REVELATION:
MORE THAN GOD'S WILL

Since this book intends to explain the Qur'an to a Christian audience, it is helpful to highlight some of the conceptual divergence between the Qur'an and the Bible at this essential juncture of understanding the content of revelation. What one believes revelation to reveal will ultimately shape and direct one's response to that revelation.

From a Christian perspective, it has become apparent that the doctrine of revelation according to the Qur'an stops short of what the Bible claims to reveal. As the previous section concluded, the Bible teaches that God has actually revealed himself, and has done so in the most intimate of ways. The book of Exodus shows God entrusting his personal name to a people who would be called to represent him before the nations. Likewise, through the incarnation of the Son and the sending of the Spirit, this God has revealed himself as a triune God. This self-revelation is tied to God's activity in the Gospel, which reveals him to be a God who is reconciling his creatures to himself.

Therefore, as God reveals himself, he does so through the central message of Scripture: the Gospel of God's covenant faithfulness. As one theologian, Michael Bird, states, "The Gospel is a theocentric revelation. It is a pronouncement, a proclamation, a publication of good tidings about God."[33] Bird goes on to conclude, "Evidently knowledge of God begins with knowledge of the Gospel."[34] Thus for us to distinguish the biblical teaching of revelation from the qur'anic concept is not merely splitting hairs. Rather it strikes at an essential

---

32 One especially helpful articulation of the idea that a Christian doctrine of revelation concerns God's self-revelation can be found in Michael Bird, *Evangelical Theology* (Grand Rapids: Zondervan, 2013), 164–71.

33 Bird, *Evangelical Theology,* 165.

34 Bird, *Evangelical Theology*, 165.

difference between Islam and Christianity. The following section will briefly consider some of the ways that the biblical concept of revelation diverges from what the Qur'an claims to reveal.

THE NAME OF GOD IN THE BIBLE

Like Muslims, Christians—and Jews—are cognizant of the importance of God's name. Within the biblical story, however, God's name is revealed in the context of his personal interaction with Moses, and as a precursor to God uniting himself with all of Israel in covenant. The personal name of God—YHWH—is intimately connected to the account of the Exodus. In this narrative, God extends his prior promises to Abraham, Isaac, and Jacob by establishing his covenant with the entire nation of Israel. Israel is instructed to remember YHWH's name, and in so doing, they are reminded of their unique covenant relationship to this God.

The reader encounters this story beginning in Exodus 3, where Moses encounters a bush that is burning but is not consumed. From the bush, Moses hears a voice, and it commissions Moses back to Egypt in order to liberate the Hebrews from their oppressors. This strange phenomenon is the setting, recorded in Exodus 3:14–15, in which God revels his personal name to Moses,

> God said to Moses, "I Am Who I Am." And he said, "Say to the people, I am [YHWH] has sent me to you." God also said to Moses, "Say this to the people of Israel: 'The Lord [YHWH], the God of your fathers, the God of Abraham, the God of Isaac, and the God of Jacob, has sent me to you.' This is my name forever, and thus I am to be remembered throughout all generations."

In this encounter, YHWH provides his personal name to his servant Moses and to the people with whom he will make his covenant after the exodus event. This name indicates his character, but it also instantiates a unique relationship between the Israelites and the God of the universe.

The importance of the divine name is made even more personal in the New Testament. Not a few scholars and pastors have pointed to the shocking manner in which Jesus instructs his followers to pray in Matthew 6 and also in Luke 11. The fact that Jesus encourages his followers to address God as "Father" is scandalously inappropriate for a Muslim considering how to conceive of God. Even for Muslims who contend that God can be known through his revelations in the Qur'an, the idea that he might be intimately known in filial terms is far removed from the Islamic understanding of humans relating to God as servants relate to masters.

In fact, though some authors have compared *al-Fatiha* to the Lord's Prayer, Islamic teaching departs from the material in the Lord's prayer at the point of the initial address: "Our Father." For example, Muhammad Abdel Haleem writes,

> A Muslim would view the content of the *Fatiha* as being acceptable to Christians. There are, however, elements in the Lord's Prayer that pose difficulties for a Muslim nurtured on the *Fatiha*, which is universal. "Our" limits God to a particular community and to a particular relationship of fatherhood, compared to "the Sustaining Lord of all the Worlds" not the Lord of the Muslims or the Arabs. And although "father" is a very intimate term to Christians, Muslims would not speak of God as a "father" or a "son."[35]

Thus, even with the extensive list of attributes of God that one might collect throughout the Qur'an, God is not conceived of as a being to be known intimately. Rather, he is a God to be obeyed, served, and praised by virtue of his sovereign power as creator and his eternal worth.

Furthermore, at the end of Jesus's ministry, after his death and resurrection, Jesus refers to the divine name in a commissioning that is not unlike Moses's commissioning. In Matthew 28:19, Jesus instructs his disciples to go and make disciples of all nations, and then

---

35   Haleem, *Understanding the Qur'an*, 25.

to baptize them into the name of the Father, the Son, and the Holy Spirit. By bearing this triune name, Christians testify to the fact that they believe God is both transcendent and imminent, and that he has condescended to dwell among his people, making it possible to be known by them and among them.

This vision of God dwelling amidst his people comes to its full expression in the final vision of biblical hope. In John's eschatological vision recorded in Revelation 21:3–4, the Christian knowledge of God is most clearly seen as immediate, personal, and intimate as one reads, "Behold, the dwelling place of God is with man. He will dwell with them, and they will be his people, and God himself will be with them as their God. He will wipe away every tear from their eyes, and death shall be no more, neither shall there be mourning, nor crying, nor pain anymore, for the former things have passed away." Such a vision and expectation of God's immediate presence dwelling amidst his creation is absent from the Qur'an's depiction of paradise.

BIBLICAL COMPASSION AND MERCY

The immediacy of God's presence among his people also affects how the Bible presents God's mercy and compassion. In contrast to the Qur'an's view of God's compassion and mercy, the Bible connects God's compassionate love for his creation with his willingness to condescend and reveal himself personally. The Qur'an's message appears similar at first glance, because it involves God's compassionate revelation of his will and merciful provision of guidance to the otherwise-wandering human race. However, since God sends down this revelation of his will as mercy rather than coming down as mercy himself, the conceptual distance is far greater than what it originally appears.

Again, evidence for this distinction comes from the Exodus account, among other places. Prior to God speaking to Moses from the burning bush, Exodus records an account that reveals God's compassion and mercy, and which compels him to draw near to his people. Exodus 2:23–25 provides insight into what prompted God's encounter with Moses as it reads,

> During those many days the king of Egypt died, and the
> people of Israel groaned because of their slavery and cried
> out for help. Their cry for rescue from slavery came up to
> God. And God heard their groaning, and God remembered
> his covenant with Abraham, with Isaac, and with Jacob.
> God saw the people of Israel—and God knew.

The verbs employed in this passage indicate God's intimate knowledge of his people's situation. His "coming down" emphasizes his willingness to intimately enter into and relieve the suffering they were enduring as an expression of his compassion and mercy.

The ensuing exodus from Egypt and eventual deliverance to the land of promise is explicitly connected to God's compassion for his purposes and his people in Psalm 78. In this psalm, Asaph recounts the Lord's faithfulness to deliver his people from bondage and to provide a means of atoning for their yet-sinful hearts. In Psalm 78:37–38 he states this baldly, writing, "Their heart was not steadfast toward him; they were not faithful to his covenant. Yet he, being compassionate, atoned for their iniquity and did not destroy them; he restrained his anger often and did not stir up all his wrath." God's compassion in the Bible leads him to atone for their sins.

Furthermore, the Old Testament explicitly and repeatedly states that it is God's purpose to dwell among his people. The proximity of God's presence—specifically his righteousness and holiness—to a stiff-necked, sin-stained people necessitates the meticulous process of substitutionary blood-wrought atonement described in the Pentateuch.[36] Yet the Bible is clear in repeatedly affirming that it is YHWH himself who purposes to dwell among his people. Thus it is unsurprising that the New Testament continues the theme of God's presence with his people.

That God's compassion would result in his presence among his people is perhaps most visible in the New Testament through the

---

36   See Exod. 29:45–46; Lev. 9:22–24; 16:3–17:11–14; 23:26–32.

incarnation and sending of the Holy Spirit.[37] Such an immediate experience with the very presence of God is characteristic of the biblical story and hope, yet intimate relationship with God remains outside of the qur'anic teaching and expectation.

BIBLICAL JUDGMENT, PRAISE, AND GUIDANCE

As discussed above, *al-Fatiha* reveals God's will in connection with the promises of blessings and the warnings of judgment that pervade the Qur'an. Additionally, the Qur'an establishes that it is God's will that humanity should praise and worship God, as he alone is the creator of worlds. In order to do so, the Qur'an provides guidance and reminder of how to walk on the straight path of adherence to God's will.

In these three ways, then, a Christian might notice that the Bible appears to exhibit significant overlap with the Qur'an. The Bible establishes God as the creator who is worthy of human praise and worship in places such as Psalm 33, which calls for praise to be offered to God who has made everything by the power of his word. Likewise, one reads reminders to recall the commands of God, such as Deuteronomy 4:9, which states, "Only take care, and keep your soul diligently, lest you forget the things that your eyes have seen, and lest they depart from your heart all the days of your life. Make them known to your children and your children's children." And throughout Scripture God guides his people to walk before him.

Yet, as seen above, the Bible goes beyond merely promising judgment for bad behavior. The Qur'an presents instructions on how to find and walk the straight path. In so doing, it assumes human ability to follow the instructions sufficiently enough to find their way. However, the Bible reveals the law as the straight path in

---

37   The "tabernacle" of the Old Testament was the locus of God's presence dwelling with his people as the objects of his compassion. Such language reappears in John 1:14, "The Word became flesh and dwelt among us." The word that is translated "dwelt" is the verbal form of the Greek word that the LXX uses to translate the word "tabernacle" in the Old Testament. Likewise, this same word appears in the eschatological vision of Revelation 21:3, "And I heard a loud voice from the throne saying, 'Behold, the dwelling place of God is with man. He will dwell with them and they will be his people, and God himself will be with them as their God.'"

order to demonstrate human inability to guide themselves back. For instance, as Paul reflects on the role of the law in its biblical context, he is convinced that the instructions given in the law prove only to expose human sin and depravity. For example, he writes in Romans 7:10–11, "The very commandment that promised life proved to be death to me. For sin, seizing and opportunity through the commandment, deceived me and through it killed me." Thus, the law simply lures human sinfulness into view in order to expose our inability to live according to God's ways on our own.

The difference, then, between the Qur'an as an ethical guide and the Bible's ethical guidance is that the Qur'an is optimistic about human ability to follow its guidance, offer pleasing worship, and avoid divine judgment. The Bible, on the other hand, presents a catalogue of ways that humanity has fallen short—and always will fall short—of perfect obedience and pleasing worship. The Bible provides its ethical teaching in order to confront the reader with his or her own failings, and to cause them to cry out for God's mercy and grace in the Gospel to do that which fallen humans are incapable of accomplishing for themselves.

CONSIDERATIONS FOR PRACTICE: REVELATION AND THE REAL-LIFE MUSLIM

This book is intended to introduce a Christian reader to the Qur'an with an eye to understanding their Muslim friends and neighbors. By necessity, much of the investigation will take the more formal approach to the material illustrated above in order to orient the Christian to the Qur'an and its teaching as objectively as possible. However, it is important to step aside briefly at the conclusion of this chapter to recognize that an academic study of Islamic teaching is only part of understanding and engaging Muslims.

In reality, all formal theology is finally embedded, embodied, and expressed in particular person or community. As a result, one might encounter those who describe themselves as Muslims but who live out their Islamic convictions in ways that deviate from the academic or traditional expressions of Islam and the teachings of the Qur'an.

Below are a conversation-deepening questions that can help you apply the information gleaned above in conversations over a fence, over a meal, or over an open Bible.

What Does the Qur'an Reveal About Knowing God?

As noted briefly above, within popular expressions of Islam, many Muslims believe that God has ninety-nine names derived from the attributes given to him throughout the Qur'an. Many Muslims today would also see no problem in viewing these names of God as ways of actually knowing God. Likewise, some of your Muslim friends might even assume that "Allah" is God's proper, personal name despite of the discussion above regarding the etymology of Allah.[38] In spite of the questions raised by Islamic theology and philosophy regarding how God's attributes relate to his essence without compromising his singularity, most of your Muslim friends will simply take the Qur'an's descriptive language at face value.

However, even Muslims who claim to know God through his attributes will eventually depart from the Christian claim that God has revealed himself intimately and interpersonally. In other words, many Muslims read the Qur'an as providing revelations about God's personal qualities and will, yet not as a means of inviting humanity into an interpersonal relationship with a heavenly father.[39]

In conversation with your Muslim neighbor, then, you might find it fruitful to ask what God has revealed in the Qur'an. This allows you to hear from your friend's perspective what they expect to find when they pick up and read their holy book. Likewise, it can provide

---

38 Haleem, *Understanding the Qur'an*, 16. Even the Islamic scholar Haleem writes, "In Islam, 'Allah' is the name of God in the absolute sense, the only 'personal' name. All other 'beautiful' names are adjectives or attributes." Though Haleem includes "personal" in scare quotes, many practicing Muslims would acknowledge that Allah is a proper name for God rather than a title for the one and only divine being.

39 See chapter 9 in Gabriel Said Reynolds, *Allah: God in the Qur'an* (New Haven, CT: Yale University Press, 2020), 203–32. Reynolds shows significant similarity between the personal attributes of God in the Qur'an and in the Bible. However, he concludes the chapter by citing Fazlur Rahman's contention that the Qur'an admits nothing of God that would make it proper to view him as relating to creation as a Father relates to his children.

opportunity to explain the biblical concept of revelation is directly connected to the Christian claim that God has revealed himself—most clearly in Jesus Christ, the incarnate Son.[40]

What Does the Qur'an Reveal About Relating to God?

Regardless of whether a Muslim claims to know God or merely to know God's will, the Islamic doctrine of *tawhid* is explicitly incompatible with the biblical God's trinitarian nature.[41] One result of this conception of God, is that the Qur'an also rejects the idea that God relates to creation in the intimate manner described in the Bible. The God of the Qur'an is the sovereign creator and master of the universe. Yet, he will not be addressed as Father, nor is he a God that created in order to develop a loving relationship with his creatures.

To the contrary, one of the indicators we have in the Bible as to why God created us is the often-repeated declaration that he intends to dwell with his people as their God.[42] For our Muslim friends, the idea that the perfect, holy, and righteous creator intends to dwell in the midst of his people is as foreign as it is shocking. Yet the Bible repeatedly and unambiguously reveals a God who, though ontologically transcendent, is relational, present, and imminent.

This imminence is, again, perhaps nowhere clearer than in the incarnation of the Son in John 1:14, which states, "And the Word became flesh and dwelt among us, and we have seen his glory, the glory of the only Son from the Father, full of grace and truth." In conversation with Muslims, then, it might be fruitful to ask what the Qur'an reveals about how humanity is supposed to relate to God. Pointing them to the places in Scripture that show God's stated declaration to dwell among his people can indicate a more personal knowledge of God than admitted by the Qur'an. Yet God's own declared intention to be "God with us" produces significant complications for the qur'anic remedy to human

---

40   For instance, see passages such as John 1:14–18; 1 Cor. 4:6; Heb. 1:1–2.

41   Isma'il al-Faruqi, "Tawhid: The Quintessence of Islam," *The Journal of South Asian and Middle Eastern Studies* 8 no. 4 (Summer, 1985), 9.

42   See for example: Gen. 17:7–8; Exod. 6:7; Ezra 34:24; 36:28; Jer. 30:22; 32:38; Rev. 21:3.

sinfulness. If the holy and perfect God intends to draw near, impurity and imperfection cannot remain in humanity.

What Does the Qur'an Reveal About How God Forgives Sin?

In light of the preceding discussion, it is clear that when a Christian engages in explaining the Gospel to a Muslim neighbor, the discussion will inevitably encounter different understandings of revelation. The qur'anic God does not create in order reveal himself to his creation, nor to dwell amongst his creatures. Rather, the qur'anic God creates in order to test humanity to see whether they will submit to his will or not.[43] Moreover, when the qur'anic God wills to demonstrate his compassion, he does not come as a savior to rescue his people. Rather, he sends guidance and reminder so people can rescue themselves.

Yet, if this is God's revealed purpose—to be "God with us"—the implications of our imperfection are profound. As less-than-righteous creatures, the Bible presents humans as being in need of more than guidance and reminder in order to be made suitable for the holy and righteous presence of God. Humanity is in need of a savior who can provide an unsullied righteousness to a sin-stained and imperfect people.

Thus, a question that naturally arises from this understanding of what the Qur'an reveals might be, "Have you followed God's will perfectly? If not, what does the Qur'an reveal about how God forgives sin?" The Qur'an contends throughout its pages that repentance is sufficient for God to overlook and forgive human sin. However, the Qur'an stops short of explaining how God's righteous wrath against sin can be satisfied while yet providing merciful rescue for sinners. In other words, the biblical formula for atonement in which God's justice and mercy can be satisfied through a substitutionary sacrifice is absent from the pages of the Qur'an.[44]

---

43 Qur'an 2:155: "We shall indeed test you with some (experience) of fear and hunger, and loss of wealth and lives and fruits. But give good news to the patient, who say, when a smiting smites them, 'Surely we (belong) to God, and surely to Him we return.'"

44 For an exhaustive treatment of the Qur'an's teaching on "atonement" for sin compared with the biblical concept, see Matthew Bennett, *Narratives in Conflict: Atonement in Hebrews and the Qur'an* (Eugene, OR: Pickwick, 2019).

CONCLUSION: DIFFERENT
EXPECTATIONS OF REVELATION

This chapter has explored the concept of revelation provided by the Qur'an. Primarily, it has concluded that the Qur'an reveals God's will and a variety of attributes that are understood to more or less describe God. Though there is certainly conceptual overlap in what is revealed in the Bible and the Qur'an, the Bible is keen to reveal God himself in a way that the Qur'an does not. The Qur'an's reticence to introduce God intimately and interpersonally is connected to the qur'anic doctrine of *tawhid*, which sets God apart from humanity in a more absolute sense than does the Bible. This distinction is most pronounced in the fact that the Bible repeatedly presents God's intention to be "God with us."

What the Qur'an most clearly and consistently reveals is the will of God. The Qur'an presents this revelation of God's will as a merciful means of guidance and reminder for the faithful believer. In order to inspect the specific content of God's will, the following chapter will unpack some of the Qur'an's central themes and teachings. This survey will help a Christian to understand some of the practices and convictions exhibited by their Muslim neighbor and where they arise from the teaching of the Qur'an.

3

THE INSTRUCTION OF THE QUR'AN

*Those who have believed and done righteous deeds —
We shall indeed settle them in exalted rooms of the
Garden, through which rivers flow, there to remain.
Excellent is the reward of the doers [of righteous
deeds], who are patient and trust in their Lord.*

Qur'an 29:58–59

The Qur'an repeatedly refers to itself as a book of guidance[1] and remembrance,[2] having been sent down in clear Arabic[3] as an instruction for those who believe in Allah. The previous chapter explained that the Qur'an serves as God's merciful provision of a remedy for human weakness of will and memory. The Bible likewise presents God's moral law to the reader, however it repeatedly demonstrates that unredeemed humanity is incapable of perfect and pleasing obedience. Biblical law, then,

---

1   See examples in Qur'an 2:2–5; 12:111; 16:64; 20:123.
2   See examples in Qur'an 16:43; 20:124–26; 38:1, 8.
3   See examples in Qur'an 16:103; 26:195.

provides evidence of human imperfection and reveals humanity's need for a savior.

Contrary to such a pessimistic estimation of human morality, the Qur'an presents moral law and religious reminder from a more optimistic posture. In fact, the Qur'an purports to reveal God's will sufficiently for a human to respond appropriately to his instruction and live according to his will. The Qur'an refers to this human capacity for pleasing obedience by employing the word *taqwa*, which calls believers to exhibit a "God consciousness" that implies obedience and submission to God's commands.[4] In fact, Islamic scholar Fazlur Rahman views *taqwa* as the most important single term used by the Qur'an.[5]

Thus, though Muslims and Christians share similar ethical convictions, the role of ethics in each system functions differently. For the Christian, pleasing God by one's ethical living is possible only after regeneration through faith in Jesus as savior. For the Muslim, however, ethical living is the means to pleasing God and humanity is capable of following this law on their own strength and power. With this underlying distinction in mind, the present chapter will provide an overview of the specific themes and instructions revealed within the Qur'an.

THE QUR'AN: GOD'S GUIDANCE
AND HUMAN *TAQWA*

Throughout the Qur'an one finds the word *taqwa* and its cognates occurring more than 250 times, in order to call the reader to Godward piety.[6] For instance, Qur'an 33:70–71 states, "You who believe! Guard (yourselves) against [Lit. Have *taqwa* for] God, and speak a direct word. He will set right your deeds for you, and forgive you your sins. Whoever obeys God and His messenger has attained a great

---

4   Clinton Bennett, "A–Z Index of Key Terms and Concepts," in *The Bloomsbury Companion to Islamic Studies,* ed. Clinton Bennett, 327–74 (New York: Bloomsbury, 2015), 369.

5   Fazlur Rahman, *Major Themes of the Qur'an* (Chicago: Chicago University Press, 2009), 28.

6   John Esposito, ed., *The Oxford Dictionary of Islam* (New York: Oxford University Press, 2004), 314.

triumph." Likewise, Qur'an 19:72 promises, "Then We shall rescue the ones who guarded (themselves) [Lit. "who have *taqwa*"], and leave the evildoers in it (on) bended knees." Both of these passages exhibit the struggle to adequately represent the concept of *taqwa* in English, yet both also speak to the qur'anic promise that exercise of *taqwa* produces forgiveness and rescue for the faithful.[7]

Despite the difficulty in finding an English equivalent, the concept of *taqwa* can clearly be seen as the counterpart to the qur'anic doctrine of divine revelation. If God has mercifully revealed guidance to the straight path, it is incumbent upon human agents to exercise *taqwa* in pursuit of submitting to this revelation. In other words, the Qur'an views humanity as desperately in need of divine guidance, but also as capable of responding to it when it is granted.

Before proceeding, it may be helpful to recognize that both the Qur'an and subsequent Islamic theology are concerned with pious actions and with faithful belief. While the outward displays of piety can cause an observer to conclude that Islam is more concerned with outward action than inward faith, it would be an error to see it as merely a religion of orthopraxy. Therefore, as the following chapter inspects the specific instructions given by the Qur'an, we will first consider how *taqwa* results in right belief—orthopraxy—and then also the ways in which it results in right practice—orthopraxy.

QUR'ANIC INSTRUCTIONS ON BELIEF

The Qur'an is everywhere interested in calling the reader to a recognition that God is sovereign and worthy of worship and service. As the previous chapter indicated, the English words "worship" and "serve" can both express the meaning of the Arabic word *'abd*, which

---

7   The idea of *taqwa* has connections with guarding oneself against wrong action and also can be roughly equivalent to the idea of reverently fearing God. Various translations attempt to make sense of this word in English to varying degrees of success. See also Qur'an 49:13b, which represents the basic qur'anic teaching regarding moral effort when it records, "Surely the most honorable among you in the sight of God is the one among you who guards (himself) most. Surely God is knowing, aware." The phrase rendered "guards (himself) most" is a form of the word *taqwa* and could thus be rendered, "who has the most *taqwa*."

features in many of the Qur'an's instructions regarding how humanity is to relate to God.[8] Thus, an individual who wishes to exhibit *taqwa* in pious action must be prompted to such action by proper belief.[9]

Reflecting this faith-foundation for faithful action, the Qur'an concerns itself with instructing and guiding its audience to proper belief, as indicated by the opening verses of Qur'an 2:2–4, which state,

> This is the Book—(there is) no doubt about it—a guidance for the ones who guard (themselves) [*mutaqin* which is a nominal/adjectival form of *taqwa* that could be rendered "those who have *taqwa*"],[10] who believe in the unseen, and observe the prayer, and contribute from what We have provided them, and who believe in what has been sent down to you, and what was sent down before you, and they are certain of the Hereafter.

While this list includes several actions, it also refers to "belief in the unseen." Such belief is presented through various themes in the subsequent verses of the sura and expanded upon throughout the rest of the Qur'an. In order to properly exhibit *taqwa*, the Qur'an calls faithful Muslims to begin with their underlying beliefs which the Qur'an also appears to

---

8 This word may be familiar to readers with Muslim friends named Abdullah, which means "slave/servant/worshipper of God."

9 One such instance of *'abd* in connection with the concept of *taqwa* can be found in Qur'an 2:21, which states, "People! Serve [plural imperative of *'abd*] your Lord, who created you and those who were before you, so that you may guard (yourselves) [plural verbal form of *taqwa*]." According to Qur'an commentator, Abdullah Yusuf Ali, *The Qur'an: Text, Translation, and Commentary* (Elmhurst, NY: Tursile Tahrike Qur'an, 2005), 21n40, this verse connects the ideas of belief and works, saying, "Adoration is the act of highest and humblest reverence and worship. When you get into that relationship with God, Who is your Creator and Guardian, your faith produces works of righteousness."

10 See Ali, *Qur'an*, 17n26. "*Taqwa* and the verbs and nouns connected with the root, signify: (1) the fear of God which, according to the write of Proverbs (1.7) in the Old Testament is the beginning of Wisdom; (2) restraint, or guarding one's tongue, hand, and heart from evil; (3) hence righteousness, piety, good conduct. All these ideas are implied. In translation, only one or the other of these ideas can be indicated, according to the context."

include within the concept of *taqwa*. In fact, later Islamic theology has identified six major aspects of belief derived from the Qur'an's teaching that have come to be known as the six articles of faith.[11]

The Oneness of God: Tawhid

The previous chapter introduced the concept of *tawhid* as being essential to Islam, and it features as the first of six articles of faith in Islamic belief.[12] Despite the fact that the word *tawhid* is not found in the Qur'an, there is arguably no more important and formative concept within Islam than the oneness of God. Much like the Christian doctrine of the Trinity, later Islamic theological reflection on the Qur'an's teaching about God provides contemporary Muslims with the vocabulary of *tawhid* as shorthand for this essential belief.

One important eighteenth-century work that explains the doctrine of *tawhid* is Muhammad Ibn 'Abd al-Wahhab's *Book of Tawhid*. From al-Wahhab's work, three important categories of *tawhid* emerge.[13] First, belief in *tawhid* binds a believer to understand that God alone is the possessor of the attributes and characteristics mentioned in the Qur'an. Furthermore, these characteristics must not be likened to the characteristics of created things.[14] Second, *tawhid* includes recognition that "Allah is the sole Lord of creating, providing, originating, the One who nurtures all creation with its bounty, and nurtures some of His creation—they being the prophets and their followers—with

---

11   Ibn Taimiyah, *Sharh al-Aqeedat-il-Wasitiyah*, trans. Muhammad Khan (Riadh, KSA: Darussalam, 1996), 28. Ibn Taymiyah cites a hadith recorded in the collection of Muslim that records the following six articles of faith, then goes on to comment, "Unless one had faith in these six things in accordance with the Qur'an and the *Sunnah*, his faith will not acquire perfection."

12   Ibn Taimiyah, *Sharh Al-Aqeedat-il-Wasitiyah*, trans. Muhammad Khan (Riyadh, KSA: Darussalam, 1996), 28, lists the traditional six articles of faith as (1) faith in Allah (*tawhid*); (2) angels; (3) heavenly books (Torah, Psalms, Gospels, and Qur'an); (4) messengers of Allah (all the prophets, including biblical and extrabiblical prophets, culminating in Muhammad, the seal of the prophets); (5) life after death (resurrection); (6) good and bad destiny (fate or *qadr*).

13   'Allamah 'Abd al-Rahman al-Sa'di, *An Explanation of Muhammad ibn 'Abd al-Wahhab's Kitab al-Tawhid,* trans. Abu Khaliyl (Birmingham, UK: Al-Hidayah, 2003), 26–28.

14   Al-Sa'di, *Explanation*, 26–27. Sa'di designates this aspect *tawhid al-Asma' wa l-Sifat*—oneness of names and characteristics.

correct creed, beautiful morals, knowledge that provides benefit, and
righteous deeds."[15] And third, *tawhid* requires a believer to worship
God alone as the natural outworking of the first two categories of
tawhid.[16]

For a Christian considering this doctrine, one important qur'anic
passage leading to *tawhid* is found in Qur'an 4:171:

> People of the Book! Do not go beyond the limits in your re-
> ligion, and do not say about God (anything) but the truth.
> The Messiah, Jesus, son of Mary, was only a messenger of
> God, and His word, which He cast into Mary, and a spirit
> from Him. So believe in God and His messengers, but do
> not say, "Three!" Stop! (It will be) better for you. God is
> only one God. Glory to Him! (Far be it) that He should
> have a son! To Him (belongs) whatever is in the heavens
> and whatever is on the earth. God is sufficient as a guardian.

This passage not only defends the concept of *tawhid*, but it also rejects Christian christological teaching and the biblical presentation
of God as Trinity.

Related to the distance between Islamic monotheism and
Christian trinitarianism, belief in *tawhid* also has implications for
understanding the extent of the transcendence of God. Though
some Muslims claim that God can be identified and known by the
perfections the Qur'an lists as his names and attributes, Daud Rahbar criticizes this reading in his book *God of Justice.*[17] Gabriel Said
Reynolds, a renown scholar of Islamic studies, helpfully summarizes
Rahbar's work on this point, writing,

---

15 Al-Sa'di, *Explanation*, 27. Sa'di designates this aspect *tawhid al-Rububiyah*—oneness
    of Lordship.
16 Al-Sa'di, *Explanation*, 27. Sa'di designates this aspect *tawhid al-'Ibadah*—oneness of
    worship.
17 Daud Rahbar, *God of Justice* (Leiden: Brill, 1960). I'm indebted to Gabriel Said Reyn-
    olds's book cited below for this reference.

Rahbar makes the important observation that the Qur'an on occasion gives pairs of divine names that would seem to affirm both one thing and its opposites. For example, Allah is "the one who honors" and "the one who humiliates," "the one who grants" and "the one who causes distress," "the one who guides" and "the one who leads astray." In other words, these names simply make the point that God is responsible for everything. They do not define his character or disposition in any particular way. Indeed, they would seem to keep God's nature a mystery.[18]

To this same point, Seyyed Hossein Nasr distinguishes this cognitive knowledge about God from intimate, relational knowledge of God, writing, "The Divine Essence (*al-dhat*) remains absolutely transcendent and no religion has emphasized the transcendent aspect of God more than Islam."[19] In other words, belief in *tawhid* precludes one from believing in a God who would be so imminent as to dwell among his people in the fashion celebrated throughout the Bible.

Not only does the Qur'an discuss the oneness of God, but it also prohibits any belief that might associate partners with God. Such association of partners with God is known as the sin of *shirk* and is often thought to be the one sin that will not be forgiven. An instance of this instruction to maintain the purity of *tawhid*, in Qur'an 4:36, reads, "Serve [*'abd*] God, and do not associate anything with Him." Through positive commands to believe in God's oneness and also by prohibiting the associating any partners with God, then, the Qur'an calls its audience to believe in *tawhid*.

The Heavenly Books and the Prophets
The Qur'an is consistent in calling believers to recognize that God has revealed his will as a matter of mercy and guidance. The vehicles

---

18   Gabriel Said Reynolds, *Allah: God in the Qur'an* (New Haven, CT: Yale University Press, 2020), 49.
19   Seyyed Hossein Nasr, *Ideals and Realities of Islam* (San Francisco: Aquarian, 1994), 18.

of such revelation come in two forms: heavenly books and prophetic messengers. According to the Qur'an, all true prophets—from Adam to Muhammad—have essentially proclaimed the same message. That message could be variously summarized as a call to submission (*islam*) to the One True God, the maker of worlds.

The Qur'an makes this claim explicit in several key places, perhaps none more crucial than in its treatment of Abraham.[20] For instance, in Qur'an 2:124–37 the reader encounters an extended presentation of Abraham and Ishmael that is intent on establishing them as pro-Muslim. Such a presentation comes to its climax through the words the Qur'an's author places on Abraham's own lips in Qur'an 2:128: "Our Lord, make us both submitted [*muslimayn*] to you, and (make) from our descendants a community submitted [*umma muslima*] to You."[21] As Abraham makes this petition, he asks that he and his son would be made Muslims and that a community of Muslims would derive from his offspring. The Qur'an drives this point home further in Qur'an 3:67, which states baldly, "Abraham was not a Jew, nor a Christian, but he was a *hanif*, a Muslim. He was not one of the idolaters." This passage illustrates how the Qur'an intends to revere biblical prophets while also recasting them as protagonists in its own story and for its own purposes.

Abraham is not the only prophet that is drawn up into the Qur'an's orbit. The Qur'an also discusses Adam as one who received prophetic words from God.[22] It endorses Moses as a prophet.[23] Also, Jesus is recognized as a prophet who has received a message from God in

---

20 The Qur'anic/Arabic name for this character is Ibrahim. While there is perhaps reason to distinguish between the Abraham character in the Qur'an and the similar character in the Bible, I have chosen for ease of reading to retain the anglicized name that the Christian will recognize.

21 A. J. Droge, *The Qur'an* (Bristol, CT: Equinox, 2015), 13n154. The reader will note that the request to be made submitted ones is in Arabic a request to be Muslims. Muslim derives from the Arabic root word that includes the idea of submission. Likewise, Abraham prays that his offspring would form a community of Muslims when he prays for an *umma muslima*.

22 Qur'an 2:34–38.

23 Qur'an 2:51–57, 87.

various places throughout the Qur'an.[24] As will be discussed further in subsequent chapters, it is important to note that Jesus is viewed as a highly revered prophet, but nothing more. The qur'anic Jesus is not the incarnate Son of God, not worthy of worship, nor does he bring a message that is any different than that of the prophets who went before him.

The Qur'an does not only require belief in the prophets who delivered God's message to his people. It also includes injunctions to believe in the books of revelation that precede the Qur'an. For instance, Qur'an 2:97 says, "Say: 'Whoever is an enemy to Gabriel—surely he has brought it down on your heart by the permission of God, confirming what was before it, and as a guidance and good news to the believers." Though somewhat cryptic in its language, most scholars believe that this verse refers to the manner in which the Qur'an confirms the Torah of Moses and the Gospel of Jesus.[25]

Chapters 4 and 5 of this book will explore the implications of this claim and will treat some of the intertextual relationships that exist between the Qur'an and the Bible at length. Therefore, it is sufficient for the purposes of this section to simply note that most Muslims would agree that they are commanded to recognize all of the biblical prophets as true prophets of God and the previous writings of the Torah, Psalms, and Gospel—in their original and uncorrupted forms—as true communication from God.

Angels, the Day of Resurrection, and Fate

The final three articles of faith that the Qur'an teaches believers to cling to are belief in angels (*malak*), the Day of Resurrection (*yom aq-quiyyama*), and fate or predestination (*qadr*). These three beliefs correspond to one another in a number of ways. While angels appear to have a variety of roles, one of their tasks is ushering in the Day of Judgment wherein human fate is most clearly revealed. It behooves

---

24 Qur'an 2:87
25 Droge, *The Qur'an*, 11n118. Droge summarizes the standard understanding here, citing corroborating passages such as Qur'an 3:3; 5:48; 35:31; and 46:30 as making similar claims.

us to consider these three articles together as we continue to explore the content of the Qur'an's instruction.

Due to the fact that angels feature in several crucial elements of the Qur'an's teaching, it is unsurprising that Islamic tradition puts such a high value on believing in angels. For instance, Qur'an 2:97–98 credits Jibril—identified by Islamic tradition as the angel Gabriel from biblical accounts—as the one who revealed the Qur'an to Muhammad.[26] Thus, the Islamic belief in angels is connected to their activity in revealing God's instructions to humanity.

Additionally, the Qur'an teaches that some angels are tasked with guarding hell and overseeing the eschatological events that prepare the way for the day of resurrection and the final judgment.[27] Further connecting the call to belief in angels, the Qur'an indicates that angels will continue to have interactions with humans after the the Day of Judgment. Qur'an 13:23–24 teaches that angels will provide comfort to believers in paradise and in Qur'an 6:93 will heighten the suffering of those who are experiencing hell's fires.[28]

The Day of Judgment—alternatively referred to as the day of resurrection or the hour—is another essential component of Islamic belief that is part of the exercise of *taqwa*. Reinforcing the importance of the coming reckoning, the Qur'an includes ubiquitous reminders of impending eschatological judgment. Furthermore, while belief in a coming day of reckoning is part of the *taqwa* of right belief, it also motivates believers to more seriously consider how they are exhibiting *taqwa* in their actions, since those actions will be uncovered on the Day of Judgment.

Fazlur Rahman explains why the Qur'an is so concerned to remind believers of the coming judgment, writing, "Man is generally so absorbed in his immediate concerns, particularly selfish, narrow, and

---

26   Droge, *The Qur'an*, 441n96.
27   Qur'an 69:13–18; 74:26–31; 89:21–23. Again, see the treatment of Kaltner and Mirza, *The Bible and the Qur'an*, 22.
28   See the treatment of these angelic activities helpfully summarized in John Kaltner and Younus Mirza, *The Bible and the Qur'an: Biblical Figures in Islamic Tradition* (New York: T&T Clark, 2018), 21–22.

material concerns, that he does not heed the 'ends' of life [al-akhira] and constantly violates moral law."[29] In other words, the Qur'an teaches believers to have faith in the coming judgment so that they might be further motivated by the fear of their deeds being exposed to live according to God's will in the present.

Related to the Day of Judgment and eschatological reckoning, the Qur'an also calls the reader to believe in fate, or *qadr*. While various forms of this belief chart the narrow course between fatalism and sovereignty, Ziuaddin Sardar provides a representative expression of how this article of faith works itself out in the Muslim mind, writing, "Muslims believe that their destiny is firmly in the hands of God. The outcome of every effort, every good intention and action is subject to the will of God."[30]

Without delving into the intramural debates over how to understand the extent of God's active role in predestining the events of history, it is instructive to consider where and how the Qur'an discusses *qadr*. In Qur'an 97 one finds a short sura—it consists of only five verses–that is named after the idea of *qadr*. This sura describes the night on which the Qur'an was revealed to Muhammad as a night of *qadr* which is alternatively translated as the night of power, destiny, measure, or decree.[31] In this sura, the translation decree appears to be most fitting for the understanding of *qadr*, as the sura celebrates God's act of making his will known and providing a means of measuring one's life to humanity. Likewise, in Qur'an 97:4 we read that it is "by the permission of their Lord" that the angels and spirits are able to unveil his commands and his revelation. Thus, even those supernatural agents who deliver God's word cannot do so without being granted leave to do so by God's authority.

Furthermore, this view of God's sovereign, determinative power is reinforced in Qur'an 25:2, which refers to God's *qadr*, saying, "To

---

29   Fazlur Rahman, *Major Themes of the Qur'an* (Chicago: University of Chicago Press, 2009), 106.

30   Ziauddin Sardar, *What Do Muslims Believe? The Roots and Realities of Modern Islam* (New York: Walker, 2007), 45.

31   Droge, *The Qur'an*, 442n1.

Him (belongs) the kingdom of the heavens and the earth. He has not taken a son, nor has He any associate in the kingdom. He created everything and decreed it [*faqaddrahu*] exactly."[32] Here we see that all of creation is subject to God's authoritative decree as a result of the exercise of his creative power.[33]

The word *qadr* and its derivatives also appear in multiple other places with slightly different nuance. For instance, in Qur'an 2:236 the word is used to identify the financial means allotted to a person, when it says, "(There is) no blame on you if you divorce women whom you have not touched, nor promised and bridal gift to them. Yet provide for them rightly—the wealthy according to their his means [*qadruhu*], and the poor according to his means [*qadruhu*]." This indicates a form of *qadr* that pertains to the allotment of finances measured to a person by God, and can reinforce God's activity in determining a person's economic status.

And finally, in some places God exercises *qadr* in ways that appear to impinge upon human choice. For instance, Qur'an 15:49–60 records messengers from God speaking with Abraham about their plans to rescue Lot and his children. In the context of revealing what was about to transpire, Qur'an 15:58–60 records, "Surely we have been sent to a people who are sinners, except for the household of Lot. Surely we shall indeed rescue them—all (of them)—except his wife. We have determined [*qaddarna*] that she indeed (will be) one of those who stay behind." This verse indicates that Lot's wife is not independently making the decision to remain in Sodom, but that it has been determined for her.

While some Islamic presentations of *qadr* tend towards a more fatalistic view of God's predetermination of all things, it appears from most of the qur'anic instances that the idea of *qadr* relates to God's role as the creator who has the right and authority to decree and determine things as they are to be. Later Islamic reflection on *qadr*

---

32   In this verse, the conjunction "and" is more typically seen as a causative conjunction and might better be understood as "so." This implies a more direct correlation between the Qur'an's view of God as creator and therefore as the one who gives creation its decree. "He created everything so he has decreed [*qadr*] it."

33   Cf. Qur'an 10:5; 41:10; 56:57–60.

often extrapolates on the extent to which God's active determination of all things conflicts or is compatible with human free choice.[34] It appears that the Qur'an at least intends to remind the reader that God is sovereign, he is the creator, and it is his proper role to determine how his creation will proceed.[35] Fazlur Rahman helpfully cautions against the tendency towards fatalism and hard determinism as he writes,

> All things have potentialities, but no amount of potentiality may allow what is finite to transcend its finitude and pass into infinity. This is what the Qur'an means when it says that everything except God is "measured out" (*qadar* or *qadr, taqdir*, etc.), and is hence dependent upon God, and whenever a creature claims complete self-sufficiency or independence (*instighna, istikbar*), it thus claims infinitude and a share in divinity (*shirk*). When God creates anything, He places within it its powers of laws of behavior, called in the Qur'an "guidance," "command," or "measure" whereby it fits into the rest of the universe.[36]

Thus, Rahman sees *qadr* as being inextricably related to the first article of faith: protecting the concept of *tawhid*. For a Muslim intent on exercising *taqwa* in and through what they believe, these six qur'anic teachings prove indispensable. However, *taqwa* of belief is only part of the call to being a faithful Muslim. We must also consider what the Qur'an teaches about *taqwa* of action through its regular instructions regarding ethical living.

---

34   For a helpful introduction to the history of the debate, see Alexander Treiger, "Origins of *Kalam*," 27–43 in *The Oxford Handbook of Islamic Theology*, ed. Sabine Schmidtke (Oxford, UK: Oxford University Press, 2016). See especially the section entitled "II Origins of the *Qadar* Debate," 34–38.

35   See the definition given for *Jabr* and *Qadr* in John Esposito, *Oxford Dictionary of Islam* (New York: Oxford University Press, 2003), 153. Esposito notes, "The Qur'an is not decisive on the question of free will and predestination. Many passages uphold the former and many passages uphold the latter. The Qur'an is uncompromising, however, on the absolute power of God, without whose permission or creative act nothing at all occurs."

36   Rahman, *Major Themes of the Qur'an*, 67.

QUR'ANIC INSTRUCTIONS ON PRACTICE

As has already been noted, the Qur'an is intent on calling the reader to submission of belief and body. The Qur'an aims to bring human beliefs about the world into submission while also instructing the human will and action according to God's proper order. Fazlur Rahman is again instructive as he notes that within the Qur'an, "[*Taqwa*] means to be squarely anchored within the moral tensions, the "limits of God," and not to "transgress" or violate the balance of those tensions or limits."[37] We've considered the anchor of the internal *taqwa* of belief. We now turn to consider how that *taqwa* manifests itself in measured living that does not violate the ethical limits set for humans by God. To do so, we will look briefly at the Qur'an's teaching on individual piety, family relationships, and community expectations.

INDIVIDUAL PIETY

The Qur'an teaches that humanity is in need of guidance and reminder. These reminders occur in both individual lives and in the corporate life of the Islamic community. As a result, the Qur'an provides humans with various rituals that aim at punctuating one's life and filling society with reminders of God's will.

Salat *Prayers*

Perhaps most obviously, the Qur'an prescribes regular prayers (Ar. *salat*) as means by which believers are to interrupt the routine of each day to remember God and prostrate humbly before him. The importance of this daily ritual for Muslim practice is evident, as Mark Anderson writes, "[Prayer is] the daily practice that is the heart and soul of Muslim spirituality. Indeed, together with faith and alms-giving, prayer may almost be said to define true *islam*."[38] It would be impossible to speak of personal *taqwa* without recognizing the centrality of the *salat* prayers.

---

37   Rahman, *Major Themes of the Qur'an*, 29.
38   Mark Anderson, *The Qur'an in Context* (Downers Grove, IL: IVP Academic, 2016), 166. Anderson goes on to reference Qur'an 27:3, 31:4, and 98:5 as verses that reference prayer and almsgiving as being definitive of what it means to be a faithful believer.

These ritualized prayers occur five times per day in mosques—and in living rooms, in offices, and in streets—all around the world. While the Qur'an prescribes such *salat* prayers in various places and at various intervals, it is later tradition that formalizes the obligation to pray five times per day.[39] Regardless of frequency, the Qur'an instructs ritual prayer as an indispensable part of individual *taqwa*.

In the preceding paragraphs, the reader might note the repeated clarification that *salat* prayers are ritualized prayers. This is an attempt to distinguish the obligatory *salat* from the more extemporaneous idea of *du'a* prayer within Islam. The purpose of *salat* prayers is not to draw near to God as Father, nor is it explicitly tied to the idea that one might approach God with personal concerns. Rather, *salat* is a ritual that is designed to interrupt the activities of each day to encourage and remind Muslims of their submission to God. Such submission is reinforced through recited prayers and prostrated posture. *Salat* is a part of *taqwa* that is designed to help believers remember God and to counteract the great human problem of forgetfulness.

At the individual and corporate level, then, prayer is injected into daily life as a reminder to believers that they are subjects under the watchful gaze of an all-powerful master and that they owe him a debt of gratitude for creating them. *Salat* is arguably the heart of the daily practice of *taqwa*. As Mark Anderson notes, the regularity and predictability of *salat* serves a stabilizing and community developing purpose, such that, "Whatever *salat* lacks in intimacy with God it makes up for in calm predictability and . . . aesthetic power."[40] Thus, even though the performance of *salat* is an individual act of *taqwa*, it is also an act—particularly when performed in the mosque—that unifies the community around a common reminder of God's sovereignty.

---

39 For instance, Qur'an 17:78 commands sunset and sunrise prayers, stating, "Observe the prayer [*as-salat*] at the setting of the sun until the darkness of the night, and (deliver) recitation at the dawn—surely a recitation at the dawn is witnessed." Qur'an 11:114 also indicates a third time for prayer around dusk. Likewise, Qur'an 30:17–18 is traditionally understood to reference four of the five prayer times. See Droge, *The Qur'an*, 265n20.

40 Anderson, *The Qur'an in Context*, 170.

Reading and Reciting the Qur'an

Much like Christians whose devotional life revolves around prayer and reading the Bible, Muslim piety also includes the reading and reciting of the Qur'an. The Qur'an presents itself as a text that is to be read by all who would follow God's clear instruction, explaining in Qur'an 12:1–3, "Those are the signs of the clear Book. Surely We have sent it down as an Arabic Qur'an, so that you may understand. We shall recount to you the best of accounts in what We have inspired you (with of) this Qur'an, though before it you were indeed one of the oblivious." Sentiments such as this proliferate throughout the Qur'an as it presents itself as a clear, Arabic record of instruction that is given to the reader to promote understanding.

Though Muslim piety includes reading the Qur'an and even committing it to memory, the average Muslim does not read the Qur'an in the same way evangelical Christians are encouraged to read the Bible exegetically. Though the Qur'an presents itself as clear instruction, it is inextricably bound to its seventh-century Arabic form. As a result, the language itself—along with the poetics of its presentation—makes understanding a nearly impossible goal for many contemporary readers of the Qur'an. Nabeel Qureshi identifies this linguistic distance, along with several other compositional features of the Qur'an, as the reason that "the vast majority of Muslims do not directly use the Qur'an themselves for anything but liturgy: memorization and recitation for prayers."[41] Thus, when the average Muslim picks up and reads the Qur'an, they are usually not engaging in exegesis as much as they are performing ritual recitation of God's words. Many Muslims read and memorize the Qur'an to acquire religious merit.

Fighting Sin

A third—and admittedly broader—component of qur'anic instruction that pertains to individual piety is the call to fight against the sinful inclinations of the "soul" (*nafs*).[42] References to the human *nafs*

---

41   Nabeel Qureshi, *No God but One* (Grand Rapids: Zondervan, 2016), 111.
42   The breadth of discussion on the *nafs* within Islamic sources alone is wide-ranging without considering the volumes of literature that discuss the metaphysics of the human soul from theological, philosophical, and psychological perspectives. For the purposes of

appear in various places throughout the Qur'an, presenting a layered understanding of the role of the *nafs* in directing and inciting human actions. A verse that has received a lot of attention in this discussion is Qur'an 12:53, which states, "Yet I do not pronounce myself innocent, (for) surely the self [*nafs*] is indeed an instigator of evil, except as my Lord has compassion. Surely my Lord is forgiving, compassionate."

In context, this verse appears as a part of Joseph's statement of his integrity, having been exonerated from the accusation that he attempted to seduce the king's wife. For the purposes of considering the role of the *nafs*, however, it is important to note that the *nafs* is apparently at times an instigator toward evil. Such a role is reinforced in Qur'an 79:40, which envisions the human task as a restraining of the *nafs* from its inclination towards vain desires. In some ways, this use of the word *nafs* seems to have a parallel with the biblical category for the human heart, as in Jeremiah 17:9: "The heart is deceitful above all things, and desperately sick; who can understand it?"

In other places, however, the Qur'an presents the *nafs* performing a conscience-type function of accusing and convicting humans of their waywardness. Seyyed Hossein Nasr cites Qur'an 75:2 as an instance of this particular function of the *nafs*, writing, "The blaming soul (*al-nafs al-lawwamah*; 75:2), which reproaches a person for his or her evil states and forgetfulness of God, while actively attempting to effect change within that person for the better."[43] Nasr goes on to identify a third role or state of the *nafs* as being "the soul at peace (*al-nafs al-mutma'innah*; 89:27), which has conquered the lower self and resides in peace in the remembrance of God, returning to God content."[44]

There is much more that has been debated regarding a proper understanding of the role of the *nafs* in qur'anic anthropology. Yet, it suffices for our current purposes to note that there is an internal battle within humans to overcome the internal instigations to sin that arise

---

the current project, however, it suffices to note that the *nafs* performs conscience-type functions while also occasionally prompting a person toward fleshly indulgence.

43   Seyyed Hossein Nasr, ed. *The Study Qur'an: A New Translation and Commentary* (New York: HarperOne, 2015), 605n53.

44   Nasr, ed. *The Study Qur'an*, 605n53.

from the *nafs* in order to bring the *nafs* itself into peaceful submission to the ways of God. While the Qur'an also notes that humanity is beset by the wiles and temptations of the qur'anic antagonist, *Shaytan*, the human "soul" also appears at times to present a barrier to human obedience. Thus, in God's compassion and mercy he has sent along messengers and books of instruction designed to help believers subject their wayward selves to the straight path of God's revealed will.

These instructions—though often presented as broad, nondescript calls to submission—include fighting against unbelief and failing to perform righteous deeds. For example, Qur'an 13:28–29 states, "Those who believe and whose hearts are secure in the remembrance of God—surely hearts are secure in the remembrance of God—those who believe and do righteous deeds—for them (there is) happiness and a good (place of) return." A few verses later, in Qur'an 13:36, one finds similar comment regarding the overarching message of the Qur'an as a summons to obedient service: "Say: 'I am only commanded to serve God, and not to associate (anything) with Him. To Him do I call (you), and to Him is my return.'"

In fact, for most Muslims, this internal battle against sin defines the primary manifestation of the Islamic concept of jihad. While the word jihad in the Western world is likely to conjure up visions of radical violence in the name of Islam, Muslim theologians conceive of jihad in two ways: the greater jihad and the lesser jihad.[45] The greater jihad is akin to the Christian idea of the mortification of sin, while the lesser jihad is undertaken when one takes up arms either to fight in the name of Islam or to defend Islam.[46]

---

45   For a helpful perspective on how many Muslim authorities utilize these categories of greater and lesser jihad to argue against radical and violent Islam, readers might consult "Open Letter to Dr. Ibrahim Awwad al-Badri, Alias 'Abu Bakr al-Baghdadi' and to the Fighters and Followers of the Self-Declared 'Islamic State,'" www.LetterToBaghdadi. com. In this address, the writers—and subsequently the many signatories—contend, "There are two kinds of jihad in Islam: the greater jihad, which is the jihad (struggle) against one's ego; and the lesser jihad, the jihad (struggle) against the enemy." "Open Letter," 10.

46   For a helpful treatment on recent trends in understanding the role of jihad within Islam, see Syed Manzar Abbas Zaidi, "Eclipse of the Greater Jihad," *Journal of Religion, Conflict, and Peace* 3, no 1 (2009).

The traditions surrounding Muhammad's life, sayings, and ministry include countless specific ways that one might faithfully conduct such a jihad against one's ego or the aspect of the *nafs* that is involved in leading people astray. For our purposes of inspecting the Qur'an's instructions, however, it suffices to note that there is a consistent call to individuals to live out their piety as a pursuit of personal *taqwa*. The Qur'an does not restrict its ethical instructions and expectations to individual lives, however. It also includes teaching that has implications for how to order a community's broader social life.

SHARIA AND THE ETHICAL EXPECTATIONS OF THE ISLAMIC COMMUNITY

In many Western contexts, people have become accustomed to a rather sharp division between public life and private faith. Some refer to this implicit divide as the difference between the sacred and the secular spheres of life. Others may more readily refer to such a distinction by referencing the explicit and intentional separation between religious organizations (churches, synagogues, mosques, etc.) and the state functions of the government. Regardless of which nomenclature one most regularly uses, much of Western society operates under the assumption that it is possible and even advisable to divide one's religious life from one's daily life.

This potential division is not expected within Islam because the Qur'an knows no such separation. In fact, for a faithful Muslim, every aspect of life must be governed by the proper application of qur'anic and traditional instructions. Generally speaking, the instructions that guide Islamic life are known as sharia. In its qur'anic usage, sharia functions synonymously with references to the straight path of ethical living.[47] However, as the word "sharia" features in contemporary discourse, it is often understood in terms of its foundational role in establishing systems of Islamic governance. Such systems of Islamic

---

47 Consider the way that the word "sharia" is used in Qur'an 45:18: "Then We placed you on a pathway [sharia] of the matter. So follow it, and do not follow the (vain) desires of those who do not know."

communal ethics reinforce the integral connection between private *taqwa* and communal *taqwa*.

The Hijab as an Example of Communal Taqwa
Such a connection between private and communal *taqwa* drives some Muslim-majority and sharia-governed countries to mandate that women wear a traditional head covering (the hijab) in public. This specific example of public or communal *taqwa* is illustrative of the qur'anic teaching regarding the virtue of modesty which guides and shapes its approach to interpersonal interactions.

Contrary to the more oppressive interpretations of the hijab, readers may be surprised to find that the Qur'an requires both women and men to practice modesty within the Muslim community. In fact, while Qur'an 24:31 is often a point of controversy due to its call to women to wear the hijab, the preceding verse and the context in which it occurs includes instructions regarding modesty that are addressed to both men and women. Qur'an 24:30–31 reads,

> Say to the believing men (that) they (should) lower their sight and guard their private parts. That is purer for them. Surely God is aware of what they do. And say to the believing women (that) they (should) lower their sight and guard their private parts, and not show their charms, except for what normally appears of them. And let them draw their head coverings over their breasts, and not show their charms.

Traditional interpretation and application of this verse calls for women to cover not only their breasts, but also their hair and their neck in order to comply with the injunction to reserve their charms for their husbands.

However, while most contemporary attention focuses on the instructions given to women, the context clearly calls to men to likewise conduct themselves with modesty by averting their eyes and concealing their private parts. The Qur'an does not provide specifics details regarding what aspects of the human body are understood as private parts and charms. The *Sunnah*, on the other hand, includes much more detail regarding how men and women are to adorn themselves in order to comply with these instructions.[48]

Parallels with Biblical Ethics
Such an injunction regarding dress code is an example of how the Qur'an defines and guides proper interpersonal conduct. Other examples include avoiding frivolous talk, giving alms, and keeping pledges and promises.[49] Still other places in the Qur'an contain lists of ethical expectations that seem to echo biblical instructions such as the ten commandments. For example, Qur'an 2:83–84 records,

> (Remember) when We took a covenant with the Sons of Israel: 'Do not serve (anyone) but God, and (do) good to parents and family, and the orphans, and the poor, and speak well to the people, and observe the prayer and give the alms.' Then you turned away in aversion, except a few of you. And when We took a covenant with you: 'Do not shed your (own) blood, and do not expel your (own people) from your homes,' then you agreed (to it) and bore witness.

This passage appears to remind the audience of the specific instructions given to the Sons of Israel. Yet, the various instructions contained within these verses appear to be binding for all time since similar instructions to these are repeated in various places throughout the Qur'an.

In addition, several early Muslim exegetes argue that since the Qur'an is the extension of God's communication to humanity through the Jews, Christians, and now the Muslims, it has also preserved and extended for all time what is necessary of those early commands.[50] One commentator even claims that one of the tablets given to Moses

---

48   See for example, Al-Bukhari, *Sahih al-Bukhari*, https://sunnah.com/urn/44370, book 65 (§4759).
49   Qur'an 23:1–11.
50   For a thorough treatment of the decalogue and the Qur'an, see Sebastian Günther, "O People of the Scripture! Come to a Word Common to You and Us (Q. 3:64): The Ten Commandments and the Qur'an," *Journal of Qur'anic Studies* 9, no. 1 (2007): 31.

confirmed the instructions and covenant of God while the other tablet recorded an early version of the Islamic the testimony that there is no God but God (*Allah*).[51] While the *Sunnah* and later Islamic traditions add significant layers of detail to the instructions for ethical living contained in the Qur'an, many of the basic values that it teaches can be connected to biblical parallels.

For these reasons, many outside observers make connections of similarity between Islam and Christianity at the point of their ethical overlap. Such shared moral convictions do often allow Christians and Muslims to link arms in the public square regarding issues of religious liberty, definition of marriage, and even abortion. However, while there are similar conclusions regarding ethical living, this chapter has shown that the concept of *taqwa* that underlies and drives Islamic ethics maintains a different expectation of human capacity for moral living.

INSTRUCTION AND *TAQWA*: FORMULA FOR A PROPER RESPONSE

For Muslims, the Qur'an is a book that is filled with guidance, re-minder, and instruction. It lays the foundation for what has become the vast body of literature and legal rulings on how to live and believe rightly in the eyes of God. As noted above, many of the particular instructions for Islamic *taqwa* have biblical parallels. Such parallels, however, can often obscure the vast difference between what the Qur'an teaches and what the Bible reveals about human capacity to please God through obedience.

In defining *taqwa*, Fazlur Rahman provides a helpful summary of how humans are both capable of and called to respond to the Qur'an's revealed instructions. Rahman states,

> The best way to define *taqwa* is to say that, whereas action belongs to man, real and effective judgment upon that

---

51   Günther, "The Ten Commandments and the Qur'an," 33. Here Günther cites Ibn al-Nadim as saying that one of Moses's tablets contained the covenant while the other contained the confession.

action, as well as the standard whereby that action is to be judged, lie outside of him. Similarly, in the case of the collective performance of a society, both the final criterion of judgment and the judgment itself transcend that society. When a man or a society is fully conscious of this while conducting himself or itself, he or it has true *taqwa*. This idea can be effectively conveyed by the term "conscience," if the object of conscience transcends it. This is why it is proper to say that "conscience" is truly as central to Islam as love is to Christianity when one speaks of the human response to the ultimate reality—which, therefore, is conceived in Islam as merciful justice rather than fatherhood.[52]

In this statement, Rahman's comments belie the Islamic belief that when the human conscience is aided, reminded, and guided by revealed will of God, humans have sufficient moral capacity to choose to submit themselves appropriately to God's guidance. The Islamic understanding of God as a just judge—but not as a loving father— is matched with the expectation that through the Qur'an and the conscience, humanity is able to live in such a way as to please God.

This human capacity for pleasing obedience stands in stark contrast to the biblical understanding of the human condition after Genesis 3. While the Bible includes many laws and instructions for ethical behavior and ceremonial practice that have corollaries in the Qur'an, the biblical Law demonstrates the inability for members of Adam's offspring to live according to God's demands for perfection. This is the heartbeat of Paul's discussion in Romans 7:7–8, wherein he writes,

> Yet if it had not been for the law, I would not have known sin. For I would not have known what it is to covet if the law had not said, "You shall not covet." But sin, seizing and opportunity through the commandment, produced in me all kinds of covetousness. For apart from the law, sin lies dead.

---

52 Rahman, *Major Themes of the Qur'an*, 29.

Commenting on these verses, Douglas Moo identifies the thrust of Paul's argument, writing, "In 7:7–12, Paul uses a narrative to show how sin has used the law to bring death. . . . The result, then, is that the law of God, which aroused sin, is impotent to break the power of sin."[53] In other words, neither the law of God nor sinful human beings have any capacity in and of themselves to enable humans to follow and please God. Biblical law is thus not the answer to the human problem, but rather serves to highlight the human problem.

Though much more might be said regarding the biblical teaching on the effect of sin, the preceding paragraph suffices for the purpose of illustrating the distinct and divergent functions of divine law in the Bible and the Qur'an. While it is proper and often appropriate to note places of common ethical instruction between Islam and Christianity, one must do so with the underlying knowledge that such instructions are built upon different and divergent understandings of both the sin problem facing humanity and the human capacity to overcome it through mere instruction, reminder, and guidance.

---

53 Douglas Moo, *Romans*, New International Commentary on the New Testament (Grand Rapids: Eerdmans, 1996), 424.

PART 2
THE QUR'AN AS A TEXT

4

THE QUR'AN AND PREVIOUS TEXTS

*Certainly in their accounts (there is) a lesson
for those with understanding. It is not a forged
proclamation, but a confirmation of what was before
it, and a distinct setting forth of everything, and a
guidance and mercy for a people who believe.*
Qur'an 12:111

One aspect of the Qur'an's teaching that may intrigue first-time readers is its willingness to acknowledge other holy Scriptures. Throughout its pages, the Qur'an overtly recognizes the sacred texts of Jews and Christians, even going so far as to endorse their Scriptures as heavenly words. As one might notice in the verse quoted at the beginning of this chapter, Qur'an 12:111 confirms the authenticity of the message of prior Scriptures. This claim is reiterated in Qur'an 26:196–97, which states: "Surely [the Qur'an] is indeed in the Scriptures of those of old. Was it not a sign for them that it was known to the learned of the Sons of Israel?" Indeed, it appears that the Qur'an is not embarrassed in the least by the Scriptures of the Jews and Christians.

Throughout this section we will be looking at the dynamics that exist between the Qur'an and the other Scriptures that it acknowledges. This first chapter in this section will focus on the occasions when the Qur'an directly discusses the Book given to Moses and the Book given to Jesus. In considering these references, we will begin to see that, while biblical stories and characters are involved, it is too simplistic to conclude that the Qur'an endorses the Bible. Instead, we will see that the Qur'an claims to complete, extend, and perfect the heavenly revelation that Jews and Christians have received while also challenging the Bible's authority.

Following this current chapter, we will investigate the question of how the Qur'an views the Jewish and Christian communities within its contemporary setting. This investigation will shed light on the question: How the Qur'an can recognize the authenticity of the revelation given to Moses and to Jesus, when it stands in direct contradiction with the claims made by the communities of Jews and Christians to which it refers?

Finally, this section will conclude with a chapter that considers what the Qur'an does with previous texts in order to relocate their stories, themes, and characters within a wholly different context. In so doing, I will argue that the concept of a mosaic is a helpful analogy for understanding the Qur'an's creative use of previously existing material. But lest we get ahead of ourselves, let's consider where and how the Qur'an discusses prior revelation.

THE QUR'AN AND THE ARABIC BIBLE

Traditional Islamic accounts of the Qur'an's reception date the completed, written, and collated form of the Qur'an to the early-to-mid seventh century CE. Some disagreement exists between various Shia and Sunni accounts as to whether or not the Qur'an was committed to writing, collected, and canonized within Muhammad's lifetime.[1]

---

1   For an example of one who contends that Muhammad not only recited but also ordered the entirety of the Qur'an in his lifetime, see Muhammad Abdel Haleem, *Understanding the Qur'an* (New York: I. B. Tauris, 2011), 6. It should be noted that Haleem is here concerned with order of recitation, not necessarily the collation of the written materials that recorded the revelations as they were revealed to Muhammad.

Still, most Muslims of all traditions argue that by the middle of the seventh century the third caliph (successor to Muhammad), 'Uthman, had confirmed, copied, and disseminated a single authorized version of the Qur'an.[2] Thus, writers such as Muhammad Abdel Haleem contend, "The 'Uthmanic codex has remained as the only canonical text of the Qur'an that exists, recognized [by Sunni and Shia] alike throughout the Muslim world, for the last 14 centuries."[3]

Granting the mid-seventh century dating for the original compilation of the Qur'an, it is important to note that there is no evidence that copies of the Bible in Arabic were available at the time. In fact, the Qur'an appears to be the first substantial, book-length document reduced to writing in the Arabic language.[4] Thus, in his thorough treatment of the appearance of an Arabic translation of the Bible, Sidney Griffith convincingly argues that,

> The earliest time at which it would have been feasible for Arabic-speaking Jews and Christians to undertake a translation of the Bible (or parts of it) into written Arabic was the mid to late seventh century. . . . But it is more likely that the first written Bible translations were made in the eight century, and outside of Arabia.[5]

The absence of a written Arabic Bible explains why the Qur'an appears to be familiar with the teaching of the Bible in sundry ways, yet never quotes the Bible directly.[6]

---

2   See the discussion of the traditional account recorded in Muhammad Mustafa al-Azami, *The History of the Qur'anic Text* (Lahore, Pakistan: Suhail Academy, 2005), 87–108. As a helpful foil to these traditional claims, the reader should consult Ayman Ibrahim, *A Concise Guide to the Qur'an* (Grand Rapids: Baker, 2020), esp. 37–59.

3   Haleem, *Understanding the Qur'an,* 4–5.

4   Gerhard Bowering, "The Qur'an as the Voice of God," in *Proceedings of the American Philosophical Society* 147, no. 4 (2003): 347.

5   Sidney Griffith, *The Bible in Arabic: The Scriptures of the "People of the Book" in the Language of Islam* (Princeton, NJ: Princeton University Press, 2013), 90.

6   Gabriel Said Reynolds, "Biblical Turns of Phrase in the Qur'an," in *Light upon Light: Essays in Islamic Thought and History in Honor of Gerhard Bowering*, eds. Jamal Elias and Bilal Orfali, 45–69 (Leiden: Brill, 2019), 45. Reynolds writes, "The Qur'an tends

Still, the Qur'an intentionally and regularly acknowledges and engages with the stories, characters, and themes from the Bible. It appears, then, that the Qur'an was written in a situation in which there were communities of Arabic-speaking Jews and Christians who transmitted the content of the Bible orally. Endorsements of prior Scriptures appear in various places throughout the Qur'an and should be considered in their qur'anic context in order to better appreciate the Qur'an's tone and tenor as it addresses prior Scriptures. Specifically, the Qur'an refers to the Tawrat (*Tawraat*), the Zabur, and the Injil as "Books" that were given respectively to Moses, David, and Jesus. The following section will give a summary glimpse of how the Qur'an presents these Books.

THE QUR'AN AND THE TORAH (TAWRAT)

The Qur'an specifically names the Torah as an independent portion of Scripture that was revealed from heaven to Moses. Among the several places the Qur'an explicitly mentions the Torah, we see Qur'an 3:3–4 saying,

> He has sent down on you the Book with the truth, confirming what was before it, and he sent down the Torah and the Gospel, before (this) as guidance for the people, and (now) He has sent down the Deliverance. Surely those who disbelieve in the signs of God—for them (there is) a harsh punishment. God is mighty, a taker of vengeance.

The idea of prior revelation is found in multiple other places throughout the Qur'an, but this particular instance is important for at least two reasons: (1) the Torah and the Gospel are referred to as guidance

---

not to reproduce biblical passages closely. Indeed, by my reading, the Qur'an has not a single passage that we might properly consider a quotation of the canonical Bible." In footnote 2 on this same page, Reynolds notes that some scholars argue that Qur'an 21:105 includes a quotation of biblical text. Given the short phrase of relatively general content, however, Reynolds finds only resemblance to the biblical text in Qur'an 21:105 rather than direct quotation.

from God in the same way as the Qur'an refers to itself as guidance, and (2) the Qur'an confirms what has already been revealed in the Torah and Gospel.

That the Qur'an confirms the prior revelation is reiterated in another passage that provides extended treatment of Moses and his relationship to revelation. In Qur'an 2:51–90 the reader is called to remember the ways that God interacted with Moses, particularly in dispensing revelation. Verse 53 is particularly important, in that, following a reference to Moses's session on Mount Sinai, it states, "And (remember) when We have Moses the Book and the Deliverance, so that you might be rightly guided." Not only does this verse connect Moses's portion of the Book with guidance, but it also clearly recognizes it as "deliverance" in the same way as Qur'an 25:1 refers to the Qur'an.[7] The word rendered "deliverance" above is the Arabic word *furqaan*. This particular word is often translated as "criterion" by other English editions of the Qur'an.[8] Regardless of the English rendering, *furqaan* is used throughout the Qur'an to discuss God's revelation of books and signs.[9]

Furthermore, as Qur'an 2 continues to remind its audience of God's work through Moses, it recalls God's interactions with his people in the desert using the word "covenant." Qur'an 2:63 calls the reader to, "(Remember) when We took a covenant with you, and raised the mountain above you: Hold fast what we have given you, and remember what is in it, so that you may guard (yourselves)."[10]

---

7   A. J. Droge, *The Qur'an: A New Annotated Translation* (Bristol, CT: Equinox, 2015), 233n1. Here Droge clarifies that the word *furqaan* that he renders as "deliverance" is used to refer to both the Qur'an (25:1) and the Torah (21:48).

8   Cf. Seyyed Hossein Nasr, ed., *The Study Qur'an* (New York: HarperOne, 2015), 28. Also, Abdullah Yusuf Ali, *The Qur'an: Text, Translation, and Commentary* (Elmhurst, NY: Tahrike Tarsile Qur'an, 2005), 29.

9   Ali, *The Qur'an*, 29n68. Ali contends that the word *furqaan* should be understood as signs given to God's people that are distinct from the Books of revelation. That is largely because *furqaan* is used to describe something given to both Moses and Aaron in Qur'an 21:48. Since Aaron received no book, it should be viewed as a reference to signs that supplement God's revealed will in books. Ali does note, however, that other scholars view Scripture and *furqaan* as being virtually synonymous.

10 Nasr, *Study Qur'an*, 33–34nn63–64, points out that the command to "remember what is in it" refers to the content of the Torah.

The word translated covenant here is *mithaaq*. Elsewhere, the word *'ahd* is used as an apparent cognate with *mithaaq*, indicating reception of divine law, guidance, and a swearing of allegiance.[11] Thus, the use of covenant language demonstrates that the Qur'an intends to see Moses as one who has received the Torah as a covenant from God, which is to serve as deliverance from ignorance and a criterion for living as his people.[12]

As the Qur'an recognizes the authority of the Torah, it also summons its Jewish readers to consider the Qur'an in light of the Torah. For instance, Qur'an 2:40–44 addresses the Jews,

> Sons of Israel! Remember My blessing which I bestowed on you. Fulfill My covenant (and) I shall fulfill your covenant, and Me—fear me (alone). Believe in what I have sent down, confirming what is with you, and do not be the first to disbelieve in it. Do not sell My signs for a small price, and guard (yourselves) against me. Do not mix the truth with falsehood, and do not conceal the truth when you know (better). Observe the prayer and give the alms, and bow with the ones who bow. Do you command the people to piety and forget yourselves, though you recite the Book? Will you not understand?

---

11   In Qur'an 2:27, for instance, the two words are used in the same verse in relationship to one another: "who break the covenant ['*ahd*] of God, after its ratification [*mithaaq*], and sever what God commanded to be joined, and foment corruption on the earth." See also the dictionary recognition of the synonymous function of the two words in John Esposito, *The Oxford Dictionary of Islam* (New York: Oxford University Press, 2003), 9, 203. The entry for *mithaaq* refers the reader to *ahd*, which defines the terms as meaning, "Covenant or compact, as in agreement or swearing of allegiance." Additionally, corroborating the idea that *mithaaq* and *'ahd* function synonymously, the Arabic Bible uses the word *'ahd* in Exodus 19:5 to indicate God's initiation of his covenant with his people which the Qur'an references in Qur'an 2:63 using the term *mithaaq*.

12   Readers interested in the comparison of covenantal concept in the Bible and in the Qur'an are advised to read the sixth chapter of Mark Durie, *The Qur'an and Its Biblical Reflexes* (New York: Lexington, 2018), esp. 195–213. Durie convincingly demonstrates that the Qur'an conceives of a covenant in a manner that is divergent from the biblical concept.

In these brief verses, then, the reader gets a view of the Qur'an's overall posture toward the Torah as book of instruction revealed to Moses from heaven. The Qur'an acknowledges that the Torah establishes a covenant or criterion that is to be followed by the Jews, whose content is further confirmed in the arrival of the Qur'an.

As a result of this understanding of the Torah, the Qur'an warns the Jewish community to recognize that if their reading of the Book that is with them does not conform to the revelation in the Qur'an, they are guilty of misunderstanding, mixing truth with falsehood, and concealing the truth they have received. These verses prepare the reader to see how the Qur'an will address the failings of the Jews, though we will discuss the Qur'an's perception of the Jewish people in the following chapter.

THE QUR'AN AND THE PSALMS (ZABUR)

Along with the Torah that was revealed to Moses, the Qur'an also mentions Scripture given to David. The Qur'an refers to this Scripture as the Zabur. While the Torah appears nearly twenty times in the Qur'an, the Zabur is only mentioned by name on three occasions.[13] First, Qur'an 4:163 addresses Muhammad and encourages him in his own prophetic office, stating, "Surely We have inspired you as We inspired Noah and the prophets after him, and as We inspired Abraham, and Ishmael, and Isaac, and Jacob, and the tribes, and Jesus, and Job, and Jonah, and Aaron, and Solomon, and We gave David (the) Psalms." For the reader familiar with the biblical characters the Qur'an appears to be referencing, a number of things might stand out in this verse.

One such point of interest might be that the biblical account does not formally recognize most of the characters listed above as

---

13 The word *az-Zabur* appears in three places in the singular form, which is usually associated with the book given to David. However, the word appears in the plural in various other places that appear to be more general references to scriptures or sacred writ. See, for example, Qur'an 3:184 which includes references to "clear signs, and the scriptures [az-zubur], and the illuminating Book." With no reference to David, the use of the plural noun, and no direct reference to the Torah or Injil, there is no reason to restrict this usage to refer only to the Psalms.

prophets, nor as being inspired by God in the biblical sense of the term. The Qur'an, however, uses the word prophet (*nabi*) more broadly to describe men who have been tasked with bringing a message from heaven to their communities. Within the teaching of the Qur'an, the profusion of prophets is not problematic because all prophets from God have come with the singular message of submission (*slam*) to God's will.[14] In the same way as all prophets have a common divine message to proclaim, the Qur'an expects that all divine Books will likewise function as conduits of essentially the same divine message.

Another point of interest is that the characters are listed in apparently haphazard chronological order with characters like Job, Jonah, and Solomon listed after Jesus. Similar instances of chronologically confusing lists of prophets are found elsewhere in the Qur'an. For example, Qur'an 6:83–89 includes lists such as, "David, Solomon, Job, Joseph, Moses, and Aaron" and "Zachariah, John, Jesus, and Elijah." One reason that may play a factor in such disordered lists is the Qur'an's attention to a poetic meter and rhyming structure. Another possible explanation is that the Qur'an is intentionally attempting to highlight specific characters and their stories by placing them in unexpected places within the lists. We will discuss these possibilities further in chapter 6, where we will consider the parallels between a mosaic and the manner in which the Qur'an connects various characters and narratives in order to serve its own purposes and message. For the current investigation of the Qur'an's references to the Psalms, however, it suffices to note that this passage states that God gave David the Zabur.

It is worth pointing out that this verse avoids using the verb *nazal* that commonly connotes the revelation of the heavenly books.[15] Where verses that speak of the transmission of the Qur'an use *nazal* to indicate the "coming down" of the message upon the messengers

---

14   John Kaltner and Younus Mirza, *The Bible and the Qur'an: Biblical Figures in the Islamic Tradition* (New York: T&T Clark, 2018), 147–48.
15   Kaltner and Mirza, *The Bible and the Qur'an*, 148.

and prophets, this verse simply uses the verb "we gave" (*Aatina*) to indicate how David received the Zabur.[16]

The second reference to the Zabur occurs in Qur'an 17:55: "Your Lord knows whatever is in the heavens and the earth. Certainly, We have favored some of the prophets over others, and we gave David (the) Psalms." This passage again uses the verb "gave" in place of *nazal*. However, it serves to distinguish what David was given as a written book from the message given to other prophets which was primarily verbal in nature.

The final time that the reader encounters the word Zabur is found in Qur'an 21:105, which states, "Certainly we have written the Psalms, after the Reminder: 'The earth—my righteous servants will inherit it.'" This particular passage is of interest not only because it references the Psalms, but also because it is perhaps the closest the Qur'an comes to quoting the Bible. Some scholars take the phrase "my righteous servants will inherit it" to be a quotation of Psalm 37:29, which the ESV renders as "The righteous shall inherit the land and dwell upon it forever." While the sentiment is similar, this phrase is not an exact quotation.[17]

With these three appearances of the Zabur in the Qur'an, we do well to note two things that distinguish the Zabur from the Torah, Injil, and Qur'an. First, as noted above, the verb expected to describe the reception or descent of a heavenly book is *nazal*. This word is not attested in conjunction with reference to the Zabur. Second, some Islamic commentators have argued that the word Zabur refers to all the books of the prophets rather than being restricted to the Psalms.[18] This broader understanding of the meaning of the word would explain the presence of both the singular usage of Zabur and

---

16   For some references to the *nazal* word group used to describe the descent of the Qur'an, see Qur'an 20:1–4; 26:192–93; and 32:2. These references are included in Kaltner and Mirza, *The Bible and the Qur'an*, 148.

17   Gabriel Said Reynolds, *The Qur'an and the Bible* (New Haven, CT: Yale University Press, 2019), 521.

18   Said Hossein Nasr, ed., *The Study Qur'an* (New York: HarperOne, 2015), 828n105. Nasr cites Razi and Tabari as endorsers of the idea that the Qur'an uses az-Zabur to refer to the Torah, the Gospel, and the Qur'an.

the more attested usage of the plural form, Zubur in the Qur'an. Likewise, it makes sense of the occasions where the Qur'an includes references to the Torah and Gospel in the same context without also mentioning the Zabur. Regardless, it appears that the Qur'an intends to recognize David as one of the favored prophets who was given a book of revelation known as the Zabur.

THE QUR'AN AND THE GOSPEL (INJIL)

The final qur'anic endorsement of specific biblical texts involves what is likely most intriguing to a Christian reader: the Injil of Jesus. The Injil is first referenced in Qur'an 3:3–4a, which states, "He has sent down [nazal] on you the Book with the truth, confirming what was before it, and He sent down [anzal] the Torah and the Gospel before (this) as guidance for the people, and (now) He has sent down [anzal] the Deliverance [al-furqaan]." As seen here, the Qur'an almost always refers to the Gospel and the Torah together in the same context.[19]

In fact, there is only one occasion where the Gospel is treated independently of explicit mention of the the Torah. This occurs in Qur'an 57:26–27a, which reads,

> Certainly We sent Noah and Abraham, and We placed among his descendants the prophetic office and the Book. Yet (there was only the occasional) one of them who was (rightly) guided, but many of them were wicked. Then in their footsteps We followed up with Our messengers, and We followed up with Jesus, son of Mary, and gave him the Gospel, and placed in the hearts of those who followed him kindness and mercy.

Even here, the reader notes that the Torah is not far from the Qur'an's view considering that it references prophets and messengers who came before Jesus with a Book.

---

19   The word Injil occurs twelve times in the Qur'an. The Torah and the Injil are referenced in context on the following occasions: Qur'an 3:3, 48, 65; 5:43–50, 66–68, 110; 7:157; 9:111; 48:29.

This passage goes on to rebuke the recipients of divine revelation who innovated in their piety and who failed to observe God's commands as they were given. Chapter 5 will discuss the Qur'an's posture towards the communities of Jews and Christians. Still, it is helpful here to see how the Qur'an endorses the Gospel given to Jesus as true revelation, while at the same time confronting the People of the Book as those who have failed to rightly respond to revelation. Throughout its pages, the Qur'an uses nothing but respectful, honorific language to refer to the previously revealed Scriptures of the Torah, Psalms, and Gospel. Gordon Nickel notes that "the Qur'an describes the Torah as 'complete,' 'detailed,' 'guidance,' and 'a mercy' [e.g. 6:154] and the Gospel as 'guidance,' 'light,' and 'admonition' [5:46]."[20]

With such lofty language applied to the prior Scriptures, Christians often assume that the Qur'an endorses the Bible. Yet when their Muslim friends refuse to read the Bible, or seem uninterested in its teaching, confusion and frustration can follow. Before moving on to consider how the Qur'an portrays Jews and Christians as distorters of their Scripture, we need to consider where the Qur'an believes the Torah, Psalms, and Gospel to originate. Such an investigation may help to make sense of why your Muslim friend can read the Qur'an and apparently ignore the Bible that it seems to endorse.

THE QUR'AN AND THE MOTHER OF THE BOOK

One of the aspects of the Qur'an's relationship to prior Scriptures that is often missed is the fact that the Qur'an refers to the Torah, Zabur, and Injil without necessarily referring to the whole Bible. If, as was discussed at the beginning of this chapter, the Bible had not been translated and disseminated in Arabic by the time the Qur'an was written, such an omission is understandable. The content of the Bible would have been available only in oral form, and the most likely material to be discussed orally would be drawn from the historical

---

20   Gordon Nickel, "Tampering with the Pre-Islamic Scriptures," in *The Qur'an with Christian Commentary*, ed. Gordon Nickel, 142–43 (Grand Rapids: Zondervan, 2020), 142.

narratives of the Torah and the Gospel accounts of Jesus. For an Arabic-speaking community that is unfamiliar with the canonical Bible, it is plausible to think that they may refer to the compiled Christian Bible or the Jewish Scriptures by these component parts, while remaining ignorant of the various other sections of the Bible such as the prophets, wisdom writings, epistles, and apocalypse.

However, there is another potential way to understand the Qur'an's references to these specific sections of Scripture over and against the canonical Bible. As seen in the verses quoted above, the Qur'an speaks of David receiving the Zabur from heaven. It also speaks of the Torah descending to Moses and the Gospel descending to Jesus. Likewise, the Qur'an regularly refers to Jews and Christians as the People of the Book.

Such language echoes the description of how the Qur'an descended to Muhammad. For many Muslims encountering the references in the Qur'an to the Torah, Zabur, and Injil, then, the process and product of revelation is a Book directly descending upon Moses, David, Jesus, and Muhammad. Therefore, when the Qur'an speaks of these previous Scriptures, the Muslim reader is inclined to think of Moses, David, and Jesus receiving books dictated to them by angelic messengers and transmitted to their audiences via written record of what they received. While a Christian might think of Moses and David as being more directly involved in writing under the inspiration of the Holy Spirit, there is no record of Jesus leaving behind any writings of his own. A Christian use of the word "Gospel" calls to mind the four canonical books—Matthew, Mark, Luke, and John—written about the life and ministry of Jesus. From the perspective of the Qur'an, however, Jesus received a portion of the heavenly book, as did Moses and Muhammad.

The Qur'an appears to be referencing individual books revealed distinctly to Moses, David, and Jesus. Questions arise, however, when one seeks to understand the relationship between those books and the Christian Bible. Some Muslims contend that the revealed books have been lost by their respective communities as they fell away from the divine instruction they had received. Such a proposal is endorsed by

Muslim commentators such as Abdullah Yusuf Ali. In an appendix within his translation of the Qur'an, Ali writes,

> Just as the [*Tawraat*] is not the Old Testament, or the Pentateuch, as now received by the Jews and Christians, so the *Injil* mentioned in the Qur'an is certainly not the New Testament, and it is not the four Gospels as not received by the Christian Church, but an original Gospel which was promulgated by Jesus, as the [*Tawraat*] was promulgated by Moses and the Qur'an by Muhammad Mustafa.[21]

Ali continues on, contending that the Injil "spoken of by the Qur'an is not the New Testament. It is not the four Gospels now received as canonical. It is the single Gospel which, Islam teaches, was revealed to Jesus, and which he taught."[22]

For those who follow Ali's line of thought, the Injil—along with the Tawrat and Zabur—was revealed as a part of a single heavenly book. These parts have apparently been lost to history, but the basic teaching they included has been extended and confirmed through the revelation of the Qur'an. This idea is reinforced by Qur'an 3:23, which states, "Have you not seen those who were given a portion of the Book? They were called to the Book of God in order that it might judge between them." Likewise, Qur'an 4:44 reiterates this idea: "Do you not see those who have been given a portion of the Book? They purchase error and wish that you would go astray from the way." Both of these passages refer to non-Muslim communities who have received portions or parts of the one Book. Elsewhere, the Qur'an refers to this source as the Mother of the Book. Thus, one could take the Qur'an's presentation of the Tawrat, Zabur, and Injil as being chapters from the single source of divine revelation that have been lost and corrupted, but which have also found their completion and perfection in the advent of the final chapter—the Qur'an.

---

21   Ali, *The Qur'an*, 286.
22   Ali, *The Qur'an*, 287.

Why Didn't God Preserve Prior Revelation?
If one adopts the understanding that the Qur'an views the four canonical Gospels as being different than the Injil, the question yet remains, "Why did God not preserve the Tawrat, Zabur, and Injil in the same way that the Qur'an claims he has preserved the Qur'an?" Part of the answer the Qur'an gives comes through in Qur'an 13:38–39:

> Certainly We sent messengers before you, and have them wives and descendants, but it was not for any messenger to bring a sign, except by the permission of God. For every (period of) time (there is) a written decree. God blots out whatever he pleases, and He confirms (whatever He pleases). With Him is the mother of the Book.

This passage contains three essential aspects of the answer to the question of what happened to the previous revelations given to Moses, David, and Jesus.

First, these verses note that God has appointed an allotted book or written decree for every time period. This sentiment is reiterated in other places that indicate that God has provided revelation and prescribed specific rituals for various people and times throughout history. In other words, Moses provided the Jewish people with a book in the same way as Jesus provided the Christian people with a book. The Qur'an elsewhere teaches that each community has received specific rituals. For example, Qur'an 22:67 contends, "For every community We have appointed a ritual which they practice. So let them not argue with you about the matter, but call (them) to your Lord. Surely you are indeed on a straight guidance."[23] Thus, it appears that when God reveals a book he also gives specific rituals that identify the community as having authentic revelation.

Second, verse 39 indicates that God has the ability to reveal something to one community that can be nullified for another

---

23   See also Qur'an 22:34, which seems to form an inclusio with verse 67, which is quoted above in the text.

community. The phrase, "God blots out whatever he pleases" seems to correspond to the Islamic doctrine of abrogation. Abrogation is the idea that verses within the Qur'an that were revealed later in Muhammad's ministry supersede earlier verses as binding upon the community.[24] This concept of abrogation appears elsewhere, such as Qur'an 2:104–106 where one reads,

> You who believe! Do not say, "Observe us," but say, "Regard us" and hear. For the disbelievers (there is) a painful punishment. Those who disbelieve among the People of the Book, and the idolaters, do not like (it) that anything good should be sent down on you from your Lord. But God chooses whomever He pleases for His mercy, and God is full of great favor. Whatever verse we cancel or cause to be forgotten, We bring a better (one) than it, or (one) similar to it. Do you not know that God is powerful over everything?[25]

This section again connects God's omnipotence to his ability to abrogate or cancel (*naskh*) what has been previously revealed. While some might argue that abrogation indicates a change in God's mind or truth, Ali comments, "This does not mean that eternal principles change. It is only a sign of God's infinite Power." The implication of the concept of abrogation for our discussion, then, is that apparent conflicts in ritual or ethic that exist between Jewish, Christian, and Muslim communities can be explained as having been superseded by the final dispensation of revelation which has come through the Qur'an.

Third, this passage refers to the "mother of the Book." According to some Islamic scholars, this phrase refers to a heavenly and eternal source of revelation. In other words, many Muslims take this concept to mean that there exists an eternal book of revelation in heaven that

---

24   Clinton Bennett, "A–Z Index of Key Terms and Concepts," in *Bloomsbury Companion to Islamic Studies*, ed. Clinton Bennett, 327–74 (New York: Bloomsbury, 2015), 357.
25   See also Qur'an 16:101.

has been transmitted via angelic messengers to human recipients from Moses through to Muhammad. In his comments on this verse, Seyyed Hossein Nasr writes, "The *Mother of the Book* . . . refers, according to some, to the fundamental source of Divine Revelation from which the Qur'an and other Divinely revealed books are transcribed."[26] While there have been historical debates over whether or not the Mother of the Book can be coeternal with the Qur'an's monadic conception of Allah, it is broadly accepted that there is a single source from which all heavenly books have been transmitted.[27]

The Qur'an as the Eclipse of the Torah, the Zabur, and the Injil

The three insights above are instructive as we return to the question of why Muslim theology is not bothered by the idea that the Torah, Zabur and Injil have been lost or corrupted. First, the Qur'an claims in various places that it has been revealed to the Arabs in "clear Arabic."[28] Through the advent of Islam, Qur'an 5:3 states that God has perfected religion in providing Islam. Thus, for the people reading Muhammad's message, the final, universal dispensation of divine revelation has arrived and prior revelations are no longer binding or necessary. For many Muslims, then, the apparent loss and distortion of prior revelation further confirms the sinfulness and waywardness of the Jews and Christians, thus necessitating the advent of the Qur'an as the seal of revelation.

Likewise, the Qur'an contends that all true revelation has contained the same fundamental message—submission to the one true God. The various ethical and ritual differences that arise between Jews, Christians, and Muslims can be seen as specific to each time, place, and people without compromising the idea that the three faiths share the same basic content. This can be seen in Qur'an

---

26   Nsar, *The Study Qur'an*, 627n39. Nasr attributes this particular idea to al-Tabari.
27   See also the reference to the Preserved Tablet mentioned in Qur'an 85:22, which some take to indicate an actual tablet that has recorded God's revealed will and which has been the source of angelic transmission of divine revelation. Nasr, *The Study Qur'an*, 627n39.
28   Ex. Qur'an 16:103; 26:193–195

3:64—the verse underlying the recent interfaith statement "A Common Word"—which summons Jews and Christians to recognize common beliefs:

> Say: People of the Book! Come to a word (which is) common between us and you: "We do not serve (anyone) but God, and do not associate (anything) with Him, and do not take each other as Lords instead of God." If they turn away, say: "Bear witness that we are Muslims."

This passage is important in and of itself for showing how the Qur'an intends to continue in the stead of prior revelation and communities of faith. It is also important in that it sits contextually just before the Qur'an recognizes Abraham as a sort of proto-Muslim who worshipped Allah as a Muslim before the onset of Judaism or Christianity. Three verses later, in Qur'an 3:67, we read, "Abraham was not a Jew, not a Christian, but he was a *hanif,* a Muslim. He was not one of the idolaters." So, between the commonality of worshipping the one true God and the attempt to lay claim to Abraham as a model Muslim, it is not necessary for the Qur'an's purposes that the Torah, Zabur, or Injil are yet-extant sources of revelation.

Lastly, the Qur'an is the final and confirming installation of revelation which is repeatedly said to complete and confirm the prior revelation.[29] This can be seen clearly in Qur'an 3:3, which argues, "He has sent down on you the Book with the truth, confirming what was before it, and He sent down the Torah and the Gospel before this as guidance for the people, and (now) He has sent down the Deliverance." Thus, for the reader of the Qur'an, this final dispensation suffices to confirm all that needs to be known from the prior revelations.

If the Torah, Zabur, and Injil have been lost or corrupted, the Qur'an offers not only an extension of their message into the present but also the completion of what they had begun revealing. Therefore, the closing of the Qur'an serves to supersede, complete, and perfect

---

29   Ex. Qur'an 2:41, 89, 91, 97; 3:3, 81; 4:47; 10:33; 35:31–32.

all true religion in Islam.[30] The Qur'an, then, is sufficient for Muslims because, in the words of Abdullah Yusuf Ali, "The Qur'an confirms the main and uncorrupted features of previous revelations."[31] While the Qur'an does acknowledge that prior Scriptures have been given to the Jews and Christians, it does not require one to consult those Scriptures.

CONCLUSION: ISLAMICIZED BIBLICAL MATERIAL

As we conclude this chapter, it is important to note that not all Islamic scholars are convinced that the Torah, Psalms, and Gospel in the Qur'an refer to books of revelation that are totally distinct from their apparent counterparts in the canonical Bible. For example, Gabriel Said Reynolds argues compellingly that the Qur'an expects that the Christian community it addresses has access to the Gospel that it endorses.[32] He argues this from verses such as Qur'an 5:47, which states, "So let the People of the Gospel judge by what God has sent down in it." The ability to judge what is right by the contents of the Gospel indicates that the Injil is yet available to the Christians the Qur'an has in view.

Regardless of whether one takes the references in the Qur'an to refer to biblical sections of Scripture or separate books lost to history, many Muslims yet view the Bible as being worthy of respect. Prompted by Qur'an 7:157, some Muslims search the Bible in order to find evidence of prophecy that predicts Muhammad's

---

30   Qur'an 5:3 is traditionally taken to be the final verse revealed to Muhammad: "Today I have perfected your religion for you, and I have completed my blessing upon you, and I have approved Islam for your religion."

31   Ali, *The Qur'an*, 1162n3918.

32   Gabriel Said Reynolds, "On the Qur'anic Accusation of Scriptural Falsification (*tahrif*) and Christian Anti-Jewish Polemic," *Journal of American Oriental Society* 130, no. 2 (2010): 195. Reynolds writes, "If the Qur'an speaks against certain Christians, it speaks in support of the Gospel, and moreover assumes that the valid Christian revelation is still at hand in its day." Reynolds also notes that this reference seems to be peculiar to the Christians, stating that there is no comparable qur'anic statement to the Jews regarding the Torah.

ministry.[33] Even Abdullah Yusuf Ali admits that the canonical Bible likely contains at least fragments of what was given originally in the Tawrat, Zabur, and Injil. Ali writes, "Muslims are therefore right in respecting the present Bible (New Testament and Old Testament), though they reject the peculiar doctrines taught by orthodox Christianity or Judaism."[34] There is therefore neither a wholesale rejection of the Bible nor a willingness to recognize it as authoritative among Muslims today.

As we will see in the following chapter, the Qur'an both recognizes that Jews and Christians have received legitimate parts of the Mother of the Book and it addresses contemporary Jewish and Christian communities. The division between the Qur'an's high opinion of Jewish and Christian Scriptures and its low opinion of Jewish and Christian communities is due to the accusation that these communities have corrupted the revelation entrusted to them.

Such a posture allows the Qur'an to offer itself as a corrective to the Jewish and Christian use of their Scriptures by relocating the biblical material into its own narrative and for its own purposes. On this point about the Qur'an's incorporation of biblical material, Griffith concludes,

> Given the concomitant Islamic contention that the earlier scriptures were corrupt and therefore of questionable authenticity, along with the divergent cast of many Islamic presentations of Biblical narratives, one might also speak of a simultaneous process of "Islamicizing" the biblical material.[35]

Stated differently, the ethics, characters, and stories from the previous Scriptures that the Qur'an draws up into its own purposes take on different shapes and aims as they are employed within the new qur'anic setting.

---

33 One example of many such attempts is Jamal Badawi, "Muhammad in the Bible," IslamiCity.org, http://www.islamicity.com/mosque/muhammad_bible.htm.
34 Ali, "Appendix," 287.
35 Griffith, *The Bible in Arabic*, 176.

Therefore, the Qur'an can be at one in the same time confident
in its claim that true revelation has come to the Jews and Christians
while also confronting and correcting what it believes to be inaccu-
racies and inappropriate interpretations of biblical material. Most of
these confrontations are aimed at the communities of believers who
have received the prior revelation. Before considering how the biblical
material functions within its qur'anic setting, we must consider how
the Qur'an portrays its Jewish and Christian audience.

5

THE QUR'AN AND THE PEOPLE OF THE BOOK

Surely those who believe, and those who are Jews,
and the Christians, and the Sabians — whoever
believes in the Last Day and does righteousness — they
have their reward with their Lord. (There will be)
no fear on them, nor will they sorrow.

Qur'an 2:62

Traditional Islamic accounts describe Mecca as a place permeated with polytheism. According to these traditions, the first twelve years of Muhammad's ministry were spent preaching specifically against the idolatry of these polytheists. However, despite the supposedly pagan milieu surrounding the early ministry of Muhammad, the Qur'an includes far more detailed interaction with Jewish and Christian communities and practices than it does with pagan worship and belief.

Scholars of Islamic studies such as Gabriel Said Reynolds have long recognized the curious omission of detailed interactions with paganism. To this point, Reynolds writes, "The premise that the Qur'an emerged amidst paganism has more than once left scholars confused by the fact that paganism is hardly evident in the Qur'an."[1] Reynolds goes on to note that the traditional material appears to be interested in distancing Muhammad's original audience from his monotheistic message in order to highlight the divine origins of his preaching. In other words, if Muhammad's message contrasts more starkly with the beliefs and practices of his environment, the accusation that he is merely modifying or borrowing from existing Jewish and Christian beliefs seems less likely than if he is regularly in dialogue with other monotheistic communities.[2]

While investigations into the historical setting in which the Qur'an took form are notoriously murky and inconclusive, it is important to draw attention to the fact that the Qur'an is in many places overtly engaged in discussions with Jewish and Christian communities.[3] Chapter 5 will consider how the Qur'an uses Jewish and Christian teaching, characters, and stories, but the current chapter will first investigate how the Qur'an perceives the non-Muslim monotheists with whom it engages. In the process, we will see that the Qur'an intends to embrace the Jewish and Christian communities as those who have served as conduits of truth while also chastising them for their mishandling and misunderstanding of the revelation given to them. Consideration of the particular accusations made against Jews and Christians in the Qur'an will provide insight into how the author of the Qur'an can both endorse and criticize the communities that are referred to throughout as "the People of the Book."[4]

---

1   Gabriel Said Reynolds, *The Qur'an and Its Biblical Subtext* (New York: Routledge, 2010), 33.

2   Reynolds, *The Qur'an and its Biblical Subtext*, 35. Reynolds writes, "[Muhammad's biography] goes to great lengths to emphasize Muhammad's pagan context. Thereby it emphasizes the divine origin of the Qur'an, by having Muhammad far away from the traditional centers of Judaism and Christianity, in a city that was the last, proud metropolis of paganism."

3   For investigations into the Qur'an's original audience from an orientalist perspective, see John Wansborough, *The Sectarian Milieu: Content and Composition of Islamic Salvation History* (Amherst, NY: Promethius, 2006). Also, W. Montgomery Watt and Richard Bell, *Bell's Introduction to the Qur'an* (Edinburgh: Edinburgh University Press, 1970). From a confessional perspective, see Muhammad Mustafa al-'Azami, *The History of the Qur'anic Text: From Revelation to Compilation* (Lahore, Pakistan: Suhail Academy Press, 2005).

4   The Arabic phrase, *ahl al-kitab*, appears in multiple places throughout the Qur'an to designate the Jews and Christians who have received books of divine revelation. Ex. Qur'an 2:105; 3:64–65; 4:123; 29:46; 57:29.

"THE PEOPLE OF THE BOOK" IN THE QUR'AN

At the outset of this chapter that is primarily concerned with addressing the Jews and Christians in the Qur'an, it is appropriate to note that they are not the only non-Muslim monotheists identified by the Qur'an. In several places, the Qur'an also refers to Zoroastrians (see Qur'an 22:17) and a mysterious group referred to as the Sabians (Qur'an 2:62).[5] Regardless of these communities making an appearance, the Qur'an's priority of focus is to identify and dispute the failures of Jews and Christians to responsibly handle the revelation that has come to them.

The Qur'an uses the phrase "the People of the Book" more than fifty times to describe communities that have received divine revelation prior to the advent of the Qur'an.[6] This designation reinforces the concept of a single-source of divine revelation—the "Mother of the Book"—by conflating the revelation given to the Jews and the Christians. This phrase recognizes a single, eternal, and heavenly book as the source of revelation that is distributed to distinct peoples. As such, the believing Muslim community can claim to rightly interpret and apply the true teaching that their forebearers have distorted, misunderstood, and ignored. Thus, the reference to Jews and Christians as "People of the Book" recognizes the valid revelation given to them at the same time as it chastises them for distorting the book's teaching. The Christian reader of the Qur'an does well to consider the breadth of ways that it addresses the People of the Book in order to understand how Muslim readers of the Qur'an are influenced by its teaching to assume Jewish and Christian religious shortcomings and failures.

---

5   Interestingly Qur'an 5:69 is nearly identical to Qur'an 2:62. Likewise, Qur'an 22:17 presents similar phrasing, though with the notable addition of the Qur'an's singular reference to the Magians/Zoroastrians who appear to be related to the Magi of Matthew 2:1, 7, 16. See A. J. Droge, *The Qur'an: A New Annotated Translation* (Bristol, CT: Equinox, 2015), 215n30.

6   See Sidney Griffith, *"Al-Nasara* in the Qur'an," in *New Perspectives on the Qur'an: The Qur'an in Its Historical Context 2*, ed. Gabriel Said Reynolds, 301–22 (New York: Routledge, 2011), 301.

THE JEWS IN THE QUR'AN

While the phrase "People of the Book" communicates the idea that the Jews and Christians are thought of as a singular entity, the Qur'an also addresses them as separate and distinct peoples. The Jews are noted as having received true revelation in the Torah and having taken a covenant with God. This can be seen in the first part of Qur'an 5:44, which states,

> Surely We sent down the Torah, containing guidance and light. By means of it the prophets who had submitted rendered judgement for those who were Jews, and (so did) the rabbis and the teachers, with what they were entrusted of the book of God, and they were witnessed to it.[7]

Likewise, Qur'an 2:40 calls to the Jews, "Sons of Israel! Remember My blessing which I bestowed on you. Fulfill my covenant (and) I shall fulfill your covenant, and Me—fear Me (alone)." Both of these passages affirm that the Jews have received guidance and revelation, but both are also followed by a warning to those who would sell God's signs for a small price.

THE QUR'ANIC CONCEPT OF COVENANT

The reception of revelation is not the only thing that sets the Jews apart from other peoples in the Qur'an. Beyond recognizing that the Jews have received guidance, Qur'an 2:40 twice uses the word 'ahid to convey the idea of a "covenant" made between God and Israel. The Qur'an also uses the word mithaq another twenty-two times to convey a similar concept.[8] Yet, before concluding that the qur'anic concept of covenant is a direct equivalent with the biblical concept, it is important to note some specific features of how "covenant" is used in the Qur'an.[9]

---

7   Cf. Qur'an 2:87: "Certainly We gave Moses the Book, and followed up after him with the messengers."

8   Cf. Qur'an 5:12–14, in which mithaq is used to describe a covenant or pledge taken by both the Israelites and the Christians, thus acknowledging the presence of covenant in both groups.

9   Mark Durie, *The Qur'an and Its Biblical Reflexes* (New York: Lexington, 2018), 195–213. Durie convincingly demonstrates the conceptual difference between biblical covenants and the qur'anic 'ahid and mithaq.

Within the Qur'an, a "covenant" between God and a group of people involves both parties bearing responsibility. As seen in Qur'an 2:40, God calls people to fulfill his "covenant" while also speaking about his fulfillment of their "covenant." In other places, such as Qur'an 9:12, it appears that "covenants" can also function like treaties between warring human parties.[10] Other times, as in Qur'an 23:8, "covenant" functions in a way that conveys a sense of promise that is to be kept. The biblical use of covenant has similarities, yet it is helpful to consider one further use of the word prior to concluding that the two books exhibit synonymous teaching.

The biblical concept of covenant—particularly, divinely initiated covenant—is conditioned by what occurs in Genesis 15. In this passage, Abram and YHWH enter into a covenant relationship, but it is unique from other covenants in that Abram is a passive participant.[11] Whereas covenants typically involved two parties walking in between the splayed halves of slaughtered animals as an invocation of a curse upon them should they fail to keep their side of the agreement, this covenant involved only God as a participant with Abraham merely observing. What this indicates, then, is that the biblical promise of covenant is founded upon God's own faithfulness irrespective of human unfaithfulness. Divine covenant, though it may include curses and blessings for the human parties involved, does not depend upon human faithfulness, but rather upon divine steadfastness and initiation of relationship.[12]

The distinction between this biblical vision of a divine covenant and the Qur'an's understanding is visible in Qur'an 9:111:

Surely God has purchased from the believers their lives and their wealth with (the price of) the Garden (in store) for

---

10   Cf. Qur'an 8:55–56, which says, "Surely the worst of creatures in the sight of God are those who disbelieve—and they will not believe—those of them with whom you have made a treaty, (and) then they break their treaty every time, and they do not guard (themselves)."

11   Gerhard Von Rad, *Genesis*, rev. ed. (Philadelphia: Westminster, 1972), 188.

12   See Alistair Wilson and Jamie Grant, "Introduction," in *The God of Covenant*, ed. Alistair Wilson and Jamie Grant (Leicester, UK: Apollos, 2005), 12, who write, "Covenant is all about relationship between the Creator and his creation."

them. They fight in the way of God, and they kill and are killed. (That is) a promise binding on Him in the Torah, and the Gospel, and the Qur'an. Who fulfills his covenant better than God? So welcome the good news of the bargain you have made with Him. That is the great triumph.

While there are certainly echoes of biblical covenantal concepts here in Qur'an 9:111, the qur'anic covenant functions more like a transaction of promise and purchase than the instantiation of a relationships as seen in the biblical corollary. God's requirement that his people follow his dictates—and in this specific case, to kill and be killed in the ways of God—is part of the bargain that they may receive a pleasurable eternity.

The qur'anic covenant does not anticipate God's faithful, intimate self-involvement in the daily lives of those with whom he has made a covenant. Instead, these followers are indebted to God contractually. The qur'anic use of the biblical stories of Moses and Israel and their covenants with God appear to disregard the biblical concept of covenant and the theological and relational aspects so central to it. Corroborating this, Mark Durie concludes,

> In respect of the Biblical Theology of covenant and associated divine attributes, the Qur'an shows evidence of borrowing Biblical narrative materials for covenant passages, but with loss of covenantal theology. It has borrowed the stories without awareness of or concern for the theology, and the stories are instead fitted into the Qur'an's own theological grid.[13]

Whereas the biblical covenants are completed in the person and work of Jesus Christ and the new people formed in his name, the relational and self-invested nature of the divine covenants in the Bible do not find a parallel in the Qur'an beyond the common term used by both

---

13   Mark Durie, *The Qur'an and Its Biblical Reflexes* (New York: Lexington, 2018), 212–13.

sources.[14] This recognition is important because it allows the Qur'an to accuse the Jews of failing to keep their end of the "covenant," thus prompting God to reject them and to provide another dispensation to the Christians, prior to finally to perfecting his "covenant" with the Muslims.[15]

THE JEWISH SCRIPTURES VERSUS THE JEWISH COMMUNITY

Having noted that the Qur'an acknowledges the "covenant" between the Jews and God, it is important to consider the places that the Qur'an directly addresses the Jewish community.[16] Despite the broadly positive recognition that Jews have received valid revelation, the Qur'an often appears to present the community of the Jews in a negative light.

For example, Qur'an 16:118 discusses the strict dietary laws enforced on the Jews as a curse for Jewish disobedience, as it states, "To those who are Jews, We have forbidden what We recounted to you before. We did not do them evil, but they did themselves evil." Most commentators connect this verse with Qur'an 6:146, which lists the additional dietary prohibitions given to the Jews as a punishment given for their disobedience.[17] Therefore this passage reminds the Jews that

---

14 To the point of the covenants completed in Christ, see the monumental work by Peter Gentry and Stephen Wellum, *Kingdom through Covenant* (Wheaton, IL: Crossway, 2012), 22–25.

15 Israel's rejection in the Qur'an is clearly stated in Qur'an 5:13, which states, "For their breaking their covenant, We cursed them and made their hearts hard. . . . You will continue to see treachery from them, except for a few of them." The passage goes on to accuse the Christians of consequently forgetting parts of their revealed covenant, concluding in verse 15 that the messenger of Islam has come in order to expose the impropriety of the prior communities who have distorted, forgotten, and twisted the revelation entrusted to them.

16 The Qur'an uses the Arabic word *yahud* to refer to the Jews in general and *yahudi* to refer to a single Jewish person. In addition, the Qur'an also uses the word *hada* to refer to a non-Jewish convert or proselyte to Judaism. John Kaltner and Younus Mirza, *The Bible and the Qur'an: Biblical Figures in the Islamic Tradition* (London: T&T Clark, 2018), 85. Kaltner and Mirza note that the Qur'an uses *hada* most frequently in situations where the proselyte is viewed favorably.

17 See Seyyed Hossein Nasr, ed., *The Study Qur'an* (New York: HarperOne, 2015), 689n118.

the different prohibitions levied against them are not a case of unfair treatment in light of the lesser prohibitions given to the Muslims, but rather the result of their stiff-necked disobedience. Despite the positive implications of having received revelation, even the laws revealed to them demonstrate their rebellious and wicked nature.

THE JEWISH PROPHETS VERSUS THE JEWISH COMMUNITY

The Qur'an also makes a distinction between the praise given to the Jewish prophets—Abraham, Moses, and others—and the chastisement of the rest of the Jewish people. For instance, Qur'an 61:56 shows both Moses and Jesus offering criticism of the Jews:

> (Remember) when Moses said to his people, "My people! Why do you hurt me, when you already know that I am the messenger of God to you?" Then, when they turned aside, God caused their hearts to turn aside, (for) God does not guide the people who are wicked. And (remember) when Jesus, son of Mary, said, "Sons of Israel! Surely I am the messenger of God to you, confirming what was before me of the Torah, and bringing good news of a messenger who will come after me, whose name will be Ahmad." Then, when he brought them the clear signs, they said, "This is clear magic."

In this passage one sees that the Jews are doubly condemned—first by their own prophet Moses and second by Jesus, the messenger sent to the Christians as a corrective for Jewish waywardness. Here one begins to see the Qur'an's purpose for distinguishing between the prophets and the peoples to whom the prophets are sent: to use the precedent of Jewish rejection of God's messengers in order to explain the contemporary rejection of Islam.

If the prophets sent to the Jews were rejected, then the message of the prophets can be retained while yet rebuffing the communities that failed to receive them. Furthermore, the Qur'an places on the lips of these prophets hints of a prophet yet to come. The reader sees the clearest example of this in the passage above, Qur'an 61:6, wherein Jesus predicts that a prophet named Ahmad—a name from which Muhammad derives—will come and bring the message of Islam. Qur'an 61:7 goes on to ask, "Who is more evil than the one who forges lies against God, when he is called to Islam? God does not guide people who are evildoers." The Qur'an presents the Jews as a community that, despite a few exceptions, has largely failed to recognize and follow divine guidance and therefore is rightly considered to be a community of evildoers.

JEWS AND CHRISTIANS NEGLECTING THEIR BOOKS

Amidst the critique of the Jews, the Qur'an also charges the Christian community with negligence of their responsibility to follow the guidance sent down to them. For instance, Qur'an 5:64 calls the Jews "fomenters of corruption" as it addresses them, saying,

> The Jews say, "The hand of God is chained." (May) their hands (be) chained, and (may) they (be) cursed for what they say! No! Both His hands are outstretched: He gives as He pleases. What has been sent down to you from your Lord will indeed increase many of them in insolent transgression and disbelief. We have cast enmity and hatred among them until the Day of resurrection. Whenever they light the fire of war, God extinguishes it. But they strive (at) fomenting corruption on the earth, and God does not love the fomenters of corruption.

At the peak of its accusations against the Jews, then, the Qur'an declares that the Jews have determined God to be chained, have fomented corruption, and are not God's beloved people. This is a scathing rebuke of the Jewish community for walking away from the truth that has been revealed to them.

While the passage above directly addresses the Jewish community, the broader context of Qur'an 5 is replete with illustrations of how the Christians have likewise failed and may also be guilty of fomenting corruption. For example, prior to this passage, Qur'an 5:17 has already addressed the blasphemy of the Christians who point to Jesus's divinity, stating, "Certainly they disbelieve who say, 'Surely God—He is the Messiah, son of Mary.'" Thus, both the Jews and the Christians provide for the Qur'an a foil against which to compare those who would believe God's messengers and follow his guidance. Still, the Qur'an appears slightly more inclined toward Christians than it is toward Jews. It is important, then, to turn attention to those places that the Qur'an directly addresses its Christian audience.

THE CHRISTIANS IN THE QUR'AN

The Qur'an regularly discusses the People of the Book in general, and Jews specifically, though it also devotes significant attention to directly addressing Christians. The most common term used to refer to Christians is *nasara*, which is traditionally understood to derive from Jesus's association with Nazareth.[18] In recent years, drawing on the first letter of the word *nasara*, the Arabic letter *nun* (ن) has been used broadly to identify Christians. Beginning with the Islamic State's use of the letter to mark Christian homes for attack, the *nun* has been widely incorporated throughout the Christian world as a way of self-identifying as a Christian and standing in solidarity with persecuted Christians in the territory ravaged by the Islamic State.

The Qur'an refers to Christians as the *nasara* in places such as Qur'an 2:62 which reads, "Surely those who believe, and those who are Jews, and the Christians (*an-nasara*), and the Sabians—whoever believes in God and the Last Day, and does righteousness—they have their reward with their Lord. (There will be) no fear on them, nor will they sorrow." This is one of three places that the Qur'an uses the word *an-nasara* to refer to Christians positively.[19]

---

18 Kaltner and Mirza, *The Bible and the Qur'an*, 29–30. Kaltner and Mirza also note that the singular form is *nasrani*. A wooden translation might be the Nazarenes/a Nazarite, serving as an adjectival descriptor of people connected with Nazareth.

19 Kaltner and Mirza, *The Bible and the Qur'an*, 30. The authors also mention Qur'an 5:69 and Qur'an 5:82, which will be considered shortly.

There are also references to Christians that identify them as the People of the Gospel. One important instance of this occurs in Qur'an 5:46–47, which reads,

> And in their footsteps We followed up with Jesus, son of Mary, confirming what was with him of the Torah, and We gave him the Gospel, containing guidance and light, and confirming what was with him of the Torah, and as guidance and admonition to the ones who guard (themselves). So let the People of the Gospel judge by what God has sent down in it. Whoever does not judge by what God has sent down, those—they are the wicked.

This passage is characteristic of what has been noted above: The Qur'an is keen to acknowledge the heavenly origin of the Gospel while still recognizing the Christian responsibility to adhere to the Qur'an's interpretation thereof. The Christians are the People of the Gospel, but their understanding of the Gospel must be shaped and conditioned by qur'anic instruction.

This passage goes on immediately to address the Muslim community that has now received a Book that confirms the Gospel and the Torah, and provides the final litmus test for proper interpretation. As such, the People of the Gospel are expected to judge their interpretation of the Gospel by the final dispensation of the heavenly Book now available through the Qur'an. Qur'an 5:49 calls its readers to judge the interpretations of the Jewish and Christian communities by what has been revealed in the Qur'an:

> (So) judge between them by what God has sent down, and do not follow their (vain) desires, and beware of them in case they tempt you (to turn away) from any part of what God has sent down to you. If they turn aware, know that God intends to smite them for some of their sins. Surely many of the people are wicked indeed.

The Qur'an recognizes that the Christians have true revelation, as do the Jews, but they are always in danger of chasing vanities and twisting interpretations. Therefore, the Qur'an presents itself as the final arbiter of proper interpretation of heavenly revelation.

CHRISTIANS VIEWED MORE FAVORABLY THAN JEWS

Still, the Christians mentioned in the Qur'an often appear in a slightly more positive light than do their Jewish counterparts. For instance, Qur'an 5:82 contrasts the character of the Jews and the Christians directly, stating,

> Certainly you will find that the most violent of people in enmity to the believers are the Jews and the idolaters. Certainly you will find that the closest of them in affection to the believers are those who say, "We are Christians." That is because (there are) priests and monks among them, and because they are not arrogant.

The passage goes on in optimistic tones regarding the likelihood of Christians hearing the Qur'an, recognizing its truth, and asking to be listed among those who bear witness to it. In fact, Qur'an 5:85 states, "So God has rewarded them for what they have said (with) Gardens through which rivers flow, there to remain. That is the reward for the doers of good." It is worth noting that there is ambiguity as to whether this passage has in mind Christians who rightly follow their Book or former Christians who have officially converted to Islam. Nonetheless, it has led some Muslims to speculate that God will admit Christians who are faithful to share in the Garden paradise that they hope for as well.[20]

---

20   See Nasr, *The Study Qur'an*, 319–321nn82–83. Nasr notes that al-Tabari argued that if Christians remained Christians while yet admitting that the Qur'an is from God and Muhammad is a messenger, then this verse indicating divine blessing and favor applied to them. See also Gabriel Said Reynolds, *The Qur'an and the Bible: Text and Commentary* (New Haven, CT: Yale University Press, 2018), 211, who notes, "This passage is meant to distinguish Christians, some of whom recognize the Qur'an's prophet, from the Jews, who are categorically opposed to him."

AWARENESS OF CHRISTIAN THEOLOGY

Not only does the Qur'an recognize the Christian community, but it also demonstrates more familiarity with and awareness of Christian theology than it appears to have regarding Jewish or pagan beliefs. One instance that illustrates such theological awareness comes from Qur'an 4:171 as we discussed on page 74, which contends,

> People of the Book! Do not go beyond the limits in your religion, and do not say about God (anything) but the truth. The Messiah, Jesus, son of Mary, was only a Messenger of God, and His word, which He cast into Mary, and a spirit from Him. So believe in God and His messengers, but do not say, "Three." Stop! (It will be) better for you. God is only one God. Glory to Him! (Far be it) that He should have a son! To Him (belongs) whatever is in the heavens and whatever is on the earth. God is sufficient as a guardian.

The command to avoid saying "Three" is a clear reference to the doctrine of the Trinity. Likewise, even though the Qur'an argues against associating Jesus with God, this argument itself demonstrates a clear knowledge that Christians believe that Jesus is the Son of God, the second person of the Trinity. Though the Qur'an demonstrates an awareness of Jewish dietary laws, and references many of its prophets, there are few instances within the Qur'an that admit of a similarly detailed knowledge of Jewish belief.

Instead, the Qur'an often appears to view accounts of biblical stories through the lens of a Christian interpretation. One might see this in the important passage found in Qur'an 3:67, which states, "Abraham was not a Jew, nor a Christian, but he was a *hanif*, a Muslim. He was not one of the idolaters." Though this verse clearly teaches that Abraham provides an archetype of the ideal Muslim, the impulse to seeing Abraham as one commended by God prior to the law of Judaism is reflected in the New Testament. For instance, Paul writes of Abraham in Galatians 3:6–9 that Abraham was commended for his faith—counted righteous—before the law was ever given. This is reiterated in Romans 4:1–12 as Paul reminds his readers that Abraham was counted righteous by his faith, not even by circumcision as a mark of the covenant. The New Testament seizes on the fact that Abraham was deemed righteous prior to the coming of the law upon which Jews were inclined to rely for their own righteousness. In a similar way, the Qur'an views Abraham as a prototypical predecessor of its own religious advent.

Likewise, there are places where the Qur'an contains instructions that seem to view the Jews in the same way as the New Testament views the unbelieving Jews, Pharisees, and scribes. Consider Qur'an 5:70, where the Qur'an accuses the Jews of killing the prophets sent to them, saying, "Certainly We took a covenant with the Sons of Israel, and We sent messengers to them. Whenever a messenger brought them what they themselves did not desire, some they called liars and some they killed." This is not substantially different than Matthew 23:33–34 where Jesus chastises the scribes and Pharisees, saying, "You serpents, you brood of vipers, how are you to escape being sentenced to hell? Therefore, I send you prophets and wise men and scribes, some of whom you will kill and crucify, and some you will flog in your synagogues and persecute from town to town." As such, it appears that the Qur'an is keen to present similar accusations against the Jews as did Jesus. Still, the Qur'an attributes its own existence to the fact that Christians have distorted the truth.

CHRISTIANS IN NEED OF CORRECTION

On many occasions, the Qur'an chooses to discuss the community of Christians as those who have distorted, misunderstood, rejected, or hidden the revelation for which they are accountable. As the Jews are often addressed as those who rejected Moses's teaching, so too the Christians are often addressed as those who distorted Jesus's teaching. For example, Qur'an 9:30–31 mocks the Christian community for their apparently foolish understanding of Jesus as the divine son of God when clearly he is merely the human son of Mary.[21] Likewise, Qur'an 5:116–117 records Jesus's denial that he ever sought worship from those of his followers who insist on worshipping him.

Relatedly, Qur'an 57:27 addresses the fact that, though Jesus received the Gospel and passed it on to his followers, some of them added unhelpful innovations as it affirms, "We followed up with Our messengers, and We followed up with Jesus Son of Mary, and gave him the Gospel, and placed in the hearts of those who followed him kindness and mercy. But monasticism, they originated it. We did not prescribe it for them." While accusations of innovative monasticism may not appear to be a scathing rebuke, Qur'an 9:31 identifies a tendency to elevate monks to the role of Lords, thus making them guilty of the cardinal sin of *shirk*: "They have taken their teachers and their monks as Lords instead of God." Thus, these unprescribed innovations are viewed as first steps down the slippery slope of disobedience and disbelief. Since both Jews and Christians have been accused of having abandoned or distorted their revelation, the Qur'an presents itself as a final corrective to the People of the Book who have wandered from their books.

CONCLUSION: THE QUR'AN AS CORRECTIVE TO THE PEOPLE OF THE BOOK

Though there is much within the Qur'an that presents the People of the Book in a positive light, the final conclusion concerning how Muslims are to relate to their Christian and Jewish neighbors is not favorable. In Qur'an 5:51 the Muslims are instructed clearly, "You who believe! Do not take the Jews and Christians as allies. They are allies of each other. Whoever of you takes them as allies is already one of them. Surely God does not guide the people who are evildoers." It goes on in verse 57 to caution further, "You who believe! Do not take those who take your religion in mockery and jest as allies, (either) from those who were given the Book before you, or (from) the disbelievers."

---

21   Chapter 8 will discuss this passage in depth in order to consider some of the proposed interpretations of how to understand this singular use of the phrase *ibn Allah*.

Instead of affirming the Jews and Christians, the Qur'an consistently presents itself as a final correction of the distortions that the Jews and Christians have introduced to their portions of the Book. Qur'an 13:36–37 confirms this as it chastises the Jews and Christians, stating:

> Those to whom We have given the Book rejoice in what has been sent down to you, though some among the factions reject part of it. Say: "I am only commanded to serve God, and not to associate (anything) with Him. To Him do I call (you), and in Him is my return." In this way, we have sent it down as an Arabic judgment. If indeed you follow their (vain) desires, after what has come to you of the knowledge, You will have no ally and no defender against God.

This passage confirms that the Books that have been revealed previously have come from God. However, it also accuses some of the former recipients of having rejected parts of it. Such is the justification of the final revelation in the Qur'an, given in Arabic as a corrective of Jewish and Christian tampering with their holy books.

Lest the Jewish and Christian communities dispute the argument that they have tampered with their books by providing evidence that it has been unchanged, this passage continues in Qur'an 13:38–39 to say, "For every (period of) time (there is) a written decree. God blots out whatever He pleases, and He confirms (whatever He pleases). With Him is the mother of the Book." Therefore, whether the Jews or Christians can be proven guilty of altering their Scriptures, the Qur'an is God's final dispensation of the mother of the Book. It alone is binding upon the Muslim community, and all who would dispute it or its relevance are counted among the unbelievers—even if they are among the People of the Book.

Ultimately, the Qur'an is inclined to endorse the prior Scriptures and the communities that follow them only insofar as they reinforce and submit to the message of the Qur'an. It envisions communities of Jews and Christians hearing its message and realizing that they were Muslims all along, as seen in Qur'an 28:52–35: "Those to whom

We gave the Book before it—they believe in it. When it is recited to them, they say, 'We believe in it. Surely it is the truth from our Lord. Surely we were Muslims before it.'" For all who fail to recognize the Qur'an's truth due to a misunderstanding of prior Scriptures, the Qur'an assigns the label of unbeliever. As the Qur'an picks up teachings, characters, and stories that have their origin in the prior books it is important to consider how its integration of these stories into its own concerns needs to be considered. The next chapter will address the way that the Qur'an uses the material of the previous books to reinforce its own message.

6

THE QUR'AN AS MOSAIC

*And Mary, daughter of 'Imran, who guarded her
private part: We breathed into it some of Our spirit,
and she affirmed the words of her Lord and His Books,
and became one of the obedient.*

Qur'an 66:12

The previous chapters highlight the fact that the Qur'an is intentional in presenting itself as a continuation of the same message as recorded in the previous books. The continuity of message is reinforced further by the idea that all of the heavenly books belong to the Mother of the Book: the single, unified, eternal record of God's revealed will to humanity. This is the claim repeated in various ways throughout the Qur'an's pages.

It remains, however, to press past the mere claim of continuity and to consider the particular references to shared history, characters, and teaching within the Qur'an. Given the regular insistence that the Qur'an completes the revelation that was given before, one would expect to find similarity of concern, detail, and content within its pages. If the Qur'an is a sequel to the prior Scriptures, then the main characters, personalities, messages, and storylines should be cohesive with previous records. While the Qur'an undoubtedly exhibits points of obvious similarity, it is the various points at which the Qur'an presents differences from the Bible that have caused scholars of Islam to propose various theories of explanation.

One instance of apparent difference can be seen in Qur'an 66:12, the verse cited at the head of this chapter. A reader familiar with the biblical story is likely to see in this verse the apparent conflation of Miriam—the daughter of 'Amram and the sister of Moses and Aaron (Exod. 6:20)—and Mary the mother of Jesus.[1] This conflation is all the more pronounced in Qur'an 19:16–28 where the Mary discussed is clearly the mother of 'Isa, but is also referred to as the "sister of Aaron" in 9:28.

At this point, the question presents itself, "If the Qur'an perfectly continues the divine revelation given prior, what do we make of apparent errors, contradictions, and conflations of the previous material that are found within its pages?" While each particular instance presents its own unique questions and multiple potential answers have been proposed, it is important to consider these points of apparent discord in developing an understanding of exactly how the Qur'an intends to relate to the prior revelations it claims to complete.

For confessional Muslims, most such points of discord are resolved by appealing to the final authority of the Qur'an and the potential of the biblical sources having undergone corruption.[2] Scholars of a less pietistic bent have at times simply attributed such anomalies

---

1   See Gordon Nickel, ed., *The Qur'an with Christian Commentary* (Grand Rapids: Zondervan, 2020), 83n3.25. By referring to Mary as the daughter of 'Imran—here in Qur'an 66:12 and also in 3:35–62—the Qur'an seems to present Mary the mother of Jesus as a daughter to 'Amram, the father of Moses, Aaron, and Miriam (see Exod. 6:20).

2   Given the specific example of Mary the mother of Jesus referred to as the sister of Aaron, many scholars would also suggest that this language is not intended to represent an immediate biological relationship. Instead, "sister" should be understood to highlight a genealogical association with one known for righteousness and a key role in the history of the people of the Book in previous days. This way, taking "sister" as a general reference to "descendent/relative" does not involve a difference of contradiction, but might be compared to the way that the Bible refers to Jesus as a Son of David (Matt. 1:1). Likewise, just because 'Amram and 'Imran likely derive from the same name, it does not mean that Mary's father was not also named 'Imran. Some such apparent discrepancies can be explained with plausible suggestions while others are perhaps more difficult to navigate.

to Muhammad's partial apprehension of the biblical material being related and conflated through orally transmitted retellings.

Yet giving devoted deference to the Qur'an when faced with its apparent historical contradictions of biblical material or dismissing its historical errors as evidence that its author was misinformed are not the only possible explanations. In fact, both of these explanations presume that the Qur'an intends its accounts primarily to be understood as historical records and that these records have been appropriately analyzed through the lens of later traditional Islamic theology. However, much of these extra-qur'anic traditions and the hermeneutical lens they provide have been demonstrated to be unreliable, uncorroborated, and inadmissible as historical records.[3] Recent scholarship has shown fruitful engagement with the text of the Qur'an freed of the imposition of later, biased, and historically dubious traditional interpretations.[4]

In following the promising light provided by these recent interpretive proposals, this chapter will investigate a mosaic reading of several points of apparent historical discord in the Qur'an's content. These sections will be useful in demonstrating the fruitful interpretive results that come from viewing the Qur'an as a sort of subversive mosaic. By viewing the genre of the Qur'an as a biblically conscious mosaic, the points of apparent conflict might not be dismissed as mere errors, but can be seen as instances of an intentional subversion of the traditional Jewish and Christian interpretations of biblical material. I want to argue that inspecting the Qur'an as a theologically subversive mosaic alleviates the interpreter of the burden to reconcile the apparent historical discrepancies presented within the Qur'an and instead focuses

---

3   Gabriel Said Reynolds, *The Qur'an and Its Biblical Subtext* (New York: Routledge, 2010), 3–22; Mark Durie, *The Qur'an and Its Biblical Reflexes* (New York: Lexington, 2018), 8–20. See also the collection of critical writings in the volume Karl-Heinz Ohlig, *Early Islam: A Critical Reconstruction Based on Contemporary Sources* (Amherst, NY: Prometheus, 2013). See the discussion of uncorroborated historical accounts in Nicolai Sinai, *The Qur'an: A Historical-Critical Introduction* (Edinburgh: University of Edinburgh Press, 2017), 40–58.

4   See especially Reynolds, *The Qur'an and Its Biblical Subtext*, and Durie, *The Qur'an and Its Biblical Reflexes*. Their proposals will be explored in greater detail in what follows.

on the Qur'an's theology. Prior to doing so, however, it is helpful for the reader to see the interpretive importance of discerning a rhetorical genre within which to place the Qur'an.

ALTERNATIVE GENRE PROPOSALS

The expectations that a reader has for a book will inevitably shape their reception of its contents. For instance, if one were to take up a cookbook and begin to read it as if it were a novel, the measure of frustration and the lack of satisfaction with the experience would be profound. So too does one's understanding of what the Qur'an *is* affect the way that one attempts to understand what the Qur'an *says*. As non-Muslim scholarly interest has grown over the last two hundred years, multiple proposals for how to read and interpret the Qur'an have proliferated. It is important to consider some of the leading proposals in order to recognize how an understanding of the Qur'an and its genre affects one's strategy for reading an understanding it.

THE QUR'AN AS IMPECCABLE DIVINE RECORD

Most confessional Muslims approach the Qur'an as the impeccable record of what Jibril revealed to Muhammad. As discussed in previous chapters, it is the perfect and completed revelation of God's will for mankind, and its authority is final. Such a posture leads most Muslims to offer deference to the Qur'an in any situation where its historical details might differ from the biblical material. Such a willingness is amplified by the common assumption that the biblical material has been corrupted and therefore was in need of correction. Taking such a view, a reader is often unconcerned to reconcile apparent discrepancies as they are more readily dismissed as evidence of biblical corruption than qur'anic error.

Confessional approaches also often assume the basic reliability of the traditional interpretations of the Qur'an known as the *Sunnah*. This body of secondary literature bears authoritative weight in the practice of Islam by connecting verses of the Qur'an with Muhammad's biography (the biography recorded by Ibn Hisham about two hundred years after Muhammad's death is typically referred to as the *Sirat Rasul Allah*, or simply as the *Sira*) or accounts of his explanation of specific verses (short accounts of Muhammad's actions and sayings are recorded in volumes of collected *hadith* that shed interpretive light on the Qur'an and which help contemporary Muslims live out their Islamic convictions). The *Sunnah* provides a narrative frame for the historical background that the Qur'an is unconcerned to identify internally, and in so doing it applies an interpretive pressure on the Qur'an as it is written. Therefore, when a reader is interested to know the interpretation of a confusing passage, they will appeal to the *Sunnah* for a sense of context and to determine whether or not Muhammad provided an example of how to live out its specific teaching.

One of the things that the *Sunnah* is intent on establishing is the idea that Muhammad did not borrow stories and material from the Jews and Christians in the composition of the Qur'an. It teaches that Muhammad was an uneducated man—some accounts would even interpret the language to indicate that he was illiterate—and that he lived among a polytheistic people prior to receiving the revelation of the Qur'an.[5] As indicated above, however, recent scholarship has called the historical reliability of the *Sunnah* into question.

If a reader of the Qur'an were not biased by the *Sunnah* to separate the author of the Qur'an from an intentional engagement with biblical and extrabiblical materials, what impact might that have on how the Qur'an is interpreted? This is the question that has been fruitfully pursued by several recent scholars of Islam. It behooves us to consider two such approaches that intentionally read the Qur'an and the Bible as if the former is more aware of the latter than the Islamic traditions might indicate.

THE QUR'AN AS HOMILY

The first such scholar whose contributions must be considered is Gabriel Said Reynolds. Reynolds is a proponent of the idea—contrary to the assumptions of the *Sunnah*—that the Qur'an is consciously

---

5   See the discussion on the tradition of Muhammad's illiteracy in Matthew Bennett, *40 Questions About Islam* (Grand Rapids: Kregel Academic, 2020), 249.

interacting with the Bible. He contends that the Qur'an should be read as a sort of homily that is knowingly unpacking and repackaging the biblical material for a different time and day. Reynolds writes, "The Qur'an does not seek to correct, let alone replace, Biblical literature, but instead to use that literature for its homiletic exhortation."[6]

For Reynolds, the Qur'an views itself as weaving together its own distinctive—though not necessarily contradictory—teaching, presenting a fresh picture and contemporary applications by recycling and rearranging pieces of biblical material. One might think of the Qur'an's message as an image portrayed in a mosaic style. The image itself does not exist within any of the disparate parts, but as they are joined together the artist brings out her intended image through the new connections made between the parts.

Taking this approach, then, the historical inconsistencies that the Qur'an exhibits need not trouble the reader because, "For the Qur'an all that matters is the impact on the reader, the degree to which its discourse on these characters and places might lead the reader to repentance and obedience."[7] Reynolds envisions the Qur'an as an attempt to correct Jewish and Christian interpretations of the Bible while not challenging the integrity of the biblical text itself. He writes, "Through consistent references to Biblical literature the Qur'an claims a status as the proper interpreter of the Bible."[8] In the end, if stripped of its later Islamic interpretations, Reynolds concludes, "the Qur'an and the Bible, far from being incompatible or in opposition, are very much in harmony."[9]

In other words, Reynolds is optimistic that the message of the Qur'an might not be as irreconcilable with the Bible as later Islamic theology is with Christianity. Other scholars, despite a similar approach to reading the Qur'an as a commentary on biblical and extra-biblical material, however, are less optimistic regarding the potential for synthesizing and reconciling the teaching of the two books.

6   Gabriel Said Reynolds, *The Qur'an and Its Biblical Subtext* (New York: Routledge, 2009), 238–39.
7   Reynolds, *The Qur'an and Its Biblical Subtext*, 239.
8   Reynolds, *The Qur'an and Its Biblical Subtext*, 249.
9   Reynolds, *The Qur'an and Its Biblical Subtext*, 258.

THE QUR'AN AS BIBLICAL BORROWING

Mark Durie is a scholar, like Reynolds, who contends that later Islamic interpretations obscure an understanding the Qur'an on its own terms. Durie, however, proposes a more subversive understanding of the Qur'an's use of biblical material.[10] While a confessional Muslim will be unsurprised to find biblical reflections in the Qur'an due to the fact that Islam teaches that the Qur'an is the rightful inheritor and interpreter of biblical history, Durie distinguishes between inheritance and borrowing. Using the example of languages derived from a shared source, Durie defines inheritance as the incorporation of extant material into a development that retains the essential characteristics of the original paradigm.[11] Borrowing, on the other hand, dislocates something from its original context and uses it in ways irrespective of its former employ.[12]

Concluding this discussion and applying the linguistic distinctions to the relationship between the Qur'an and its appropriation of biblical material, Durie contends, "the relatedness between the Bible and the Qur'an is not due to inheritance, but to borrowing, and the Qur'an, in repurposing Biblical materials, applies them to serve its own theological agenda."[13] Such repurposing, for Durie, recognizes the biblical source for qur'anic references, but contends that such material is used to construct divergent and incompatible theologies. Reinforcing this point that biblical material is repurposed within the Qur'an, Durie agrees with John Wansbrough, who writes, "Scripture

---

10   In fact, Durie is directly critical of Reynolds' optimistic vision of a "conversation" and "harmonization" between the Bible and Qur'an. Cf. Durie, *The Qur'an and Its Biblical Reflexes*, xxxvi.

11   Durie, *The Qur'an and Its Biblical Reflexes*, xli. Using the example of languages that derive from a common source, Durie writes, "inherited similarities [are] features which two languages share because the come from the same original language." This includes sharing a similar function within the overall systems of language.

12   Durie, *The Qur'an and Its Biblical Reflexes,* xli. Using the example of borrowed language, Durie states, "Borrowing is characteristically disruptive—even destructive—of previous structural relationships. It is a process akin to plucking a brick or tile from one building and inserting it into another."

13   Durie, *The Qur'an and Its Biblical Reflexes*, lii.

was being pressed into the service of as yet unfamiliar doctrine."[14] In other words, though the Qur'an intends to use biblical material, it does so with disregard for the role that material played previously in favor of how it might be used to develop the Qur'an's independent concerns.

Having demonstrated that the Qur'an does not affirm the theological teachings of the Bible at eight significant points of shared language, Durie determines that the Qur'an shows evidence of borrowing and repurposing this biblical material but should not be understood as inheriting it.[15] As the remainder of this chapter will attempt to show, Durie and Reynolds lead in a helpful direction as they free the interpretation of the Qur'an from the shaping—and perhaps even distorting—effects of later Islamic traditions. This chapter shares Durie's skepticism that the Qur'an can be read as harmonious with the Bible. It also proposes a more intentional and subversive relationship to the biblical material by using the analogy of a subversive mosaic.

A SUBVERSIVE MOSAIC

Within the Qur'an, one finds not only biblical material, but also extrabiblical material that circulated in writing in the third and fourth centuries. As the Qur'an employs these references from biblical and extrabiblical sources, it often conflates different stories, drawing together otherwise discrete incidents in order to reinforce its own teaching.[16] This rhetorical approach creates a resonance with the original referents while also engaging in the creation of new meaning. As alluded to above, I find it helpful to illustrate the difference between

---

14   Durie, *The Qur'an and Its Biblical Reflexes,* xxxvi, draws his citation from John Wansbrough, *Qur'anic Studies: Sources and Methods of Scriptural Interpretation* (Oxford: Oxford University Press, 1977), 20.

15   Durie, *The Qur'an and Its Biblical Reflexes,* liii. Durie lists the topoi for consideration at the close of the introduction: Christology, Pneumatology, Divine Presence, Holiness, Satan and "satans," Covenant, Narratives of the Fall, and Warfare. Through the investigation of the qur'anic use of these topoi, Durie convincingly demonstrates systemic inconsistency between biblical theology and qur'anic theology at these key points.

16   John Wansbrough, *The Sectarian Milieu: Content and Composition of Islamic Salvation History* (Amhurst, NY: Prometheus, 2006), 11.

biblical history and the Qur'an's use of biblical history by referring to the difference between a jigsaw puzzle and a mosaic. A jigsaw puzzle is made up of interlocking pieces that display a single, complete picture when each piece unites its contribution with the adjacent pieces, demonstrating an apparently preexisting relationship between the individual pieces. A mosaic, on the other hand, brings together pieces that would otherwise bear no obvious relationship to one another in order to manifest an image that exists in the mind of the artist. Despite the production of an image through the collection and arrangement by the artist, the pieces of a mosaic remain discrete and artificially connected to adjacent pieces in an effort to produce an image that is not native to any of the individual parts. To apply this distinction to the Bible and the Qur'an, one might see the Bible presenting historical pieces as parts of a jigsaw puzzle while the Qur'an uses biblical history as pieces in a mosaic that displays an image of its own making.

The Qur'an's mosaic use of biblical material exhibits itself in several ways. As we will see below, the Qur'an occasionally conflates biblical accounts in an apparent effort to demonstrate that the characters—though far removed from one another chronologically—illustrate the same teaching or warning that the Qur'an is keen to highlight. Such instances may be generally in keeping with biblical teaching, such as the warning to those who would be placed in leadership and yet pridefully fail to submit themselves to God as their authority. Other uses of mosaic construction of biblical material, however, may intend to undermine or subvert biblical teachings.[17] For instance, as we consider the implications of non-chronological lists of biblical characters there is reason to see the Qur'an subtly dethroning Jesus from his place in biblical history in order to prepare

---

17   On the topic of subversion, see the helpful work of Daniel Strange, *Their Rock Is Not Like Our Rock* (Grand Rapids: Zondervan, 2014), 285–302. While Strange's work contends that the Gospel subversively fulfills alternative worldviews and non-Christian religions, it is important to see that other faiths might similarly be engaged in a similar attempt. Islam presents itself as a fine candidate for such subversion as its advent postdates Christianity. Chapter 9 will discuss Strange's work more extensively in relation to the Gospel and the Qur'an.

the way for the prophet of the Qur'an. The following examples will illustrate the fruitfulness of this approach to the Qur'an's curious use of biblical material.

A MOSAIC READING: HAMAN, PHARAOH, AND A TOWER TO HEAVEN

One instance of the apparent conflation of biblical stories is found in the qur'anic references to Pharaoh, Haman, and Korah. These three characters are listed together in Qur'an 40:23–24, which states, "Certainly we sent Moses with our signs and clear authority to Pharaoh, Haman, and Qarun [Korah], but they said, 'A magician and a liar!'" This section parallels with another qur'anic account of Pharaoh's interactions with Haman, including Pharaoh issuing a command to Haman to build him a tower that would reach into heaven and allow him to expose the lies of Moses regarding his God (cf. Qur'an 28:36–39; 40:36–37).

Furthermore, listed alongside of Haman, Qarun—or Korah— appears in Pharaoh's court in Qur'an 29:39–40:

> And Qarun [Korah], and Pharaoh, and Haman—certainly Moses brought them the clear signs, but they became arrogant on the earth. Yet they did not outrun (Us). We seized each one for his sin. We sent a sandstorm against one of them, and another of them was seized by the cry, and We caused the earth to swallow (yet) another of them, and We drowned (still) another of them. Yet God was not one to do them evil, but they did themselves evil.

If one compares this qur'anic passage with the biblical accounts of Pharaoh and Korah deaths, it seems likely that the drowning is meant to refer to Pharaoh's death in the Red Sea (cf. Exod. 14:28) and Korah's death corresponds to those who were swallowed into the earth (cf. Num. 26:10). The references to a sandstorm and being seized by the cry are perhaps more obscure, though Seyyed Hossein Nasr suggests that the "sandstorm" might also be translated as a hailstorm of rocks or a torrent of stones which would be reminiscent of the fate of those who opposed Lot (cf. Qur'an 15:74; 29:33; 54:34).[18] An observant reader who is biblically aware will likely detect echoes of several disparate stories in these verses. First, Moses and Pharaoh's showdown seems to be in view as Pharaoh resists the command of YHWH to release the Hebrew people (cf. Exod. 7–10). Second, the character of Haman who accompanies Pharaoh in the Qur'an does not appear in the biblical narrative, yet the exact form of this name is a central character in the book of Esther (Esther 3). Third, Korah and the reference to being swallowed by the earth recalls Korah's rebellion in the wilderness long after the exodus (cf. Num. 16:1–35). Fourth, one might also detect an allusion to the tower of Babel narrative from Genesis 11:1–9. In light of the apparent synthesis of these four stories, a reader might be tempted to arrive at a number of conclusions.

First, an historical-critical reading might account for this novel narrative by appealing to mistaken transmission of disparate oral stories. If Muhammad was illiterate and uneducated, he would have had no means of confirming the narratives he heard against the details of the biblical account. Confessional Muslims, on the other hand, might be inclined to point to the fact that Haman and Korah could share their names with other characters in the biblical account but remain otherwise independent of them. Biblical silence regarding the names of those who might have been a part of Pharaoh's court is by no means a denial of their existence.

Still, if the Qur'an has exhibited mosaic tendencies in other places, there may be a way that we might see the Qur'an intentionally referring to the biblical characters from disparate stories without being accused of error. If the Qur'an knowingly draws these characters together in circumstances that are not necessarily historical, what theological purpose might that serve? Is there any reason that

---

18   Seyyed Hossein Nasr, *The Study Qur'an* (New York: HarperOne, 2015), 976n40, writes, "A torrent of stones (cf. 17:68; 67:17) was sent against the people to whom Lot preached (see 15:74; 29:33; 54:34)."

the Qur'an might want to appropriate these four events in order to reinforce a shared theme?

As this passage continues in Qur'an 29:41–44, each of these four biblical stories are shown to be illustrative of a common lesson:

> The parable of those who take allies other than God is like the parable of the spider: it takes a house, but surely the house of the spider is indeed the most feeble of houses—if (only) they knew. Surely God know whatever they call on instead of Him. He is the Mighty, the Wise. Those parables—we strike them for the people, but not one understands them except the ones who know. God created the heavens and the earth in truth. Surely that is a sign indeed for the believers.

What the reader encounters as the Qur'an employs these chronologically distant narratives in a single occasion is the same basic teaching that emerges from the other places that the Qur'an refers to these characters: arrogance leads creatures to try to replace the Creator.[19] This is clearly articulated in Qur'an 28:39 as it exposes the underlying problem exhibited by Pharaoh: "He and his forces became arrogant on the earth without any right, and thought that they would not be returned to Us."

In each of these passages also, Pharaoh and Haman and Korah stand in contrast to Moses who is one to whom God has given a Book of instruction and guidance. It appears, then, that the Qur'an intends to demonstrate that Pharaoh is not the only exhibition of arrogant rejection of God's message. Instead, each of the characters and stories reinforce this same idea. The people at Babel attempted to make a name for themselves in arrogant self-confidence and in rejection of God's command to fill the earth and multiply. Korah and his community stubbornly resisted the commands of God and the one whom God had commissioned to lead his people. And Haman attempted to set himself up as one worthy of esteem and honor at

---

19   Qur'an 28:6–8; 40:36–37.

the expense of the Hebrew people. Reynolds states it this way, "Nimrod [of the Babel account] and Pharaoh in the Qur'an represent the same type, the ruler who challenges God's sovereignty."[20] Thus, like Pharaoh resisting the words of God in preference to his own wisdom and desire for attention and authority, all of these accounts prove the folly of rejecting God's word and God's messengers.

A MOSAIC READING: DAVID, SAUL, GOLIATH, AND GIDEON

Another place that the Qur'an appears to conflate biblical stories is found in Qur'an 2:246–51. In this passage the reader encounters references to Israel's first king, Talut—assumed to be the biblical Saul from 1 Samuel 10—to king David, and also echoes of the story of Gideon's army and hints at the battle with Goliath, whom the Qur'an refers to as Jalut.[21] Despite the length of the passage, it is worth quoting it in full here prior to unpacking the potential interpretations involved in this account.

> Have you not considered the assembly of the Sons of Israel after (the time of) Moses? They said to a prophet of theirs, "Raise us a king for us, (and) we shall fight in the way of God." He said, "Is it possible that, if fighting is prescribed for you, you will not fight?" They said, "Why should we not fight in the way of God, when we have been expelled from our homes and our children?" Yet when fighting was prescribed for them, they (all) turned away, except for a few of them. God has knowledge of the evildoers.

> And their prophet said to them, "Surely God has raised up for you Talut as king." They said, "How can he possess

20 Gabriel Said Reynolds, *The Qur'an and Its Biblical Subtext* (New York: Routledge, 2010), 103.

21 Nasr, *The Study Qur'an*, 108nn249–51. See the defense of the translation of Talut as "Saul" and Jalut as "Goliath." Likewise, Nasr notes the apparent correlation of the Gideon account, but dismisses the similarity as an event that could have occurred both for Gideon and for Saul.

the kingship over us, when we are more deserving of the kingship than him, and he has not been given abundant wealth?" He said, "Surely God has chosen him (to be) over you, and has increased him abundantly in knowledge and stature. God gives his kingdom to whomever He pleases. God is embracing, knowing."

And their prophet said to them, "Surely the sign of his kingship is that the ark will come to you. In it is a Sakina from your Lord, and a remnant of what the house of Moses and the house of Aaron left behind. The angels (will) carry it. Surely in that is a sign indeed for you, if you are believers."

When Talut set out with his forces, he said, "Surely God is going to test you by means of a river. Whoever drinks from it is not on my side, but whoever does not taste it is surely on my side, except for whoever scoops (it) up with his hand." But they (all) drank from it, except for a few. So when he crossed it, he and those who believed with him, they said, "We have no strength today against Jalut and his forces." But those who thought that they would meet God said, "How many a small cohort has overcome a large cohort by the permission of God? God is with the patient." So when they went forth to (battle) Jalut and his forces, they said, "Our Lord, pour out on us patience, and make firm our feet, and help us against the people who are disbelievers." And they routed them by the permission of God, and David killed Jalut, and God gave him the kingdom and the wisdom, and taught him about whatever he pleased. If God had not repelled some of the people by means of others, the earth would indeed have been corrupted. But God is full of favor to the worlds.

The echoes of Gideon's story occur in the reference to Saul leading his forces to a river, testing them to see who will drink from their hands or refrain from drinking altogether. Though not an exact retelling of the account of Gideon's army, the significant parallels evoke the story while being applied in a time well after Gideon's day.

On the surface, one can see why Gideon and Saul and David might be used by the Qur'an to mutually reinforce one another as symbols of the same teaching. As leaders of God's people, Gideon, Saul, and David all are looked to as examples of leadership under God's authority. At the beginning of Gideon's leadership, God demonstrated that it would be YHWH's favor that granted victory to Israel, not Gideon's strength or cunning. Judges 7:1–8 recounts the story of Gideon's army being culled to three hundred men on the seemingly arbitrary distinction made between how the men drank water from the spring. This reduction of force is explicitly tied to the recognition that it is not Israel's might that would save them, but Israel's God.

Saul's appointment to the throne was likewise marked by dependence upon the Lord. As Samuel was sent to the house of Benjamin, to a man named Kish who was wealthy. Despite this Saul himself initially protests this appointment to king, saying, "Am I not a Benjaminite, from the least of the tribes of Israel? And is not my clan the humblest of all the clans of the tribe of Benjamin?" Despite the lowly status of Saul's family, Samuel is directed to anoint him as king and the Spirit of God rushes upon him (1 Sam. 10:10). And even though a portion of the people were inclined to reject him, Saul kept his peace, indicating a deference to the will of the Lord over and against his popularity among the people.

Finally, Saul's trust of the Lord culminates biblically with his willingness to send David—a youthful shepherd—out to do battle against Goliath an the Philistine armies (1 Sam. 17). In the biblical account, David has already been anointed king but has not attempted to usurp Saul's leadership. Furthermore, when David volunteers to confront Goliath, he does so on the explicit conviction that the Lord will be the one who will deliver Goliath into David's hand. Again, this victory is not one that is achieved by human strength, popularity, or cunning, but on the basis of the Lord's provision. Thus, all three leaders—despite each one's biblical failures—are taken by the Qur'an as exemplars of faithful trust in the strength and wisdom of God. For the Qur'an to make the parallel is therefore justified as it seeks to reinforce the idea that it is God who fights on behalf of his people who humbly submit themselves to his guidance.

But there is another aspect of this qur'anic portrayal that seems to harken back to biblical concepts that are reappropriated to serve the Qur'an's purposes. That is the reference in Qur'an 2:248 to the *Sakinah* from the Lord that will validate Saul's kingship and recall Moses and Aaron's ministry. While some translations render *Sakinah* as "tranquility"[22] or "security,"[23] though A. J. Droge leaves untranslated to indicate the lack of consensus regarding what this word should be understood to indicate. In so doing, Droge highlights for the English reader the similarity between this Arabic term and what might be a Hebrew cognate: *shekinah*. The postbiblical Hebrew term *shekinah* is associated with the descent and presence of God's glory among his people, a Talmudic term that expresses a biblical concept central to the work of Moses, Aaron, and the ark of the covenant.[24]

Furthermore, as Gordon Nickel points out, the Qur'an uses *Sakinah* in six places.[25] Of these other occurrences, Qur'an 9:40 is perhaps most intriguing as it indicates the *Sakinah* apparently falling on Muhammad while he and Abu Bakr were hiding in a cave, avoiding the Meccans who were seeking to kill him.[26] The remainder of the occasions refer to the provision of the *Sakinah* to believers who are in need of assurance and increase in their faith (48:4), success in battle (48:18) and the hope of entering the sacred Mosque (the Ka'ba) following the victory over the Meccans (48:26–29). Thus, Qur'an 2:248

---

22 Nasr, *The Study Qur'an*, 107n248.

23 Abdullah Yusuf Ali, *The Qur'an: Text, Translation, and Commentary* (Elmhurst, NY: Tahrike Tarsile Qur'an, 2005), 99n282.

24 Nickel, *The Qur'an with Christian Commentary*, 71n2.248. Cf. Gabriel Said Reynolds, *The Qur'an and the Bible: Text and Commentary* (New Haven, CT: Yale University Press, 2018), 95–96. Cf. Ali, *The Qur'an*, 99n282. Ali specifically notes, "Later Jewish writings use the same word for a symbol of God's Glory in the Tabernacle or tent in which the Ark was kept, or in the Temple when it was built by Solomon."

25 Nickel, *The Qur'an with Christian Commentary*, 72n2.248. Nickel notes Qur'an 9:26, 40; 48:4, 18, 26 as other occurrences of *Sakinah* where it is associated with success in battle being divinely granted.

26 Nasr, *The Study Qur'an*, 518n40. See also the references to the *Sakinah* being given to both Muhammad and the believers in Qur'an 9:26, 48:26.

is the only reference to the *Sakinah* that is applied to biblical figures. The qur'anic concept of *Sakinah* appears to have a connection with divine protection and assurance being given to the faithful as they trust in God to deliver them in battles, but rather than presenting itself as a new innovation in divine relationship with his people, Qur'an 2:248 links the *Sakinah* with Moses, Aaron, Gideon, Saul, and David.

What appears to be in view, then, is not a reference to the Hebrew concept of the Glory of God dwelling in the midst of his people.[27] Rather, there is a parallel with those saints of old who faced opponents that were likely to overwhelm them, and yet God fought on their behalf. Moses and Aaron before Pharaoh saw God providing victory and deliverance. Likewise, Gideon faced extermination and found himself hiding in a winepress in fear of his numerous enemies, yet God provided demonstration of his deliverance. So too did Samuel, Saul, and David find themselves outnumbered and yet victorious by the work of God on their behalf. The *Sakinah* is what God delivered to assure these faithful men that God would act on their behalf against all odds to the contrary.

While it might be tempting to see the Qur'an assimilating a biblical vision of the presence of God assuring the hearts of his people with qur'anic teaching, it is important to note that Qur'an 2:248 indicates that the *Sakinah* that would come to Saul would be in the ark of the covenant.[28] Drawing on Exodus 25:10–22, one notes that the contents of the ark of the covenant include Jesse's budded staff, some of the manna of God's provision, and the tablets of the law given on Mount Sinai. Thus, it seems more likely that the Qur'an intends to use *Sakinah* as a reference to God's comforting words of instruction and law that assure the believing communities that he will act on their behalf.

Moses, Aaron, Gideon, Samuel, Saul, and David have all given testimony in their lives of having received words from the Lord

---

27   On the topic of the Presence of God in the Qur'an, see the helpful study of Durie, *The Qur'an and Its Biblical Reflexes*, 175–80.

28   The Arabic phrase clearly indicates that the *Sakinah* is in the *taabut* (ark of the covenant).

that have promised their protection despite dire circumstances. Therefore, as Muhammad likewise receives instructions from God, mediated through Jibril's transmission of the Qur'an, assurance of success over their enemies builds their faith and results in comfort in the face of adversity. If the Qur'an intends this mosaic synthesis of the Gideon-Samuel-Saul-David stories, it thus provides a platform upon which to demonstrate that Muhammad inherits this same *Sakinah* and its corresponding divine endorsement. In other words, Muhammad is counted among those leaders of God's people who demonstrate faith in the midst of adversity and who are granted assurance of success by the sending of God's word.

A MOSAIC READING: CHRONOLOGICALLY NON-SENSICAL LISTS

A third place where the Qur'an might demonstrate a type of mosaic approach to its use of biblical material can be seen in several of the lists of biblical characters that are given with no reference to chronological order.[29] For instance, Qur'an 6:83–89 provides the longest list of prophets in any one place in the Qur'an, listing eighteen names traditionally associated with biblical characters: [30]

> That (was) our argument. We gave it to Abraham against his people. We raise in rank whomever We please. Surely your Lord is wise, knowing. And We granted him Isaac and Jacob—each one We guided, and Noah We guided before (them)—and of his descendants (were) David, and Solomon, and Job, and Joseph, and Moses, and Aaron—in this way We repay the doers of good—and Zechariah, and John, and Jesus, and Elijah—each one was of the righteous—ad Ishmael, and Elisha, and Jonah, and Lot—each one We

---

29 Not all lists appear with disregard for the chronological appearance of the referenced characters. Qur'an 3:84 lists Abraham, Ishmael, Isaac, the tribes, Moses, and Jesus according to the biblical order.

30 John Kaltner and Younus Mirza, *The Bible and the Qur'an* (New York: T&T Clark, 2018),146.

favored over the worlds—and some of their fathers, and
their descendants and their brothers. We chose them and
guided them to the straight path. That is the guidance of
God. He guides by means of it whomever He please of
His servants. If they had associated, what they did would
indeed have come to nothing from them. Those are the ones
to whom We gave the Book, and the judgment, and the
prophetic office. If these (people) disbelieve in it, We have
already entrusted it to a people who do not disbelieve in
it. Those are the ones whom God has guided, follow their
guidance. Say, "I do not ask you for any reward for it. It is
nothing but a reminder to the worlds."

While those listed here are but a partial list of all those referred to as
prophets in the Qur'an, the representative sample and the seemingly
arbitrary order of their groupings and listings reinforce the qur'anic
prophetology that it is everywhere keen to present.

This chronologically disordered list highlights the fact that for
the Qur'an, the prophetic message remains essentially singular and
basically static despite the various particulars of its expression that
were assigned to the Jews and Christians. Thus, since the basic message
issued by each prophet is the call to submission, whether a prophet
precedes or follows another historically is somewhat inconsequential.
Furthermore, the specific names chosen within these lists seem to
indicate an even more direct attack on the Christian idea of a christocentric and historically developing redemptive history.

Consider the various groups of names included above along with
the interjections after each. The first group is the pair of Isaac and
Jacob. The Qur'an confirms that both were guided. Similarly, Noah
is noted as having been guided before these two. Following Noah, are
those of a second group, consisting of six names—David, Solomon,
Job, Joseph, Moses, and Aaron. Of these six, the Qur'an refers to the
fact that God rewards doers of good. The third and fourth groups each
include four names. In the former, we find Zachariah, John, Jesus,
and Elijah, followed by the note that each one was righteous. The

final group includes Ishmael, Elisha, Jonah, and Lot, and interjects that each one was favored over the worlds. Each of these epithets is instructive to hearing the Qur'an on its own terms as it develops its own concept of the prophetic office. As the final verses quoted above summarize the role of prophet, however, it seems apparent that the various interjections might apply to all prophets to whom God gives guidance, the Book, and the prophetic office.

But there is perhaps a deeper intention behind the ordering of the names that simply reinforcing their shared prophetic task. Significant for Christians, the fact that when Jesus is mentioned his name is followed by Elijah, giving a sense of chronological disruption to one reading an otherwise-sequential list of four names. The New Testament authors routinely put Jesus at the end of the lists of forerunners, reinforcing the fact that he was the one to whom the prophets pointed. Stephen and the author of Hebrews trace the prophetic messages and redemptive history of the Hebrew scriptures to their culmination in Jesus (Acts 7; Heb. 11–12). And Jesus himself—having declared, "It is finished" from the cross—teaches his followers to see the prior Scriptures pointing to his life, death, and resurrection in Luke 24. There is nothing biblically that would anticipate the coming of another prophet after Jesus's ascension, thus the addition of Elijah after Jesus in Qur'an 6:85 seems awkward and out of place to a reader soaked in the biblical narrative.

Yet the Qur'an clearly teaches that neither was Jesus the final prophet, nor was the closing of the biblical canon the end of divine revelation. Here in this list of names, the Qur'an may be placing Elijah after Jesus in order to recall the prophecy of Malachi 4:5–6:

> Behold, I will send you Elijah the prophet before the great and awesome day of the LORD comes. And he will turn the hears of fathers to their children and the hearts of children to their fathers, lest I come and strike the land with a decree of utter destruction.

Of course, during Jesus's transfiguration in Matthew 17:1–21, Moses and Elijah appear with him in his glory. When they inquire about the fact that Elijah has not yet come, Jesus responds by saying, "Elijah does come, and he will restore all things. But I tell you that Elijah has already come, and they did not recognize him, but did to him whatever they pleased." Matthew inserts an interpretation of Jesus's comments, noting in Matthew 17:13, "Then the disciples understood that he was speaking to them of John the Baptist."

Returning to the list of names in Qur'an 6:85, one finds Zachariah, John—traditionally understood to be John the Baptist—Jesus, and Elijah grouped together. It may be that the Qur'an is attempting to correct Matthew's interpretation of the Malachi prophecy in order to show that the Elijah of the Day of the LORD comes after Jesus, not before him. Therefore, when Matthew records Jesus saying "he will restore all things" in a future sense, there is yet one who comes after Jesus. Considering the fact that Qur'an 61:6 records its Jesus character prophesying the advent of Ahmad, it is not unlikely that this order is intended to reinforce the qur'anic teaching that Jesus is just another one of the prophets, and also that Jesus anticipates one more prophet to follow him and conclude divine revelation.

If this grouping is not a haphazard recollection but is an intentional instance of mosaic structure used to reinforce qur'anic teaching, then the other name groupings might likewise produce similar meaning upon inspection. Suffice it to note, however, that the initial dismissal that some readers of the Qur'an might be inclined to give to its ahistorical rendering could obscure some of the intended meaning and could also miss the impact of this sustained construction of qur'anic prophetology.

While the Bible is a book that appears to bear significant conceptual similarity with the Qur'an, we do the Qur'an injustice if we require it to report its message in the same way that the Bible instructs its audience. If we see that the Qur'an expects its readers to be familiar enough with the biblical material to recognize that it is doing something new with old material, then we begin to be primed to hear it on its own terms. In fact, as seen through the exercises above, on many occasions it appears that the Qur'an marshals its references to biblical characters and concepts in service of its own biblically subversive teaching.

CONCLUSION

In each of these curious accounts in the Qur'an, a reader familiar with the Bible will undoubtedly encounter some interpretive tension. However, prior to dismissing the Qur'an as simply mistaken in its conflation of biblical-historical details, it can be fruitful to pause and consider whether the Qur'an intends to employ this material as unified history or if, in its synthetic arrangement of various narratives, it is weaving together a different story altogether. With Durie, I believe that it is important to note when we encounter these biblical stories that, "It seems to have been important to the Qur'anic Messenger and his community that the text of the Qur'an should sound and feel like a Jewish or Christian text, yet it has its own distinctive theological character."

Specifically in regard to the Pharaoh-Haman-Babel account, Reynolds likewise concludes that the Qur'an may be telling its own theological story without intending its readers to attempt to reconstruct a new historical narrative. Reynolds writes,

> The argument that the Qur'an is somehow wrong or confused by placing Haman and Qorah in Egypt . . . seems to me essentially irrelevant. The Qur'an's concern is not simply to record Biblical information but to shape that information for its own purposes. The more interesting question is therefore *why* the Qur'an connects Haman and Qorah with the story of Pharaoh.[31]

With Reynolds and Durie, this chapter has sought to answer the more interesting question of *why* the Qur'an might conflate various biblical episodes. Further, it is important to then consider what impact such a reading has on the Qur'an's audience and how it might shape a subsequent encounter with biblical stories, teachings, and claims that involve the same characters and accounts.

Investing time to consider the impact of the Qur'an on Muslims is often received as a demonstration of love, but it is also a preparation

---

31   Reynolds, *The Qur'an and Its Biblical Subtext*, 105.

for communication. If one is naive to the impact that the Qur'an has already had on a Muslim neighbor, it is unlikely that the Christian will be sensitive to the likely miscommunication that is occurring. Thus, a Christian engaging in ministry among Muslims will benefit from developing a familiarity with the Qur'an.

However, while familiarity with the Qur'an will help Christians develop their understanding of their Muslim friends, some will inevitably encounter the apparently shared characters, themes, and teachings of the Qur'an and find themselves inclined to affirm these teachings as common ground. Having surveyed the way that the Qur'an utilizes biblical concepts and characters to advance its own message, we must also avoid using superficial bridges to the Gospel that either exhibit an offensive treatment of Muslim scriptures or silently smuggle in Gospel-contrary baggage. Especially in the subtle ways that the previous section demonstrates the Gospel-subversive mosaic use of biblical material, it is important for a Christian to develop a meaningful awareness of the influence that the Qur'an exerts over apparently shared concepts and characters. It is the task of part three of this book to explore and explain these premises further.

PART 3

THE QUR'AN AND THE CHRISTIAN

7

SHOULD CHRISTIANS READ THE QUR'AN?

*Do you then believe in part of the Book
and disbelieve in part? What is the payment for
the one among you who does that,
except disgrace in this present life, and
on the Day of Resurrection they will be
returned to the harshest punishment?
God is not oblivious of what you do.*

Qur'an 2:136–137

As the final installment of heavenly revelation, the Qur'an—and specifically the verses quoted above—chastises the Jewish and Christian communities who would receive their preferred parts of the revelation while yet rejecting the Qur'an, the advent of Islam, and the ministry of its prophet—all of which the Qur'an contends are predicted within the biblical material. The warning of Qur'an 2:136–37 couldn't be clearer as to the consequences of such rejection: disgrace in the present and punishment in the afterlife. For many Muslims, then, they wonder why their Jewish and Christian neighbors have so long neglected to take up and read this final chapter of the heavenly revelation. Why would Jews and Christians risk being disgraced and tormented because of a refusal to consider the final dispensation of God's word?

For Christians, the question of whether or not to read the Qur'an is met with more complicated answers. On the one hand, many Christians do not read the Qur'an because of an outright refusal to acknowledge its claims to be divine revelation. Having already read Jesus's cry from the cross, "It is finished!" and having read Revelation's warning, "If anyone adds to these words of prophecy, God will add to him the plagues that are written in this book," many Christians see no reason to approach the Qur'an at all. After all, Jesus is clear that his work of redemption has been completed, and John testifies that anyone who would add prophecy beyond what has already been written will be cursed. Why should a Christian, then, spend the time to read a book that has nothing to add to Christ's accomplished work and can only invite a curse with its claims to correct, clarify, and add to prior revelation?

On the other hand, some Christians refuse to read the Qur'an due to the belief that it comes from a satanic source and as such might pose a spiritual danger to them. For instance, I regularly assign sections of the Qur'an to students in my World Religions class as we discuss the topic of Islam. At times, some of these students have approached me and questioned the wisdom of inviting people to open up and read what they understand to be a Satan-inspired work that undermines the Gospel. Their question is often, "Isn't it inviting demonic danger for us to dabble in a text that is custom built to reject the Gospel?"

While I never encourage anyone to violate their conscience if they have a genuine concern, I believe there are many reasons that a Christian should familiarize themselves with the Qur'an. I would argue that Christians should read the Qur'an in order to better understand their Muslim neighbors, to better communicate with them, to engage in comparison between the Qur'anic stories and their biblical counterparts. This chapter, then, will be a long-form answer to those who wonder why a Christian should read a book that distorts the Gospel and which can't add anything to the finished work of our God.

READ THE QUR'AN FOR UNDERSTANDING

The first reason that a Christian should read the Qur'an has to do with gaining understanding. As we have already noted, a person looking at the Qur'an's role within Islam from a distance might be tempted to simply assume that the Qur'an is the Islamic version of the Bible.[1] This is only true insofar as both the Bible and the Qur'an are texts with religious value to their respective faith communities. Upon closer inspection, however, the Bible plays a very different role in the life of a Christian than the Qur'an plays in the life of a Muslim.

By reading the Qur'an personally, the Christian accomplishes several things that will prove vital to their ability to understand and relate to their Muslim neighbor. First, they begin to get a feel for how the Qur'an functions in their Muslim neighbor's life. Second, they glimpse the implicit vision of how the Qur'an expects its readers to relate to God. Third, by reading the Qur'an's instructions for oneself the Christian acquires a sense of the expectations for faithful worship and living that are impressed upon their Muslim friends. By hearing the Qur'an speak of worship and faithfulness in its own way, the Christian will become familiar with the fact that worship, piety, and faithfulness for the Qur'an are shaped according to its own unique concerns. Therefore, in conversations with Muslims influenced by the qur'anic perspective on such ideas, Christians need to know how their use of language will be received in order to make sure that what they desire to communicate is in fact what is heard. Let's unpack each of these three doorways to understanding in a little more detail.

THE QUR'AN'S FUNCTION

As the previous chapters have detailed, reading the Qur'an is a unique endeavor that requires an atypical approach to interpreting. For readers of sacred texts who are used to encountering sections of historical narrative, linear development of argumentation, or a progression from

---

1   Ayman Ibrahim, *A Concise Guide to the Qur'an* (Grand Rapids: Baker Academic, 2020), 3. Ibrahim recounts an encounter with an atheist neighbor who believes that the Qur'an is "the Bible of Muslims."

a clear beginning to a definitive end, the Qur'an will present some initial confusion and possibly even some frustration. Such a response results from the fact that the Qur'an is not designed to be read as a novel, nor does it always present proofs and warrant to reinforce its various claims and perspectives. The Qur'an is often satisfied to simply make claims from the perspective of God that should be received by the faithful as authoritative and true.

Such a distinct presentation of its contents threatens to lead new readers of the Qur'an to conclude with Voltaire that "the Qur'an is rhapsody without liaison, without order, without art; it is said nevertheless that this boring book is a very beautiful book—I am referring here to the Arabs, who pretend it is written with an elegance and a purity that no one has approached since."[2] Other Western scholars have expressed a similar critique of the aesthetics and literary construction of the Qur'an. The prolific scholar of the Middle East, F. E. Peters, writes, "There is much in the Qur'an to baffle the reader . . . the work seems to have been only marginally affected by a literary sensibility. There has been some cutting and pasting to be sure, and, for reasons we cannot fathom, some very unliterary arrangements."[3]

While the first-blush read—particularly in translation—might produce sympathy with these conclusions in an uninitiated reader, it should not be taken as a reason to simply dismiss the effort to seek understanding. First of all, as chapter 5 argued, there is more work to be done in recognizing the message that the Qur'an intends to communicate that lies behind its creative references to familiar materials. This requires a more intentional reading than what can be done in a quick pass over the text. Indeed, if the Qur'an intends itself to be read in a particular fashion, it cannot be criticized for being hard to understand when it is read contrary to its intent.

---

2   As cited in Raymond Farrin, *Structure and Qur'anic Interpretation* (Ashland, OR: White Cloud Press, 2014), xiii.
3   F. E. Peters, "The Poet in Performance: the Composition of the Qur'an," in *Sacred Books of the Three Faiths: Judaism, Christianity, Islam,* ed. John Reeve (London: British Library, 2007), 26, 28.

If one is to levy a true critique of the Qur'an's message, it should come from a careful inspection of the internal structures that are less overt but which more helpfully guide the reader to hear and see what it intends to communicate. It may be that a more careful reading will produce a more coherent picture of the Qur'an's arrangement and lead us to see that its structure—rather than presenting a barrier to interpretation—is actually a key aspect of the Qur'an's presentation of its message.[4] The structural and rhetorical features of the Qur'an must be taken into account as one seeks understanding of its message.

RHETORICAL QUESTIONS

One way that the Qur'an regularly utilizes structural and rhetorical features to convey its message is by presenting the reader with questions that the text does not explicitly answer. For example, when discussing resurrection, Qur'an 19:66–67 invites the reader to affirm resurrection without explicitly doing so itself, as it records, "The human says, 'When I am dead, shall I indeed be brought forth alive?' Does the human not remember that We created him before, when he was nothing?" The passage goes on to discuss an eventual gathering of humans and satans together, presumably following the implied resurrection, in order to face the judgment of God. While human resurrection is explicitly affirmed elsewhere in the Qur'an, this verse provides an example of a common way that the Qur'an presents its arguments indirectly. One reason that it is important to note this common rhetorical feature is that there is much said by inference and implication that cannot be ascertained through a concordance. Thus, a Christian is well served to read the Qur'an rather than merely use it as a reference text to be consulted for its teaching on a particular topic.

---

4   This is the essential argument of Raymond Farrin, *Structure and Qur'anic Interpretation*, xvi, whose book aims, "To refute—indeed, to lay to rest the longstanding criticism of 'disjointedness' and to encourage in its place an increased appreciation for the organization of the Qur'an. Second, insofar as structure can serve to frame meaning, it aims to show how a better understanding of the Qur'an's structure may, in fact, ais in our interpretation of the text."

Elsewhere the Qur'an utilizes rhetorical questions to oppose its audience and to imply their folly. For instance, Qur'an 19:77–80 records,

> Have you seen the one who disbelieves in Our signs, and says, "I shall indeed be given wealth and children"? Has he looked into the unseen, or has he taken a Covenant with the Merciful? By no means! We shall write down what he says, and We shall increase the punishment for him. We shall inherit from him what he says, and he will come to Us alone.

Rather than merely presenting the erroneous logic of an opponent's argument, these questions press further to pointing to the absurdity of their position. This passage does not deny that some will receive blessings and offspring despite their unbelief. However, it leaves the reader with the impression of how absurd it is to deny the only one who is capable of providing the benefits for which one pines.

Reading the Qur'an, then, allows the Christian reader to both hear the Qur'an's claims and to enter into the experience it invites. As the environment created by these rhetorical features shapes the manner in which our Muslim friends come to theological discussions. The Christian reader of the Qur'an, then, should be familiar not only with the arguments and contents of the Qur'an, but also its mood. The only means by which to acquire such familiarity is through reading the Qur'an for oneself.

AFFIRMATIONS VERSUS SILENCE

Another aspect of the Qur'an's structure that affects meaning is its use of affirmation and silence. While we will consider this idea further below, a key place this silence comes into play is in answering the question of whether the Qur'an teaches that Jesus died. An often-discussed verse, Qur'an 4:157 contradicts the claims made by its Jewish audience that "'surely we killed the Messiah, Jesus, son of Mary, the messenger of God'—yet they did not kill him, nor did they crucify him, but it (only) seemed like (that) to them. Surely those who differ about him are indeed in doubt about him. They have no knowledge about him, only the following of conjecture. Certainly they did not kill him." While most Muslims believe that the following verse indicates that God assumed Jesus to heaven prior to his death,[5] others have noted the problem with this interpretation presented by Qur'an 19:33, in which Jesus says, "Peace (be) upon me the day I was born, the day I die, and the day I am raised up again."[6]

An overall consideration of the Qur'an's teaching on Jesus's death must again deal with an ambiguous hypothetical question whose answer is not provided in the text. This occurs when one brings Qur'an 5:17 into the discussion: "Certainly they disbelieve who say, 'Surely God—he is the Messiah, son of Mary.' Say: 'Who could do anything against God if He wished to destroy the Messiah, son of Mary, and his mother, and whoever is on the earth—all (of them) together?'" While this verse does not explicitly state that God brought about Jesus's death in the same way as he brings about other deaths, it is strongly implied by the context.[7]

A superficial reading of Qur'an 4:157—especially if influenced by Islamic tradition—seems to imply that Jesus never died at all. Yet, considering the rest of the qur'anic testimony, the reader is invited to take a closer look to determine whether or not the passage necessarily denies Jesus's death or simply denies that the Jews could claim responsibility. It is possible to understand Qur'an 5:17 as affirming the fact that the Jews cannot take credit for Jesus's death while not denying that Jesus died. Jesus's own claim in John 10:17–18, then,

---

5   Gordon Nickel, ed., *The Qur'an with Christian Commentary* (Grand Rapids: Zondervan, 2019), 127n4.158.

6   See Gabriel Said Reynolds, "The Muslim Jesus: Dead or Alive?" *Bulletin of the School of Oriental and African Studies* 72, no. 2 (2009): 237–58.

7   Reynolds, "The Muslim Jesus: Dead or Alive?," 239. See also the discussion within the Islamic community as to how to interpret the verb *tawaffa* as it occurs in Qur'an 3:55 and 5:117 in relation to Jesus. Qur'an 5:117 presents Jesus as saying, "And I was a witness over them as long as I was among them. But when you took me [*tawaffaitani*], you became the Watcher over them. You are a Witness to everything." Nickel, *The Qur'an with Christian Commentary*, 156n5.117 states, "The Arabic verb here, *tawaffa*, is the same verb that causes the confusion at 3.55. In all occurrences not relate to 'Isa, *tawaffa* is commoly translates 'cause to die.' . . . Perhaps in an effort to be consistent with Muslim beliefs about 'Isa, most translations render 5.117 with expressions like 'when you took me.'"

could be reconciled with this denial that anyone other than Jesus is responsible for his death: "I lay down my life that I may take it up again. No one takes it from me, but I lay it down of my own accord. I have authority to lay it down, and I have authority to take it up again." Such an understanding of this well-known text should be bolstered by the recognition that the affirmations made by this verse do not preclude the understanding that Jesus could have died.

A FEEL FOR ITS FUNCTION

As we saw in chapter 5, an attentive reading to the mosaic structure of the accounts recorded in the Qur'an might prove to be more insightful in understanding the qur'anic meaning than a casual reading might produce. Thus, if our intention is to develop an understanding of the Qur'an and the influence of its message, we do well to spend time reading it for ourselves in order to get a sense for how its cadence, its patterns, and its postulates affect its readers and disseminate its message.

But beyond understanding the Qur'an on its own terms—and perhaps even more importantly for developing an understanding of our Muslim friends and neighbors—we need to consider how Muslims use the Qur'an and what role it plays in their religious lives. In practice, the Qur'an is appreciated more for the beauty of its form than for the accessibility of its message.[8] Reinforcing this fact, one of the chief ways that the Qur'an is employed in the life of a Muslim is through the pious act of committing its lines to memory. Memorization is a pious task that can be undertaken whether or not one understands the content of what is recited. But the impact of what is recited and the experiential contact with a text that is believed to exhibit a beautiful and inimitable aesthetic quality leads believers to overlook some of the difficulty in understanding the meaning in favor of embracing the experience of hearing and being carried along by the poetics of the text.[9]

---

8   Farrin, *Structure and Qur'anic Interpretation*, xii, quotes William Graham and Navid Kermani on this point, writing, "The recited Qur'an is and has ever been the epitome of aesthetic as well as spiritual perfection for the faithful."
9   Ibrahim, *A Concise Guide to the Qur'an*, 24–28. In this chapter, Ibrahim addresses the traditional claims regarding the beauty and inimitability of the Qur'an's Arabic as one

Furthermore, reading the Qur'an will reveal the truth of what Muhammad Abdel Haleem states: "The Qur'an is not an academic thesis, but a book of guidance and has its own methods of *targhib* (instilling desire) and *tarhib* (instilling fear) so that they act together."[10] As much as the words themselves convey meaning, reading the Qur'an is intended to be a visceral experience in which one encounters the terror of divine punishment along with the sweet rewards of divine blessing. All of the direct instructions about how the devout are to conduct themselves under God's watchful eye are situated contextually in the experience of having fear of punishment and hope of reward awakened. The Qur'an—its function reinforced by its form—is a book that invites its reader to soak in its proposals, appreciate its rhythmic presentation, and contemplate how to live according to the straight path of God's will so as to avoid his judgment.

Reading the Qur'an, then, will help the Christian to understand the role it plays in the lives of Muslims, and it will also help to convey the experiential nature of sitting under its message. In so doing, the reader will also immediately recognize that much of the Qur'an is written from the perspective of God as the speaker. Part of the impact of this direct divine address, then, is the implicit apprehension of how the reader is expected to relate to this God. This leads us to a second way that reading the Qur'an can help us to better understand our Muslim neighbors.

THE QUR'AN'S GOD

Many times throughout the Qur'an, the reader is addressed with commands and declarations that appear to have come directly from

---

of the chief apologetics used to defend its veracity and inspiration by faithful Muslims. However, Ibrahim also includes significant reason to critique the traditional approach to the "inimitable beauty" argument. Among other criticisms of the traditional trope, Ibrahim notes that there is no evidence that the supposedly renowned Meccan poets existed, let alone that they were awed and silenced by the Qur'an's perfection. Likewise, he points to literary critics—and even some Muslim scholars—who have shown that the language of the Qur'an is flawed.

10 Muhammad Abdel Haleem, *Understanding the Qur'an: Themes and Style* (New York: I. B. Tauris, 2019), 12.

God.[11] For example, Qur'an 2:40 addresses the Jews saying, "Sons of Israel! Remember my blessing which I bestowed on you. Fulfill My covenant (and) I shall fulfill your covenant, and Me—fear Me—alone)." Likewise, the reader is directly addressed by God in Qur'an 2:104 which says, "You who believe! Do not say, 'Observe us,' but say, 'Regard us,' and hear. For the disbelievers (there is) a painful punishment." And again, the Qur'an addresses the believers with direct instructions in Qur'an 2:153—157, saying,

> You who believe! Seek help in patience and prayer. Do not say of anyone who is killed in the way of God, "(They are) dead." No! (They are) alive, but you do not realize (it). We shall indeed test you with some (experience) of fear and hunger, and loss of wealth and lives and fruits. But give good news to the patient, who say, when a smiting smites them, "Surely we (belong) to God, and surely to Him we return." Those—on them (there are) blessings from their Lord, and mercy. Those—they are the (rightly) guided ones.

Such statements and propositions are interjected throughout most every sura. Modern readers are confronted by these warnings and commands addressing them directly as those counted among the believers and who are receiving instruction directly from God. These addresses, often stated as imperatives and directives, condition the reader to understand that they are subjects who are properly commanded to submit to God's will.

Certainly this idea of God as the ultimate authority and law-giver is not foreign to readers of the Bible. Christians throughout the ages have recognized that humans as creatures are subject to their creator. The idea of God as the true master of believers is reinforced by the Pauline idea, "You are not your own, for you were bought with a price.

---

11   There are, of course, exceptions to this statement. For example, Qur'an 1 is written from the perspective of a worshipper petitioning God and God does not speak at all. Likewise, the first half of Qur'an 72 is apparently written from the perspective of the jinn.

So glorify God in your bodies."[12] Likewise, in Romans 6:18, Paul also calls Christians to recognize that they have been freed from having sin as their master in order that righteousness might become their proper master. The Bible certainly agrees that believers should relate to God as their holy sovereign and that the proper human posture before the Almighty is that of servant to master.

However, despite this agreement, the Qur'an does not supplement the Divine-human relationship with any of the more intimate images set forth in the biblical testimony. For instance, the Bible regularly highlights God's loving and compassionate relationship to his people. It speaks of his desire to treasure his people,[13] be a father to his people,[14] to comfort and protect them as a mother relates to her child,[15] to heal them and gather them as a shepherd does for his sheep,[16] to betroth himself to them as a husband to his bride,[17] and to dance over them with rejoicing and to quiet them by his love.[18] This love that God has for his creatures is clearly presented in 1 John 4:7–21. In this passage, John connects God's love for his people with the commands to both love him in return and to love others as an extension of divine love and verse 16 states clearly and definitively of God, "God is love."[19]

In contrast to this vision of how God relates to his creation, the intimacy of these images for the divine-human relationship is almost entirely absent from the Qur'an. In fact, beyond the implied intimacy of relationship conveyed by these various expressions, the biblical theme of God's love for his creatures is presented very differently by the qur'anic text. There are two different verbs that are used within

---

12   1 Cor. 6:19–20.
13   Exod. 19:4–6; Deut. 14:1–2.
14   Isa. 63:16–17; 64:8–9.
15   Isa. 49:15; 66:13.
16   Ps. 23; Ezek. 34:11–24.
17   Hos. 2:16.
18   Zeph. 3:17.
19   For a fantastic treatment of the concept of God's love in the biblical canon, see John Peckham, *The Love of God* (Downers Grove, IL: IVP Academic, 2015). Peckham convincingly argues that the Bible presents God as a God who, by his very nature exhibits love that is "volitional, evaluative, emotional, foreconditional, and ideally reciprocal within the context of the God-world relationship" (277).

the Qur'an to convey the idea of love: *ahabba* and *wadda*.[20] According to Gordon Nickel, the verb *ahabba* occurs with God as its subject forty-six times. Twenty-four of those occurrences speak of things or people that God does not love, while twenty-two identify the kinds of people that God loves. Nickel notes that those who are doers of good (*muhsinun*), those who act fairly (*muqsitun*), and those who guard themselves (*muttaqun*) are recognized most frequently as the kinds of people whom God loves.[21] Thus, for the Qur'an, God's love appears to be contingent upon the actions of believers.

In terms of the Qur'an's command to believers to love God, there are three verses that seems to indicate that humans should exhibit love for God.[22] While none of these verses command a believer to love God, the verse that is closest to a command is Qur'an 3:31: "Say: 'If you love God, follow me. God will love you and will forgive you your sins. God is forgiving, compassionate." Human love of God, thus, appears to be a good thing within the Qur'an's three references to it, but it is not a commanded response to God in the same way that obedience and submission are regularly required.

It is likely that a Christian reader of the Qur'an, then, will begin to sense the relative silence regarding the instruction to love God within its pages. Likewise, the omission of the expectation that God's

---

20   Gordon Nickel, "The Language of Love in the Qur'an," in *The Qur'an with Christian Commentary*, ed. Gordon Nickel (Grand Rapids: Zondervan, 2020, 560.

21   Nickel, "The Language of Love in the Qur'an," 560.

22   Qur'an 2:165: "But (there are) some of the people who set up rivals to God. They love them with a love like (that given to) God. Yet those who believe are stronger in love for God." Qur'an 5:54: "You who believe! Whoever of you turns back from his religion, God will being (another) people whom He loves, and who love Him, (who are) humble toward the believers, mighty toward the disbelievers, (who) struggle in the way of God, and do not fear the blame of anything. That is the favor of God. He gives it to whomever He Pleases. God is embracing, knowing." In Qur'an 2:177 and 76:8 one finds ambiguous references to "love of it" that perhaps refers to those who love God, though it is more likely that the referent for "it" is the riches or food that are given in charity. See the translation in A. J. Droge, *The Qur'an: A New Annotated Translation* (Bristol, CT: Equinox, 2015) and also Muhammad Asad, *The Message of the Qur'an* (London: The Book Foundation, 2003). Asad connects these two verses in a footnote, explaining that both references likely refer to the love of one's possessions that makes charity a noble act (1046n10).

love manifests itself in an intimate, divinely initiated relationship with believers will provide the reader with an appreciation for how differently the exclusive vision of God as Master shapes the reader's understanding of their relationship to God. Seeing that their Muslim friends are not regularly encouraged by their holy book consider the love of God will help a Christian understand why their neighbors are predisposed to think of God condescending to put on flesh as something wholly unbecoming of a holy and almighty creator.[23] As one reads the Qur'an and encounters a steady stream of divine commands devoid of intimate imagery for God's relationship with his creatures, one begins to grasp why scholars of Islam such as Fazlur Rahman conclude confidently that the proper relationship between God and man is merely "a relationship of the served and the servant."[24]

This is an important reality for a Christian to encounter for themselves as they read the Qur'an because it tends to diverge radically from what readers of the Bible understand as the relationship God desires with his creatures. As Gordon Nickel concludes,

> The difference between the Qur'an's material on love and biblical teaching more than simply the New Testament affirmation that the love of God is unconditional. The God who loved humanity "while we were still sinners" (Romans 5:8) is certainly quite different from the qur'anic portrait of Allah. But the biblical affirmation goes further: God demonstrated his love in history by sending his Son to die for humanity.[25]

---

23 It should be noted here that though the Qur'an may not highlight divine love for his creatures, nor encourage a cultivation of human love for God, various expressions of Islam may incorporate extra-qur'anic expectations of intimacy with God into their practice. For example, many Sufi distinctives are born of their concern to develop a love of God and even pursue a mystical union with him. So, we must be careful not to conclude that Muslims do not pursue a loving relationship with God just because it is extraneous to the Qur'an's concern.

24 Fazlur Rahman, *Major Themes of the Qur'an* (Chicago: University of Chicago Press, 2009), 3.

25 Nickel, "The Language of Love in the Qur'an," 561.

In contrast to the Qur'an, the Bible presents a portrait of God who—though he is the authoritative master of the universe—would yet also be Father to a people whom he has adopted lovingly and compassionately from the estrangement caused by their sinful rebellion.

A Christian hoping to engage in a meaningful discussion with a Muslim neighbor must be aware that the loving, sacrificial vision of a God who would condescend to take on flesh in order to redeem his beloved sinful creatures is not a vision that derives from the Qur'an, and thus is likely to require intentional conceptual development before it can be understood by a Muslim audience. Instead of assuming that the Qur'an invites the same kind of divine-human relationship—and thus similar expectations for how to respond to its message—a Christian needs to read the Qur'an to get a sense of what it expects of its readers. This brings us to a third way that reading the Qur'an can lead a Christian to a better understanding of his or her Muslim friends.

READ THE QUR'AN FOR COMMUNICATION

One of the realities that may not immediately appear for English-speaking Christians reading the Qur'an is that the language that appears familiar is often freighted with different meaning when functioning within the Qur'an and the Islamic worldview. This is especially true when considering the language required to share the biblical Gospel. Since this language—as received and used by Muslims—draws its meaning from its function within the Qur'an, it is important for a Christian communicator to see for themselves how the Qur'an employs and shapes these words. In order to illustrate this, let us consider how this plays out with two specific words and two additional concepts.

KEY WORDS AND CONCEPTS

It has long been recognized that words do not mean definitively in isolation, but in the context of sentences, paragraphs, and books. For instance, in a chapter investigating the role of context for determining meaning, Philip Gough, Jack Alford Jr., and Pamela Holley-Wilcox, write, "Context can be shown to affect the recognition of a word. For example, readers of a biology text seldom interpret the word "cell" to mean part of a jail. And you, the reader, are not likely to take mean to signify surly in the preceding sentence."[26]

The examples given in this quote demonstrate the effect of global and immediate contexts on meaning. The global context of a biology textbook provides a setting that reduces the likelihood that the reader should understand "cell" to be a reference to a prison cell. Furthermore, the word "mean" follows a noun and is preceded by the preposition "to" and is clearly functioning verbally and not descriptively. The words "cell" and "mean" can signify very different things in very different contexts, however. As readers apprehend the meaning of the sentences they encounter, however, they are rarely forced to consider the various potential meanings of each word. Rather, implicitly familiar with the context markers conventional to language, readers perceive meaning in sentences without often having to devote significant consideration to the multiple possible meanings available within each word's semantic range.

This linguistic insight is important for interpretation in general. It also demonstrates the importance of considering the way a word features not only in a sentence, but within the context of an entire written work. As in the "cell" example, the way that one author defines a specific term and uses it for purposes germane to the topic at hand may differ from the way another author uses the same lexeme. Responsible interpretation requires a reader to consider the way that the present author uses the words within the scope of the work at hand. This means that despite familiarity with a word in a different context, a reader intent on hearing a different author's message needs to take the time to hear the author quite literally on their own terms.

Additionally, language changes over time. Thus, readers of ancient texts must be cautious about the tendency to anachronistically assume that the current use and definition of a given word controls the way the ancient author understood and used it. Christian communicators

---

26   Philip Gough, Jack Alford Jr., and Pamela Holley-Wilcox, "Words and Contexts," *Perception of Print: Reading Research in Experimental Psychology,* eds. O. J. L. Tzeng and H. Singer, 85–102 (Hillsdale, NJ: Erlbaum, 1981), 86.

have a dual responsibility, then. First, the Christian communicator needs to attend to the biblical text to understand its use of terms over and against the Christian's inherited and contemporary use of similar language. Second, those same terms need to be considered as they appear in the Qur'an in order to compare the meanings text-to-text and to detect how the word will be received by an audience more familiar with the term as it functions within the Qur'an. The importance of understanding the influences our audience's context will have on their reception of our language. For a Christian, reading the Qur'an will help them to intentionally consider the way familiar words and concepts are used in unfamiliar ways. This is vital when attempting to use words like "sin," "atonement," and "salvation."

Sin

One of the words that most people associate with religion systems of all sorts is "sin." It is a word that provides English speakers of all religious stripes with a way to describe bad deeds. It will even occasionally make its way into an atheist's vocabulary, though it is perhaps there laden with irony.[27] However, it is also a word that is more complicated than its superficial familiarity might convey. In English, the word "sin" is often used to express a variety of words used by the Bible to convey transgressions against God's law.

Evangelical theologian Michael Bird notes the difficulty of defining sin exhaustively according to its biblical use. Bird writes, "It's hard to be precise [in giving a definition for sin] because there is a plethora of images for sin in Scripture."[28] He goes on to list lawlessness, transgression, rebellion, disobedience, perversion, and missing the mark as images the Bible uses. Bird goes on to write, "A full understanding of sin emerges not simply from word studies, but from the narrative of Scripture itself," and as he alludes to the first sin of Genesis 3:1–8, Bird shows that the effects of sin can be characterized as, "the seeds of

27 See the definition and use of the word sin by the self-identified Tom the Friend-ly Neighborhood Atheist, "Atheist on . . . What Is Sin?" https://www.youtube.com/watch?v=ELgA3S996Ng.
28 Michael Bird, *Evangelical Theology* (Grand Rapids: Zondervan, 2013), 667.

separation between God and humanity."[29] Since the Bible regularly presents God's desire to dwell among his people, such separation is serious insofar as it introduces a complications between God's desires and his creatures' unsuitability to those desires. Therefore, among the consequences of sin, Bird lists estrangement as central, stating, "In the end, on account of our sin, we are alienated from God. Sin brings disruption to the divine-human relationships. Because of sin, human beings are estranged from the God who made them and loves them."[30] In other words, the Bible presents humanity as having become sinful and thus separated from God as a result of a fall from their original condition in which they enjoyed the fellowship with God for which they were created.

Within the Qur'an, sin is likewise described by a variety of words. Sins are described as "evil deeds" (*sayyat*) as in Qur'an 28:84, which states, "Whoever brings a good (deed) will have a better one than it, and whoever brings an evil (deed)—those who have done evil deeds will only be repaid for what they have done." Likewise, misdeeds are described as "great sins" (*kibaar ilithm*) and "immoral deeds" (*alfawaahish*) in Qur'an 53:32 as it states, "Those who avoid great sins and immoral deeds, except for inadvertent ones—surely your Lord is embracing in forgiveness."[31] Sin is also described using the term *dhanb*, as in Qur'an 3:15b–17 which says, "God sees his servants who say, 'Our Lord, surely we believe. Forgive us our sins [*dhanubina*] and guard us against the punishment of the Fire.' (They are) the patient, the truthful, the obedient, those who contribute, the askers of forgiveness in the mornings."

Importantly, the Qur'an also appears to associate disbelief, refusal to remember God's ways, and the association of partners with God with the concept of sin. In places like Qur'an 12:103–6, these concepts

---

29   Bird, *Evangelical Theology*, 668.
30   Bird, *Evangelical Theology*, 673.
31   The translation choice represented by Droge, *The Qur'an: A New Translation and Commentary*, is a bit odd here, considering that the caveat more clearly reads as an excuse for those who will occasionally stumble in their attempts to do avoid immoral deeds. Cf. Muhammad Asad, *The Message of the Qur'an*, 9:28, who translates the phrase *illaa allamam* as "even though they may sometimes stumble."

are bound together in the statement, "Most of the people are not going to believe, even if you are eager (for that). You do not ask them for any reward for it. It is nothing but a reminder [*dhikr*] to the worlds. How many a sign in the heavens and the earth do they pass by! They turn away from it. Most of them do not believe [*ma yo'min*] in God, unless they associate [*musharikun*]." As indicated here through the language of *dhikr*, the Qur'an presents itself as a reminder of God's ways and his will to humans who are prone to forget him.

Furthermore, this passage shows the relationship between those who, on the basis of their refusal to believe in God alone, reject the reminder that the Qur'an provides. It also provides justification for those Muslim theologians like Seyyed Hossein Nasr who recognize that, for the Qur'an, the fundamental sin problem stems from forgetfulness. In contrast with the biblical conception of sin as relationship-altering disobedience, Nasr writes, "If the great sin in Christianity is disobedience, which has warped the will, the great sin in Islam is forgetfulness and the resulting inability of the intelligence to function in the way that God created it as the means to know the One."[32] Nasr goes on to connect this with Islam's greatest sin—the one referred to above as "association"—writing, "That is why the greatest sin in Islam and the only one God does not forgive is *shirk*, or taking a partner unto God, which means denying the Oneness of God, or *tawhid*."[33]

Perhaps the most important difference between the Qur'an's portrayal of sin and the biblical account, however, is its account of the first sin. In Qur'an 2:36–37, the account of Adam and his wife's[34] exile from paradise is attributed to the work of Shaytan (elsewhere referred to as Iblis): "Then Satan [*Shaytan*] caused them both to slip from there, and to go out from where they were. And We said, 'Go down, some

---

32 Seyyed Hossein Nasr, *The Heart of Islam: Enduring Values for Humanity* (New York: HarperOne, 2002), 7.

33 Nasr, *The Heart of Islam*, 7.

34 The Qur'an does not name Adam's wife, though later Islamic tradition refers to her as Hawa. As a point of interest, the Qur'an names only one woman: Mariam, the mother of 'Isa, who is mentioned specifically thirty-four times. See John Kaltner and Younus Mirza, *The Bible and the Qur'an: Biblical Figures in the Islamic Tradition* (London: T&T Clark, 2018), 112.

of you an enemy to the others! The earth is a dwelling place for you, and enjoyment (of life) for a time." The Arabic verb translated above as "caused them both to slip" is clearly intended to demonstrate that Shaytan had an active role to play in this exile from paradise.

The story is reiterated with more detail in Qur'an 7:19–23, which makes the role of Shaytan more explicit as he tempts Adam and his wife with the promise that they will become angels or immortals. In this account, Shaytan's temptation leads to Adam and his wife's disobedience and exile from paradise. It also records a request from Adam and his wife to be forgiven: "They both said, 'Our Lord, we have done ourselves evil [zhalmna anfusana]. If you do not forgive us, and have compassion on us, we shall indeed be among the losers.'" The manner in which this statement is framed proves important to our understanding of what sin is, who sin is against, and how sin functions within the Qur'an.

First, we see that the human couple understands their sin to be an offense against themselves. God is the lawgiver who has prohibited the tree and its fruit, but the offended party is not God. This can be seen in other places in the Qur'an such as 4:111 which states clearly, "Whoever earns sin, only earns it against himself." Second, the sin does need to be forgiven by God, but divine forgiveness is offered through further instruction. Qur'an 2:37–39 makes this explicit, saying,

> Then Adam received certain words from his Lord, and He turned to him (in forgiveness). Surely He—He is the One who turns (in forgiveness), the Compassionate. We said, "Go down from it—all (of you)! If any guidance comes to you from Me, whoever follows My guidance—(there will be) no fear on them, nor will they sorrow. But those who disbelieve and all Our signs a lie—those are the companions of the Fire. There they will remain."

The Qur'an's understanding of the first human sin is that it has resulted in the human need for forgiveness which can be distributed by God's merciful provision of further instruction. Thus, Qur'an 7:32 can conclude, "In this way We make the signs distinct for a people who know."

In summary, then, "sin" in the Qur'an is a failure to remember and submit to God's instructions and will. Sins, then, are individual instances of disbelief, forgetfulness, or refusal to submit to God in ways that often have biblical parallels. The qur'anic vision of the result of these sins, however, is not a breach in the relationship between God as his people as is depicted in the Bible. Instead, sin presents a situation whose remedy is presented as repentance, further instruction and more effort devoted to doing good in the future. Thus, as we saw in chapter 1, the Qur'an presents itself as the divine remedy for human forgetfulness by serving as a book of reminder and guidance.

As a result of these different conceptions of sin, long-term missionaries to Muslims like Phil Parshall conclude, "It is difficult to communicate the biblical meaning of sin to a Muslim. His outlook is horizontal rather than vertical."[35] The difficulty arises so acutely because the common language often obscures different meaning. If our Muslim friends understand us to share a largely common list of sins without acknowledging that sin itself causes relational problem between God and humanity, then the solution to sins need not be interpersonal in nature. Still, the Qur'an uses a word to discuss forgiveness that, in its biblical sense, is filled with relational implications: atonement.

Atonement

The word "atonement" is a beautiful and rich word in its biblical context. Its verbal form refers to the process whereby God provides a substitutionary way for guilty and impure sinners to be restored to a condition in which they can abide the presence of a holy and righteous God. The nominal form conveys the idea of a restored relationship between an offended party and the offender achieved by the process.[36] The Hebrew word-group *kipper* provides the foundation for this idea

---

35 Phil Parshall, *Muslim Evangelism* (Downers Grove, IL: IVP, 2003), 97.
36 See Jay Sklar, *Leviticus,* Tyndale Old Testament Commentaries 3 (Downers Grove, IL: IVP Academic, 2014), 221.

and the Greek words *hilasmos/hilasterion* convey this idea at various times within the biblical text.[37] Important for our purposes, these words are rendered with the word *kaffara* in the Arabic Bible. Despite having an Arabic cognate, *kaffara* is a problematic word in discussions with Muslims. It is not a problem due to it being an unknown word. Rather, it is problematic because of its familiarity. The idea of *kaffara* appears in the Qur'an four times as a verb and fourteen times as a noun. The nominal forms are confined to Qur'an 5 and involve the instructions as to how one will receive atonement, as in Qur'an 5:89 which says,

> God will not take you to task for a lip in your oaths, but He will take you to task for what you have pledged by oath. Atonement for it is the feeding of ten poor persons with the average (amount of poor) which you fed your households, or clothing them, or the setting free of a slave. Whoever does not find (the means to do that), (the penalty is) a fast for three days. That is the atonement for your oaths when you have sworn (and broken them). But guard your oaths! In this way God makes clear to you His signs, so that you may be thankful.

The idea of atonement as presented here is something that can be achieved by making up for one's failure to keep an oath. This process does not remove sin or impurity, but rather makes up for it with a charitable act.

Likewise, the Qur'an uses *kaffara* in its verbal form to indicate ways that a human can act to encourage God to atone for some of their sins. For example, Qur'an 39:33–35 states,

---

37   Cf. Leviticus 16–17 for a key passage discussing atonement via the Day of Atonement prescription and explanation. In the New Testament, one might find key discussion of atonement in throughout the book of Hebrews, specifically via the word *hilaskesthai* in Hebrews 2:17 and *hilasterion* in Hebrews 9:5 to refer to the mercy seat or place of atonement.

But the one who brings the truth and confirms it, those—
they are the ones who guard (themselves). They will have
whatever they please with their Lord. That is the payment
of the doers of good—so that God may absolve them [*li-
yukaffiral-lahu*] of the worst of what they have done, and
pay them their reward for the best of what they have done.

This instance of the use of *kaffara*—translated here as "absolve"—provides a good representation of how the Qur'an uses it elsewhere.[38] It
also presents clear differences with how it functions in the biblical text.

One distinct way that the Qur'an uses *kaffara* is that the Qur'an
presents God as the one who directly "atones" for human sins following repentance, martyrdom, prescribed good deeds, or charity.[39]
Additionally, the Qur'an does not present atonement as the remedy
for impurity, but rather an act required to offset a person's misdeeds.
Finally, neither sacrifice nor the presentation of blood required in Leviticus 16–17 is in view in the Qur'an's understanding of atonement.

In contrast, the biblical use of atonement involves an interces-
sor—a high priest—who is instructed to effect atonement before God
on behalf of worshippers. Furthermore, biblical atonement indicates
an understanding of sin as a complex problem involving both guilt
and impurity. Thus, atonement is a multifaceted remedy for sinners
involving a substitutionary sacrifice to remove guilt and the sprin-
kling of blood to affect cleansing of impurity.[40] This is because the
Bible teaches that sin makes humans both guilty and defiled.[41] Thus,

---

38   For an exhaustive list of occurrences of the verb and noun in the Qur'an, see Matthew
      Bennett, *Narratives in Conflict: Atonement in Hebrews and the Qur'an* (Eugene, OR:
      Pickwick, 2019), 225–29.
39   There is a single exception found in Qur'an 2:271 where it appears that the charity
      renders atonement for the giver. However, in every other instance God is the agent
      who issues atonement.
40   The concept of substitution is contested within Christian theology. However, scholars
      such as Simon Gathercole, *Defending Substitution* (Grand Rapids: Baker Academic,
      2015), provide convincing rationale for retaining substitution as a key element of
      what biblical authors understand to be necessary for atonement.
41   Mark Boda, *A Severe Mercy: Sin and Its Remedy in the Old Testament* (Winona Lake,
      IN: Eisenbrauns, 2009), 46. Boda writes, "Sin's seriousness is rooted in God's careful

the remedy for sin must be able to treat both conditions, and in the biblical context, atonement presents precisely such a remedy—one that allows Christians to speak hopefully of salvation.

Salvation
In light of the ways that sin and atonement function in the Qur'an, it may not be surprising to see that salvation is likewise a concept conceived of differently within the Islamic scriptures. Whereas salvation in the Bible is linked to a restoration and redemption of the relationship between the Creator and his creatures, the Qur'an projects a different vision and definition of salvation in eternity.

As noted in chapter 2, the Bible is everywhere concerned to demonstrate God's intention to be present among his people.[42] In fact, if you were to attempt to explain in three words the purpose of God as communicated throughout the biblical metanarrative, I would suggest that "God with us" is a fair summative reduction.[43] God's desire to be with humanity appears to be reflected in the original creation where God walked in the garden with Adam and Eve.[44] The presence of God represents the problem introduced by sin's separation of the profaned from the holy.[45] The developing story of redemption featuring God's presence in the tabernacle, in flesh, and at Pentecost,

---

attention to justice; he will not let the guilty go unpunished, meting out mitigated punishment for rebellion. At the same time, the only hope for a nation with such sinful tendencies is Yahweh's character of mercy, which dissuades him from destroying the community for their rebellion." Likewise, recognizing the impurity effected by sin along with sin's guilt, Jay Sklar concludes that biblically sin makes a person not only unfit for God's presence, but also in danger of being destroyed as guilty and defiled as a consequence of a holy and righteous God dwelling in their midst. See the sustained and convincing argument of this point by Jay Sklar, *Sin, Impurity, Sacrifice, Atonement: The High Priestly Conceptions* (Sheffield, UK: Sheffield Phoenix, 2015).

42   See the discussion on this topic in chapter 2.

43   In teaching systematic theology courses, I tell my students that each of the doctrines covered can be connected to this summary of the biblical narrative. I was delighted to find the same sentiments expressed by Ida Glaser, *Thinking Biblically about Islam* (Carlisle, UK: Langham Global Partnership, 2016), 129, who writes, "So we could say that the whole Bible is about how God fulfils his desire to live among human beings."

44   Gen. 3:8.

45   Gen. 3:22–24.

is finally consummated through the final restoration in the age to come wherein "the tabernacle of God is now with man."[46]

The concept of God dwelling with man should be taken quite literally, considering that the doctrine of the incarnation involves the second person of the Trinity—God of God—taking on flesh to dwell with and in creation in time and space. Thus, the biblical narrative is no esoteric commentary on God's spiritual-but-never-spatial presence among his image-bearers. It shows a God who would adopt a people who might enter his real presence and dare to call him "Father." The Bible portrays a God who would really, truly, and immediately live among his people. Salvation, then, involves a constitution that is restored to be able to bear the pure and righteous presence of the infinitely holy one.

Such a concept, however, is usually understood by a Muslim audience as an absurdity. Ida Glaser comments on this idea, saying, "God's fulfilling his desire to live among us can be a strange idea to Muslims, not only because the Qur'an never describes God as 'coming' to us, but also because it never tells us what God desires."[47] Glaser's reference to God's desires here should be understood to be a reference to the internal and ultimate desires of God which remain elusive in the Qur'an and Islamic theology. On a more superficial level, however, God's desires are regularly expressed through the ethical instructions he gives throughout the Qur'an as an exhibition of his merciful guidance and instruction to his forgetful and wayward human creatures.

This instruction comes through moral guidance, as recorded in Qur'an 7:27, which immediately follows the account of Adam and his wife's eviction from paradise: "Sons of Adam! Do not let Shaytan tempt you, as he drove your parents out of the Garden, stripping both of them of their clothing in order to show both of them their shameful parts." Verse 29 goes on to instruct them, "My Lord has commanded justice. Set your faces in every mosque, and call on Him, devoting

---

46   Cf. Exod. 29:45–46; John 1:14; Rev. 20:3.
47   Glaser, *Thinking Biblically About Islam*, 129.

(your) religion to Him. As He brought you about, (so) will you return." The idea of salvation, then, hinges upon human knowledge of the right thing to do, active pursuit of doing it, and willingness to seek forgiveness when they fail. Peter Riddell notes that the Qur'an views salvation primarily in terms of escape from punishment and the positive picture of what such salvation looks like is "far less clearly defined as a doctrine in the Qur'an than in the Bible."[48] Where the Bible presents salvation via connection to Jesus as the Savior, Islamic salvation is disconnected from any personal figure. Fazlur Rahman puts it this way,

> We have already said that the Qur'an rejects "saviorship." As a corollary, it equally rejects intercession. Although the Hadith literature is loaded with references to intercession of the prophets on behalf of the sinful of their communities, particularly the Prophet Muhammad's intercession on behalf of his community. . . . the Qur'an seems to have nothing to do with it. . . . The whole temper of the Qur'an is against intercession, for, to begin with, "God does not require from any person what is beyond his [or her] power."[49]

This rejection of salvific substitution grows out of the Qur'an's repeated claim that no one can bear the burden of another. This occurs in places such as Qur'an 35:18: "No one bearing a burden bears the burden of another. If one heavy-burdened calls for his load (to be carried), nothing of it will be carried, even though he be a family member."[50] The passage continues on to reiterate that a person purifies themselves for their own sake only. The implication—and the traditional

---

48   Peter Riddell, "Salvation in the Qur'an," in *The Qur'an with Christian Commentary*, ed. Gordon Nickel (Grand Rapids: Zondervan, 2019), 180.

49   Fazlur Rahman, *Major Themes of the Qur'an* (Chicago: University of Chicago Press, 2009), 31.

50   Cf. Qur'an 6:164, "Say: Shall I seek a Lord other than God, when He is the Lord of everything? No one earns (anything) except against himself, and no one bearing a burden bears the burden of another. Then to your Lord is your return, (and) then He will inform you about your differences." Cf. also Qur'an 55:38.

interpretation of this verse and the others like it—is that there is no room in the Qur'an for the idea of a substitutionary sacrifice. Likewise, Qur'an 25:70 also gives a glimpse of how salvation might come to a sinner who repents, stating,

> The punishment will be double for him on the Day of Resurrection, and he will remain in it humiliated, except for the one who turns (in repentance), and believes, and does a righteous deed—and those, God will change their evil deeds (into) good ones, (for) God is forgiving, compassionate.

The passage closes with a further promise of eternal reward for these who repent, saying in Qur'an 25:75–76, "Those will be repaid with the exalted room because they were patient, and there they will meet a greeting and 'Peace!' There they will dwell—it is good as a dwelling and resting place." Within the context of the Qur'an, however, the divine willingness to simply grant forgiveness is not problematic because we have seen that sin is conceived of differently and forgiveness is available without requiring the atoning sacrifice required in the Bible.[51] Salvation, then, can be achieved differently because it is also conceived of differently.

Ultimately, salvation in the Qur'an is conceived of as the eschatological granting of admittance into gardens of delight. For instance, Qur'an 68:34–35 records, "Surely for the ones who guard (themselves) (there will be) Gardens of Bliss with their Lord. Shall We treat those who submit like the sinners?" It is worth pausing to note briefly at this verse to show that the language rendered "with their Lord" might be understood to convey the Gardens as being inhabited by God's

---

51   Anderson, *The Qur'an in Context*, 127. According to Anderson, forgiveness, offered by God to the repentant, is "almost cosmetic, for God appears to overlook and dispense with the believer's moral faults—especially her smaller sins—as one might 'forgive' a child's inability to think of act like an adult." Anderson goes on to summarize the Qur'an's vision for forgiveness, writing, "The clear sense is that overlooking the believer's lesser sins is a minor matter, although the believer must still do her part—avoid the greater sins and do good deeds—in order for God to do his."

presence. However, in keeping with the rest of the Qur'an's teaching about the transcendence of God, it is important to note that Arabic uses this word for "with" (*'and*) to refer to a possession or thing over which a person has ownership. Perhaps a clearer rendering of the English would be, "Surely the Gardens of Bliss (that are the reward) for those who guard themselves are the possession of the Lord."[52]

Hopefully it is clear at this point that the Qur'an uses various words and concepts to convey different meaning. The reason that a Christian should read the Qur'an is to recognize the different ways that words and concepts vital to the presentation of the Gospel function within the Qur'an. This familiarity will help the Christian to understand how the shared language will be received by their Muslim neighbors and where additional clarification will need to occur for communication of the biblical Gospel. But the differences between superficial similarities are not exhausted by the words and concepts we have looked at. As chapter 5 demonstrated, the characters that inhabit the Qur'an's teaching also bear a more fundamental dissimilarity to their biblical counterparts than might initially be seen. The following section will consider two key figures and their Qur'anic appearance in order to demonstrate this divergence.

READ THE QUR'AN FOR COMPARISON

The preceding material has labored to show that a Christian should read the Qur'an in order to develop understanding of their Muslim neighbors by experiencing the style and teaching of the Qur'an. It has also argued that it is important for a Christian to see the different ways that the Qur'an employs shared terminology so as to mitigate misunderstanding when communicating the Gospel. Knowledge of how the Qur'an uses terms like "sin" and "atonement" can help to

---

52 A contemporary example of Arabic language use might be seen in the way that a person would ask a waiter at a café two questions using different forms of "with." For instance, if I want to know if the café serves my favorite drink, the question I might ask the waiter would translate woodenly into English as, "Is lemon and mint with you (*'andek*)?" However, such a question does not imply the immediate presence of the drink, but only inquires as to its availability to be offered by the café.

identify places where further biblical definition will be required than one might initially assume.

In this final section, then, it is important to consider that the Qur'an should be read in order to make direct comparison with the Bible and its teaching. While the comparison of concepts and definitions has already occurred above for the purposes of communication, the following section urges Christians to consider the roles played by important characters who are drawn out of their biblical context and into the Qur'an's horizons. Developing a familiarity with how the Qur'an uses biblical characters will help to prepare the Christian for more fruitful dialogue with their Muslim friends when the appeal to shared prophetic history arises.

KEY CHARACTERS

The Qur'an makes multiple references to important biblical characters such as Adam, Moses, Abraham, David, and Jesus. As a result, most Muslims believe themselves to be familiar with the host of biblical patriarchs and their stories. It is common, in a conversation with a Muslim friend, to hear sentiments such as, "I believe in all of your prophets—in fact, I would not be a good Muslim if I didn't believe in them."

This can initially present itself as good common ground. However, with some study of the characters cited above in the context of the Qur'an, it will become apparent that these characters play different roles on the qur'anic narrative than they do in their biblical setting. For the purposes of brevity, let us consider two such characters: Abraham and Jesus.

Abraham

Contemporary scholarship gathers Judaism, Christianity, and Islam under the shared umbrella of "the Abrahamic faiths." Where Judaism traces its covenantal lineage back to Genesis 12 and the promise of blessing and land made to Abraham, Christianity also looks back to Abraham and, with Paul in Romans 4, sees his faith in God as a prototype for Christian faith in Christ. Abraham is a key figure within the Qur'an and more broadly within the Islamic understanding of their faith's origins. Corroborating his importance within the Qur'an, Abraham (*Ibrahim*)—mentioned almost seventy times—appears more often than anyone except Moses.[53] The frequency of appearance is not the only thing that makes him a central member of the Qur'an's cast, however. His role as a prototypical Muslim is one that continues to be celebrated and immitated in contemporary Islamic practice. The reason for this celebration can be seen most clearly in Qur'an 3:67–68 which affirms Abraham as a prototype for Islamic submission, saying of him, "Abraham was not a Jew, nor a Christian, but he was a *hanif*, a Muslim. He was not one of the idolaters. Surely the people nearest to Abraham are those indeed who followed him, and this prophet, and those who believe. God is the ally of the believers."

Abraham and Muhammad

Again, in Qur'an 2:130–31, the Qur'an suggests that Abraham provides an exemplary model of a Muslim as it commends him: "Certainly We have chosen [Abraham] in this world, and surely in the Hereafter he will indeed be among the righteous. When his Lord said to him, 'Submit!' he said, 'I have submitted to the Lord of the worlds.'" In Arabic, of course, the words "Islam" and "Muslim" are drawn from the family of words related to "submission." Thus, as Abraham is portrayed throughout the Qur'an as one who submits, there is intentional interplay with the idea that Islam is the primordial religion.

In fact, scholars have noted that Abraham provides Islamic tradition with a prototype for Muhammad. As Abraham is forced to leave his homeland due to the rejection of his monotheistic preaching, so too tradition traces Muhammad's deportation from Mecca under threat from polytheists.[54] Likewise, the Qur'an relays an account wherein Abraham and Ishmael travel to what tradition

---

53   John Kaltner and Younus Mirza, *The Bible and the Qur'an: Biblical Figures in the Islamic Tradition* (New York: T&T Clark, 2018), 10.
54   Kaltner and Mirza, *The Bible and the Qur'an*, 13.

identifies as Mecca and build a house as a place dedicated to the worship of the one true God in Qur'an 2:124–29. This is mirrored by the traditional account of Muhammad growing up in Mecca and eventually cleansing the Ka'ba after his victorious return to his hometown. All this leads John Kaltner and Younus Mirza to conclude, "In the Qur'an, Abraham/Ibrahim serves as the paradigmatic believer for Muhammad and the Islamic community. He is the prototypical Muslim and every person must strive to be a *hanif* [an upright one; a monotheist] like him and avoid being a *mushrik* [one who associates partners with God]."[55] In other words, Abraham functions in the Qur'an as a model Muslim and a foreshadowing of Muhammad himself.

Abraham and Islam
While the Qur'an praises Abraham as one who submits to God in many places, it puts such submission on display most clearly in Qur'an 37:100–111. In this brief passage, the Qur'an recounts a story that bears significant resemblance to the account of Genesis 22 and what is traditionally referred to as the story of the Akedah or "Binding of Isaac." Despite its brevity, the Qur'an presents a few additional details not found in the biblical text. For instance, Qur'an 37:102, Abraham informs his son about his vision before presenting him for sacrifice. Having heard his father's dream, Abraham's son says, "My father! Do what you are commanded. You will find me, if God pleases, one of the patient." As in the Bible, Abraham is commanded to stop before he kills his son, and he hears what is recorded in verses 105–11:

> Now you have confirmed the vision. Surely in this way We repay the doers of good. Surely this—indeed it was a clear test. And We ransomed him with a great sacrifice, and left this blessing on him among the later (generations): "Peace (be) upon Abraham! In this way We repay the doers of good. Surely he was one of Our believing servants."

---

55   Kaltner and Mirza, *The Bible and the Qur'an*, 13

Several things from this passage are notable.

First of all, the Qur'an does not name the son in question. Contemporary Islamic thought nearly universally recognizes the son as Ishmael, however the earliest Islamic commentators were divided over which son was intended.[56] Contemporary opinions favor Ishmael, however, as he provides the Muslim community with a traditional lineage from Abraham to Muhammad. Second, the text clarifies that Abraham was being tested as to the extent of his faith. He is affirmed in his faithfulness and is excused from having to execute his son. However, the qur'anic account also alludes to a sacrifice that is provided as a ransom for his son in Qur'an 37:107: "We ransomed him with a great sacrifice." This verse is especially interesting within its qur'anic horizons, considering that sacrifice is never viewed as substitution but merely as a pious act.

Nonetheless, the sacrifice plays a key role in the Qur'an's presentation of Abraham as well as in contemporary Islamic practice. In Qur'an 34:78, Abraham is again called upon as an exemplar for contemporary Muslim submission as it says, "He has chosen you, and has not placed any difficulty on you in the (matter of) religion: the creed of your father Abraham. He named you Muslims, (both) before and in this." Furthermore, in the same sura, the reader is twice reminded that each people whom God has dealt with has been given a specific ritual that validates their religion. Qur'an 22:34 states, "For every community We have appointed a ritual: that they should mention the name of God over whatever animal of the livestock He has provided them. Your God is one God, so submit to Him." Similarly, Qur'an 22:67 says, "For every community we have appointed a ritual which they practice. So let them not argue with you about the matter, but call (them) to your Lord. Surely you are indeed on a straight guidance."

Connecting all of these qur'anic bits of Abraham's story and role as an exemplar, one sees in the contemporary practice of sacri-

---

56 See Jalalayn, *Tafsir Al Jalalayn*, trans. Feras Hamza, https://www.altafsir.com/Tafsir. asp?tMadhNo=0&tTafsirNo=74&tSoraNo=37&tAyahNo=107&tDisplay=yes&UserProfile=0&LanguageId=2.

fice—the central component of the 'Id al Adha ritual—as not only a rehearsal of Abraham's faith, but also as an assertion that Islam is the divinely approved religion. By rehearsing Abraham's sacrifice, contemporary Muslims recognize that they have been prescribed a ritual that confirms God's dispensation of religion upon them, as per Qur'an 22:34 and 67. However, linked with the affirmation that Abraham precedes both Judaism and Christianity, as in Qur'an 3:67, this contemporary sacrifice also lays claim to a faith that precedes Jewish and Christian religion. Therefore, the sacrifice that connects modern Muslims to Abraham as a forefather effectively reinforces the idea that Islam both precedes and supersedes Judaism and Christianity. He is the original pattern of religion for both Jew and Christian because he practices the original Islam that both communities failed to perform.

Jesus

Another figure whose appearance in the Qur'an is of central concern to Christian readers is Jesus. In the Qur'an, the Jesus character goes by the name 'Isa. This is interesting because the Arabic Bible does not use 'Isa, but refers to Jesus as Yasua' instead. [57] As with Abraham, the Qur'an includes aspects of Jesus's life that have direct biblical corroboration.

For example, Qur'an 19:16–21 describes Jesus's mother Mary as a virgin. Likewise, Qur'an 5:46 presents Jesus as a prophet who completes and continues the revelation that came before him in the Torah. Furthermore, the Qur'an presents Jesus as a moral teacher in places such as Qur'an 43:63, which confirms the heavenly origins of Jesus's wisdom, saying,

---

57   I have argued elsewhere that it can be helpful to maintain the distinction between the two characters by referring to them by the respective names assigned to them by the Qur'an and the Bible. See Matthew Bennett, "Christ in the Scripture of Islam: Remnantal Revelation or Irredeemable Imposter?" *Southeastern Theological Review* 11, no. 1 (2020): 99–117. However, for the purposes of clarity and simplicity here, I will simply use "Jesus."

> When Jesus brought the clear signs, he said, "I have brought
> you the wisdom, and (I have done so) to make clear to you
> some of your differences. Guard (yourselves) against God
> and obey me. Surely God—He is my Lord and your Lord,
> so serve Him! This is the straight path."

Along with these places of similarity, however, there are also aspects of
the Qur'an's Jesus character that are drawn from extrabiblical texts and
which seem to deviate from the portrait of Jesus on display in the Bible.

At times, even as the Qur'an confirms elements of the Bible's
teaching it adds aspects to its teaching that being to reshape the Jesus character into its own image. For instance, it confirms that Jesus
performed miracles in places like Qur'an 5:110 which states,

> (Remember) when God said, "Jesus, son of Mary! Remember
> My blessing on you and on your mother, when I supported
> you with the holy spirit, (and) you spoke to the people (while
> you were still) in the cradle, and in adulthood. And when I
> taught you the Book and the wisdom, and the Torah and the
> Gospel. And when you created the form of a bird from clay
> by My permission, and you breathed into it, and it became
> a bird by My permission, and you healed the blind and the
> leper by My permission. And when you brought forth the
> dead by My permission, and when I restrained the Sons of
> Israel from (violence against) you. When you brought them
> the clear signs, those among them who had disbelieved said,
> 'This is nothing but clear magic.'"

In this passage the reader encounters congruence with biblical teaching regarding Jesus's miracles. However, there are also extrabiblical
references included here, with the allusion to Jesus creating birds out
of clay and breathing life into them. A similar story is found in the
second-century document known as the *Infancy Gospel of Thomas.*[58]

---

58   Kaltner and Mirza, *The Bible and the Quran,* 79.

In addition, the repeated phrase, "by My permission" intentionally places Jesus's power to heal and raise the dead under the sovereign control of God rather than a power Jesus exercises for himself. While parallels could be drawn with how Jesus refers to his incarnate submission to the Father, it appears that the Qur'an is more interested in presenting Jesus as a mere human. Such an impression arises when considering that both Qur'an 2:136 and 3:84 state,

> Say: "We believe in God, and in that which has been bestowed from on high upon us, and that which has been bestowed upon Abraham and Ishmael and Isaac and Jacob and their descendants, and that which has been vouchsafed to Moses and Jesus, and that which has been vouchsafed to all the [other] prophets by their Sustainer: we make no distinction between any of them. And it is unto Him that we surrender ourselves."

In these two verses, then, Jesus is equated with the likes of Abraham, Ishmael, Isaac, Jacob, and Moses by the phrase, "we make no distinction between any of them." In other words, Jesus in the Qur'an is a prophet, a teacher, and a conduit of God for miracles. He is not, however, any different than the prophets that have come before him or the one who will come after him.

It is not simply this equation of Jesus with other prophets that provides the impression that the Jesus of the Qur'an differs substantially from the Jesus of the Bible. At least three other elements of the qur'anic Jesus demonstrate that the two books employ their Jesus character in different tasks. First, the Qur'an emphatically denies that Jesus is in any way the Son of God.[59] This denial can be seen in

---

59 It should be noted here that there are some like Abdulla Galadari, *Qur'anic Hermeneutics* (New York: Bloomsbury Academic, 2018), who would contend that the Qur'an only rejects the physical act of siring a child while yet allowing room for an ontological sonship that is compatible with biblical teaching. The following chapter will address various ways that contemporary authors have tried to reconcile the Qur'an's teaching on the sonship of Jesus with the biblical testimony. Suffice it to say here that such a reading is strained and tenuous at best.

multiple places, but perhaps the clearest rejection of Jesus as the Son of God[60] is found in Qur'an 9:30–31:

> The Jews say, "Ezra is the son of God," and the Christians say, "The Messiah is the son of God." That is their saying with their mouths. They imitate the saying of those who disbelieved before (them). (May) God fight them. How are they (so) deluded? They have taken their teachers and their monks as Lords instead of God, and (also) the Messiah, son of Mary, when they were only commanded to serve one God. (There is) no God but Him. Glory to Him above what they associate!

This passage places the claim that Jesus is the Son of God on the lips of Christians. Immediately following this, however, the Qur'an responds by condemning such a claim as an act of association (*shirk*).

Furthermore, this passage clarifies that Jesus is not the Son of God, but is instead merely the son of Mary. Throughout its pages, the Qur'an refers to Jesus as "the son of Mary" twenty-three times leading Kaltner and Mirza to conclude, "The frequent use of 'son of Mary' in the Qur'an is likely a way of underscoring the humanity of Jesus/'Isa, which is a central theme in many of the passages that refer to him."[61] With Jesus's humanity everywhere reinforced in the Qur'an, it is not surprising that the Qur'an would also omit any references to Jesus's role as the incarnate one who would die in the stead of sinners and be raised for their vindication.

As we have already seen, Qur'an 4:157–158 appears to present an account of Jesus that differs significantly from the central biblical account of the Gospel. Again, it states,

> And for their saying, "Surely we killed the Messiah, Jesus, son of Mary, the messenger of God"—yet they

---

60   In fact, this is the only place that the Qur'an uses the biblical phrase *ibn Allah*. All other references to Jesus being God's son use the word *walad Allah*, which is a term more viscerally associated with siring a child.

61   Kaltner and Mirza, *The Bible and the Qur'an*, 76.

did not kill him, nor did they crucify him, but it (only) seemed like (that) to them. They have no knowledge about him, only the following of conjecture. Certainly they did not kill him. No! God raised him to Himself. God is mighty, wise.

These verses, as noted above, might be understood in such a way as to yet allow for Jesus to have died in history. Still, the clarity of rejecting the crucifixion and the total omission within the Qur'an of the connection between Jesus's death and the remission of sins stands in irreconcilable conflict with the biblical Jesus.

Even if the Qur'an admits that Jesus died in history, it is conspicuously silent regarding his ability to offer his life as a ransoming atonement that saves sinners. Further distancing the role of the qur'anic Messiah from the biblical Jesus, Qur'an 61:6 records Jesus promising the advent of Muhammad as he is made to say, "Sons of Israel! Surely I am the messenger of God to you, confirming what was before me of the Torah, and bringing good news of a messenger who will come after me, whose name will be Ahmad." As Gordon Nickel notes, "The name of this messenger would be *ahmad*, a word that literally means, 'more praised.' Muslims have interpreted *ahmad* to be another name for Muhammad, and many have cited this verse to claim that the coming of Islam's messenger was prophesied."[62]

In summary, then, the Jesus of the Qur'an is merely human, does not lay down his life for the sins of the world, and concludes his prophetic career by pointing towards Muhammad. While the Qur'an needs to appropriate Jesus into its message in order to sustain its claim that it extends, completes, and corrects prior revelation, it is clear that Jesus in the pages of the Qur'an is a different character, playing a different role than he does in the Bible.

---

62   Gordon Nickel, ed. *The Qur'an with Christian Commentary* (Grand Rapids: Zondervan, 2020), 564n61.6.

READING THE QUR'AN FOR UNDERSTANDING, COMMUNICATION, AND COMPARISON

This chapter has attempted to lay out three reasons that it is important for a Christian to read the Qur'an for themselves. First, reading the Qur'an allows the Christian to get a feel for how their Muslim neighbors are being influenced by their religious text. Engaging with the rhetorical features, tone, and implied relationship between the reader and the Qur'an will help the Christian to develop a sense of how Muslims are being shaped under its influence.

Furthermore, we have seen that many of the words that will be necessary for having Gospel-centered conversations with our Muslim friends have cognates within the Qur'an. Despite the superficial lexical similarity, however, these words often come loaded with different meaning and impact due to their appearance and function within the Qur'an. Reading the Qur'an for yourself will allow you to recognize where there might be common words and concepts that are loaded with different meaning than what a Christian might intend or understand the word to naturally communicate. Having observed these distinctions, then, the Christian who has read the Qur'an is better prepared to sense where communication might break down and to offer biblical definition for shared terminology.

And finally, reading the Qur'an for oneself opens the door to substantive comparison. Many of our Muslim friends will be inclined to affirm that we believe in the same prophets as they do. They will likely be able to list the names of many key figures that feature in the biblical story. However, gaining familiarity with the role these characters play within the landscape of the Qur'an will allow Christians to engage in meaningful comparison between the characters who are used of the Lord to advance redemptive history and those in the Qur'an who simply serve as mouthpieces of the call to Islam.

For these reasons and more, I believe that it is important for Christians to become familiar with the Qur'an for themselves. At the same time, reading the Qur'an is different than using the Qur'an. The following chapter will address a related question: Should a Christian use the Qur'an in ministry to Muslims?

8

SHOULD CHRISTIANS USE THE QUR'AN?

If you are in doubt about what We have sent down
to you, ask those who have been reciting the Book
before you. The truth has come to you from your Lord,
so do not be one of the doubters.

Qur'an 10:94

The previous chapter argued that it is important for Christians to read the Qur'an for themselves. We saw that the Qur'an uses language, concepts, and characters that feature differently than they do in the Bible. As a result, we need to be familiar with how such concepts will need to be addressed if they are to be communicated as they function biblically.

In so doing, we highlighted some significant points of overlap between the Bible and the Qur'an. The Bible shares a great deal of ethical teaching with the Qur'an, and some of the central characters who advance the biblical storyline are viewed positively within the Qur'an. In fact, the Qur'an itself endorses the prior Scriptures. As quoted above, Qur'an 10:94 instructs Muslims to consult with People of the Book in order to better understand Muhammad's message.

This verse alone causes many Christian missionaries to wonder if the Qur'an might be the key to beginning spiritual conversations.

As a result of the Qur'an's conceptual overlap with the Bible and the generally positive posture that it takes towards the Books of the Jews and Christians, many have proposed that there might be a way to look at the Qur'an as a gateway to sharing the Gospel. Some have argued that there is good reason for Christians to not only familiarize themselves with the Qur'an, but actually to work with it as a part of their evangelistic strategy. We will look at two different types of approaches to this kind of positive use of the Qur'an in this chapter. We will also consider some contemporary attempts to reconcile the teaching of the Qur'an and the Bible that have appeared in academic circles.

These efforts are born of a desire to find fruitful ways to engage across religious lines. In the academy, much of the effort to reconcile these two books seems to be born of a desire to overcome the apparently intractable differences between the two faiths. Other approaches want to discover ways to avoid the conclusion that Muhammad was mistaken to claim that the Qur'an can extend the message of the Bible. Yet others grow out of a genuine desire to see their Muslim friends encounter the Gospel in ways that would gain more traction than they have seen through other methods.

Despite the laudable motivations, this chapter will argue that there is very little within the Qur'an that should be used by a Christian in an effort to make sense of the biblical Gospel. Apart from perhaps demonstrating awareness of the Qur'an's teaching, Christian missionaries should avoid methods and strategies that involve going to the Qur'an for positive reinforcement of the biblical message. The risks of such approaches range from confused communication to corruption of key biblical concepts and endorsing the Qur'an as revelation. In order to substantiate this claim, this chapter will look at the CAMEL Method employed by some missionaries, Insider Movement approaches to contextualization, and the academic endeavor aimed at reconciling the Qur'an and the Bible around their teachings about Jesus. While each approach raises concerns, we will begin with the least problematic and move toward the one that presents the most dangers.

THE CAMEL METHOD

The first approach that we need to consider is the one championed by Kevin Greeson in his book, *The CAMEL: How Muslims Are Coming to Faith in Christ*.[1] Therein, Greeson's proposes the mnemonic acrostic "CAMEL" (CAMEL describes Jesus as one who is: Chosen, Announced by Angels, Miracle worker, knows the way to Eternal Life) as a way of recalling important statements about the Qur'an's Jesus character.[2] Greeson is careful to note, "There is not enough light in the Qur'an to bring Muslims to salvation, but there are enough flickers of truth to draw out God's person of peace from among them. As soon as possible, you want to bridge out of the Qur'an and into the Bible where they can see the truth for themselves."[3] Still, his basic proposal is that a Christian who intends to share the Gospel with a Muslim friend should begin by reading through several passages in the Qur'an in order to prompt further inquiry into the character named 'Isa.

CAMEL IN QUR'AN 3:42–55

The CAMEL method begins by asking a Muslim friend to open to Qur'an 3:42–55 in order to ask the question, "Who is 'Isa?" The passage presents a narrative of prophecy given to Mary prior to her pregnancy as well as statements made by 'Isa himself about his calling, his message, and his miracles. For Greeson, the miracles are of special significance. Qur'an 3:49a recounts allusions to biblical and extrabiblical miracles connected with Jesus, saying,

> And (He will make him) a messenger to the Sons of Israel. "Surely I have brought you a sign from your Lord: I shall create for you the form of a bird from clay. Then I will breathe into it and it will become a bird by the permission of God. And I shall heal the blind and the leper, and give the dead life by the permission of God.

---

1   Kevin Greeson, *The CAMEL: How Muslims Are Coming to Faith in Christ,* rev. ed. (Richmond, VA: WIGTake, 2010).

2   Greeson, *The CAMEL*, 104..

3   Greeson, *The CAMEL*, 102.

Here Greeson encourages those who would employ his method to avoid pointing out the apocryphal nature of the account of Jesus creating clay birds and then breathing life into them.[4] Instead, he suggests that one might gain more traction by asking,

> Isn't it interesting that this story says 'Isa created life out of the dust by breathing life into it? How did Allah create man? . . . According to the Qur'an, 'Isa was able to do the same thing by breathing life into birds made of dust. 'Isa had the power to create life. . . . Do you know of any other prophets who had this power to create life?[5]

While these questions certainly may produce some initial traction, there are a few issues that attend this approach.

First, it is likely that your Muslim friend will point to the phrase, "by God's permission" as an easy way to explain that it wasn't Jesus who created, but it was God.[6] Second, by leaning into this account, the Christian is attempting to build a bridge to the Bible on the basis of a story that is not found in the Bible. This is problematic for two reasons. On the one hand, you may be laying the foundation for confusion later on where your Muslim friend discovers that such an account is not part of the biblical record of Jesus's life and ministry. On the other hand, you lend credence to the Qur'an as a supplementary account, thereby potentially compromising the idea of biblical sufficiency and endorsing the Qur'an as authoritative.

Regardless, Greeson's proposals are not exhausted by his reliance on Qur'an 3:42–55. Having increased curiosity about Jesus using the initial CAMEL method, Greeson proposes a secondary port of call for bridging into the biblical worldview. He refers to this aspect

---

4   The account can be found in the second century document called the Infancy Gospel of Thomas. Cf. John Kaltner and Younus Mirza, *The Bible and the Qur'an: Biblical Characters in the Islamic Tradition* (New York: T&T Clark, 2018), 79.

5   Greeson, *The CAMEL*, 135.

6   Seyyed Hossein Nasr, *The Study Qur'an* (New York: HarperOne, 2015), 145n49.

of his method as the Korbani Path drawing on the Islamic holiday called 'Id al-Korban.[7]

THE KORBANI PATH

Moving beyond the initial CAMEL sequence, Greeson goes on to employ what he refers to as the Korbani Path which continues to draw on qur'anic material while naturally bridging into biblical conversations. The Korbani Path takes its name from the Islamic holiday 'Id al-Korban—or as it is known in other parts of the Muslim world, 'Id al-Adha. He rightly notes the global importance of this holiday to the Muslim community, comparing the special nature of its festivities to those of Christmas for Christians.[8]

As we saw in the previous chapter, within Islam, 'Id al-Korban ('Id al-Adha) derives from Qur'an 37:100–111 and the account of Abraham's near-sacrifice of his son. Within the Qur'an, the account of the story includes sparse details, but it concludes with the same outcome: Abraham's sacrifice of his son is halted, and another sacrificial replacement is given. For the Christian, such a story presents itself as having an obvious link to the Gospel: a son who was spared by a ram in his place, to the Son who offered himself in our place. However, before we endorse such a move, there are two critical issues that need to be addressed.

First of all, in order to make the connection between the CAMEL method verses in Qur'an 3:42–55 and the 'Id al-Korbani story in Qur'an 37:100–111, Greeson leans on Qur'an 3:55 to tie the idea of Korbani sacrifice to 'Isa. Greeson argues that this verse should read, "Allah caused 'Isa to die" due to the presence of the word *tawaffa* which is almost always understood to be a reference to death.[9] Greeson's argument depends upon a consistent translation and interpretation of *tawaffa* to indicate a reference to God causing Jesus to die. However, that is not the traditional interpretation of this verse.

7　In parts of the Islamic world most familiar to Greeson, 'Id al-Adha is referred to as 'Id al-Korban.

8　Greeson, *The CAMEL*, 113.

9　Greeson, *The CAMEL*, 116.

Translators such as A. J. Droge follow the traditional Islamic understanding and interpretation as they render Qur'an 3:55 as follows:

(Remember) when God said, "Jesus! Surely I am going to take you (*mutawaffika*) and raise you to myself, and purify you from those who disbelieve. And I am going to lace those who follow you above those who disbelieve until the Day of Resurrection. Then, to Me is your return, and I shall judge between you concerning your differences."

As Greeson notes correctly, the Arabic text does elsewhere translate words from the verb *tawaffa* in relation to the concept of death.[10] However, most Muslims and a majority of translators understand this verse to refer to Jesus's assumption to God as a means of avoiding the cross that the Jews had intended for him in Qur'an 4:157.[11] Thus, to make the connection between this verse and Jesus's sacrificial death is a step that most Muslims will not find convincing.

Still, the biggest problem with Greeson's proposal is not convincing his Muslim audience that Jesus is the fulfillment of the 'Id al-Korbani sacrifice. Instead, it is a confused pathway from Genesis 22's account of Abram and Isaac to Jesus's atoning death. Greeson argues that the account of Abraham and his son is given to provide an understanding of God's prescribed sacrificial system. He writes,

Allah tested Ibrahim's love for Him, and Ibrahim passed the test by showing Allah how much he loved Him. A father who is willing to sacrifice his own son is revealing

---

10   Cf. Gordon Nickel, *The Qur'an with Christian Commentary* (Grand Rapids: Zondervan, 2020), 87n3.55. Nickel lists Qur'an 10:46, 104;12:101; 13:40; 16:28; and 40:77 as examples of *tawaffa* being translated in terms of death rather than being taken away. He notes, however, that most translators avoid translating *tawaffa* as death when it is used in conjunction with Jesus due to the traditional understanding that Jesus avoided death as indicated by Qur'an 4:157.

11   Ayman Ibrahim, *A Concise Guide to the Qur'an* (Grand Rapids: Baker, 2020), 114–15; Gordon Nickel, "The Death of Jesus in the Qur'an," in *The Qur'an with Christian Commentary*, ed. Gordon Nickel (Grand Rapids: Zondervan, 2020), 314.

enormous faith and love, and yet, a love of equal value is a son who is willing to be sacrificed.[12]

Greeson then suggests that the evangelist move on to say that we are in need of having our sins removed so as to enter God's holy presence. He says, "The *korbani* system is a picture revealed by God to teach us the penalty for our sins and how they might be transferred to one who is innocent."[13] And this recognition leads immediately to presenting Jesus as our great sacrifice, as Greeson writes, "With our penalty satisfied and our sins transferred to another, we are free to join Allah in heaven. . . . Allah chose 'Isa for the *korban*."[14] Finally, just prior to inviting a Muslim to consider receiving Jesus as their Korban-by-faith, Greeson suggests,

> Recall that when a Muslim practices *korban* he keeps a list of relatives' and friends' names in his pocket. When Allah performed His *korban*, He had the name of every person, past, present and future on His list. *Your name was on His list.* Allah sacrificed 'Isa, His *korban*, for you.[15]

While this approach may appear to make clear connections with the logic of sacrifice as it is presented in the Bible, it can be incredibly confusing for Muslims who do not have an understanding of ancient Israel's sacrificial system in their minds.

In fact, if we step into the biblical story at the point of Genesis 22, we realize that this is not a passage that teaches about atonement or sin offering. The Bible commends Abraham for his faith, his son is spared, and a sacrifice is provided from the hand of the Lord. Still, at this point in Genesis, the category of sacrifice is not yet developed to provide the logic of blood-bought atonement. The explanation of sacrifice and its relationship to the forgiveness

12   Greeson, *The CAMEL*, 117.
13   Greeson, *The CAMEL*, 117.
14   Greeson, *The CAMEL*, 118.
15   Greeson, *The CAMEL*, 119.

of sins is not given in full until places like Leviticus 16–17. For most Christian missionaries, the relationship between Abraham's sacrifice, the Levitical sacrificial system, and Jesus's substitutionary death is clear and beautiful. That may not, however, be the case for someone without the benefit of a biblical worldview and implicit knowledge of the biblical story.

Consider the effect of moving directly from 'Id al-Adha to Jesus on the cross. Abraham received instructions from God to put his son to death. There is no sin discussed in either the biblical or the qur'anic account for which this death is a consequence. In fact, the Qur'an explicitly states that this vision that Abraham received was a clear test of his willingness to submit to God. If that is the sum total of what they understand about sacrifice, then our Muslim friends would be justified to wonder why putting something or someone to death is God's preferred demonstration of love? Furthermore, if the event was a test of Abraham's submission, what connection is there to God sending his son to die in a way that Abraham's son was spared?

As we have already seen, the Qur'an and Islamic theology teach a different doctrine of sin. As a result, a Christian has much more groundwork to do in explaining the correlation between sin, death, and sacrifice. Without the intervening biblical explanation of sin, its separating effects, and the role of blood-atonement, jumping from Abraham's story to Jesus puts us in danger of presenting a God who shows his love by inexplicably choosing to kill his own son instead of killing us. Without the understanding of sin taught by the Bible, this God does not seem gratuitously loving, but rather seems unjust, cruel, and bloodthirsty.

Some might respond to this discussion by simply adding a stop-off in Leviticus to Greeson's four-point Korbani Path. While that might improve the presentation of biblical logic, the problem of misunderstanding is likely to persist for our Muslim friends as they are encouraged to reflect on the practice of 'Id al-Adha. This problem lingers because 'Id al-Adha is an explicitly Islamic celebration in which imitation of Abraham's submission leads away from Christ as the fulfillment of sacrificial ritual and towards human ability to please God apart from Jesus's atoning work. At the end of this chapter we will revisit this narrative in order to propose a more fruitful and faithful way to utilize it to point to Christ.

CRITICAL ASSESSMENT OF THE CAMEL

The CAMEL method is one of the more popular articulations of a particular missiological strategy that seeks to use the Qur'an in evangelism. Greeson is to be commended for his desire to find natural bridges from the Muslim worldview to biblical conversations. Likewise, he is clear in repeatedly affirming that he does not believe that the Qur'an is compatible with the biblical Gospel nor that it contains sufficient revelation to lead a person to understand the Gospel. He rightly cautions his readers about what his method does not accomplish, stating, "If a Muslim listens to you though the entire CAMEL presentation, keep in mind that he has still not heard the Gospel," but he clarifies that "A foundation for hearing the plan of salvation is now in place."[16]

These clarifications are very helpful and laudable. In fact, the CAMEL method is not far from providing helpful ways to begin sharing the Gospel with Muslims. In the following chapter we will suggest some adjustments that can overcome some of the limitations and confusions introduced by the CAMEL method. Still, while there may be some initial and pragmatic traction with this method, the handling of the Qur'an is problematic on at least two counts.

First, the passages that are recommended for use are never used by Muslims to make the points that Greeson extracts. In fact, to the point of Jesus's miracles noted above, the caveat that the Qur'an includes—"by God's permission"—is taken universally to be an affirmation that Jesus was simply the conduit of God's signs. As stated elsewhere, the Qur'an makes it clear that 'Isa is just one of the prophets, among whom there is no distinction.[17]

---

16   Greeson, *The CAMEL*, 111.
17   See Qur'an 3:58, which equates Adam and 'Isa's natures. Also, Qur'an 2:136, 285; 3:84; 4:152; 21:92, which state that there is no distinction between the various messengers of God.

206 PART 3: THE QUR'AN AND THE CHRISTIAN

Secondly—and more problematic for long-term ministry—is the manner in which the Qur'an is recognized as providing truth leading to the hope of salvation. Greeson suggests two openings for how to begin using his method conversationally, one of which is: "I have been reading the Qur'an and have discovered an amazing truth that gives hope of eternal life in heaven. Would you open your Qur'an to *surah al-Imran* 3:42–55 . . . so we can talk about it?"[18] Even if this particular entre into the conversation is adapted, the method leans into the qur'anic account to determine 'Isa's uniqueness, affirm what the Qur'an says about him even when some details are extrabiblical, and it culminates with a comparison to the Islamic festival of 'Id al-Adha.

As we saw in the previous chapter, within the Islamic worldview 'Id al-Adha provides a foreshadowing of Islam, not of Christ. The continued interweaving of Islamic forms and qur'anic foundations into the attempted retelling of the Abraham story and its relation to biblical redemptive history presents both immediate and long-term confusion over which sources are to be trusted to provide truth about Jesus and human responses to his Gospel. Despite this critique, Greeson's CAMEL method represents a method of using the Qur'an that recognizes its incompatibility with the biblical Gospel. Other approaches to using the Qur'an in evangelism and discipleship argue that it might not be as incompatible as it is often made out to be.

THE QUR'AN AND INSIDER MOVEMENTS

Many missionaries who would make use of the CAMEL Method likely view the Qur'an as nothing more than a conceptual bridge to the Bible. As one does not linger on a bridge but instead uses it as a means of reaching a desired destination, so too the Qur'an provides a means of transferring a person from their Islamic world and to the intended destination of the Bible. Once it has served its purpose of transporting a person from its pages and into the biblical text, it is no longer active in the process.

---

18 Greeson, *The CAMEL*, 106. To be fair, the second opener is much less affirmative of the Qur'an and its message, noting only that the speaker has found "some very interesting things about 'Isa" in the suggested verses.

Over the last three decades, however, there have been some missionaries who have offered an approach to the Qur'an that goes beyond bridging. Many of these advocates are proponents of strategies for missionary contextualization that are broadly defined as Insider Movements (IM). While it is difficult to provide a definition that would satisfy all those who adhere to the underpinning philosophy of IM, Rebecca Lewis—a prolific author and advocate of IM strategies—offers this description: "Believers retain their identity as members of their socio-religious community while living under the Lordship of Jesus Christ and the authority of the Bible."[19] In another article, Lewis further expands upon what she means in terms of retaining a Muslim identity, writing,

> The new spiritual identity of believing families in insider movements is in being followers of Jesus Christ and members of His global kingdom, not necessarily in being affiliated with or accepted by the institutional forms of Christianity that are associated with traditionally Christian cultures. They retain their temporal identity in their natural socio-religious community, while living transformed lives due to their faith in Christ.[20]

In other words, Lewis and other IM advocates often refer to a person's socio-religious identity in an effort to acknowledge the fact that Muslim-majority cultures cultivate identities that are both religious and extrareligious in nature. By being born in a Muslim society, given an Islamic name, and recognizing the social importance of the mosque, even an atheist can retain something of a Muslim identity while rejecting the specifically religious elements of the label.[21] So

---

19 Rebecca Lewis, "Insider Movements: Retaining Identity and Preserving Community," in *Perspectives on the World Christian Movement,* eds. Ralph Winter and Steven Hawthorne, 4th ed. (Pasadena, CA: William Carey, 2009), 673.

20 Rebecca Lewis, "Insider Movements: The Conversation Continues/Promoting Movements to Christ within Natural Communities," in *International Journal of Frontier Missiology* 24, no. 2 (2007): 76.

21 See the argument of Harley Talman, "Muslim Followers of Jesus, Muhammad, and the Qur'an," in *Muslim Conversions to Christ,* eds. Ayman Ibrahim and Ant Greenham, 123–38 (New York: Peter Lang, 2018), 124.

too can a person be a cultural Christian in the United States without ever darkening the door of a church.

Further, many IM advocates recognize that the word "Muslim"—though typically associated with the contemporary understanding of Islam as a distinct religious system—simply derives from the Arabic concept of submissions. As a result, IMs typically encourage those who put their faith in Christ to continue identifying themselves as Muslims—submitted ones. If the word "Muslim" merely means "one who is submitted," then a person submitted to Jesus as Lord is a Muslim of sorts, and can retain this identifier and the relational connections that come with it can be utilized as opportunities to share their faith in 'Isa. There is much to be discussed about IMs in general, though for our purposes, we must consider what ongoing role the Qur'an plays within these contextualization strategies.[22]

CONTINUED DEVOTIONAL USE

One approach to the Qur'an taken by some IM advocates is to allow the Qur'an to remain a part of a Muslim follower of 'Isa's life as long as it does not usurp the Bible. Some even include readings from the Qur'an within the worship services conducted by groups of believers from a Muslim background. For such strategists, whatever cultural or even spiritual role it played in the life of a Muslim prior to their decision to place their faith in Christ can be retained as long as its teaching does not contradict biblical teaching. The Qur'an can thus continue to play a role in the devotional life of an 'Isa Muslim.

For some IM proponents, the idea of retaining the Qur'an as an active part of a person's spiritual life is not viewed as a problem because it can be reinterpreted in novel and unattested ways that allow it to be reconciled with Christian teaching. For instance, Harley Talman writes,

---

22   For those interested in further reading on the subject from the perspective of advocates of IMs, see Harley Talman and John Jay Travis, eds, *Understanding Insider Movements: Disciples of Jesus within Diverse Religious Communities* (Pasadena, CA: William Carey Library, 2015). For a compilation of important critiques of IM, see Ayman Ibrahim and Ant Greenham, *Muslim Conversions to Christ: A Critique of Insider Movements in Islamic Contexts* (New York: Peter Lang, 2018).

Unfortunately, most Muslim clerics interpret and teach the Qur'an in ways that contradict some fundamental teachings of the Bible. As a result, most Christians completely reject the Qur'an. But I believe that if more Muslims would interpret the Quran in ways that affirm biblical teachings (which is what the Qur'an says its purpose is), then many Christians may begin to view Muhammad's prophetic mission much more positively.[23]

There are many curiosities about such a sentiment that deserve significantly more attention than can be given here.[24] But it is important to see this type of claim for what it is. It is a bold claim issued to 1,400 years of scholars, clerics, and Muslims that they have been misreading and misunderstanding their holy text.

Even if one sets aside the audacity and offense of such a claim, however, the danger these ideas represent come from the unspoken assumption that seems to motivate a person to invest time and energy into producing such reinterpretation: the Bible may not be sufficient to meet the spiritual needs of a believer from a Muslim background.

Most IM proponents who support or allow for the inclusion of the Qur'an will yet make a caveat that the Qur'an is only useful insofar as it reinforces or does not contradict biblical truth. Still, the overwhelming majority of Islamic interpreters have argued for nearly a millennium and a half that the Qur'an teaches that Jesus did not die for anyone's sins. The Qur'an does not teach about a God who loves his creation and demonstrates it by taking on flesh and living among his creatures. The Qur'an does not teach that Jesus's atoning

---

23 Harley Talman, "Rehabilitating Our Image of Muhammad: A Concluding Response to Ayman Ibrahim," *International Journal of Frontier Missiology* 33, no. 3 (2016): 121–35.

24 One wonders how likely it is that a new believer will convince his or her Muslim neighbors that they—along with the last 1,400 years of Islamic scholars—have been misunderstanding the Qur'an. If it is unlikely that this type of fresh reading of the Qur'an will help in evangelism, one still must wonder what reason a believer in Jesus might have for exerting the effort to reinterpret a book in fresh ways so as to make it cohere with the Bible.

blood adopts rebellious sinners back into the family of the triune God. The Qur'an does not teach that the Holy Spirit has been sent to encourage, convict, illuminate, and guide believers into the truths of Scripture and their application in contemporary life. With all of these omissions, it is difficult to see what benefit might remain that would make it worth the risk to encourage the Muslim to continue reading a book that needs to be reinterpreted against the current of historical and contemporary understanding.

Perhaps the most common answer is that the Qur'an can be retained because it can be helpful in further evangelism. In fact, statistics can be marshalled to show that many believers in Christ from Muslim backgrounds point back to the Qur'an as the place that they were introduced to Christ. Therefore, despite the potential risk, I advocates often see great evangelistic reward in reading the Qur'an christocentrically in order to view it as a sort of *preparatio evangelica* for Muslim peoples.

PREPARATIO EVANGELICA: A CHRISTOCENTRIC READING OF THE QUR'AN

Proposals for "christocentric" readings of the Qur'an have been made as ways to not only justify the retention of the Qur'an in the life of a believer from a Muslim background, but to admonish the reading and use of the Qur'an in evangelism and as a book largely compatible with the central teachings of the Bible. Relating an anecdote about a woman who came to faith from a Muslim background, Harley Talman writes,

> Another Muslim who came to faith in Christ married a Christian worker and could not remain an insider, but is sympathetic with insiders she has met. I observed her ask some Christians, "Why do Christians hate Muhammad so much? This is against the Gospel! Does not Jesus command us to love everyone?" Then she added soberly, "I hate to think where I would be today without Muhammad." (She would not have known about Christ and become

his disciple, but would instead be an ignorant pagan and polytheist.) The same is true of many insiders who view Muhammad and the Qur'an as instrumental in pointing them to Christ and as playing an essential role in their coming to faith.[25]

Citing research conducted by David Garrison, Talman reiterates, "Garrison's research showed that the witness of the Qur'an brought many Muslims in South Asia to initial faith in Christ who then led them to the Bible for a clearer understanding."[26] With multiple testimonies providing similar evidence, it is not surprising to find missiologists who are optimistic about the prospects of using a christocentric reading of the Qur'an as an evangelism pathway.

The problem is that the Qur'an is not a christocentric book, while the Bible explicitly is. Luke 24:44–49 shows that Jesus understood the entire Bible to be pointing to him. Jesus's own hermeneutics were christocentric, and the reader of the Bible is justified in following suit to discover that the whole book centers on Christ.[27] Such a claim cannot be made of the Qur'an.

It is possible to conduct a christo-exclusive reading of the Qur'an wherein all of the passages that discuss 'Isa are highlighted. But what one finds in consulting those approximately twenty-seven passages is that the Qur'an's Jesus character is not portrayed as a long-awaited savior whose life, teaching, and Gospel culminate the story told through the Scriptures of the prior 1,500 years.[28] And as the previous chapter noted, these passages will also include the Qur'an's teaching that indicates that Jesus was not crucified and therefore raised again

---

25   Talman, "Muslim Followers of Jesus, Muhammad, and the Qur'an," 130.
26   Talman, "Muslim Followers of Jesus, Muhammad, and the Qur'an," 130.
27   See the helpful works on this point such as Craig Bartholomew and Michael Goheen, *The Drama of Scripture*, 2nd ed. (Grand Rapids: Baker, 2014); Matthew Emerson, *The Story of Scripture* (Nashville: B&H, 2017); Trent Hunter and Stephen Wellum, *Christ from Beginning to End* (Grand Rapids: Zondervan, 2018); Bruce Ashford and Heath Thomas, *The Gospel of Our King* (Grand Rapids: Baker, 2019).
28   For further elaboration, see Matthew Bennett, "Christ in the Scripture of Islam," *Southeastern Theological Review* 11, no. 1 (Spring, 2020): 99–117.

three days later. And it will include the passages in which Jesus predicts that Ahmad will follow him as a messenger of God. Therefore, while the Qur'an does uphold Jesus as a key figure and as a messenger of God, it does so exclusively on its own terms and for its own purposes.

Stated bluntly, the Qur'an does not look to Jesus to save nor does it allow him to save. Only the Jesus of the Bible is presented as a worthy object of faith because the Jesus of the Qur'an is a mere messenger, undifferentiated from others. While certain testimonies may continue to proliferate wherein people associate the Jesus of the Qur'an with their now-saving faith in the Jesus of the Bible, it should not be employed as a part of missionary strategy to utilize a book that wrenches Jesus from his salvific role in order to prepare the way for another human messenger.

MUSLIM IDIOM TRANSLATIONS OF SCRIPTURE

As an extension of the desire to see those familiar with qur'anic language engaging with the Gospel, some missiologists have proposed the production of new translations of the Bible, often referred to as Muslim Idiom Translations (MIT). Such proposals are born of the recognition that Islamic Arabic has its own contours, conventions, vocabulary, and register that are used to discuss religious topics. MIT advocates encourage the production of translations that capture the expectation for religious dialogue that are native and familiar to Muslim societies.

Such translation proposals emerge from underlying translation theories—particularly the theory of Dynamic Equivalence (DE). Briefly stated, DE translation theory intends to render the text in such a way as to create the same impact on the reader as it would have had on its original audience. Such an approach can be as seemingly inconsequential as rendering weights and costs according to contemporary units of measure. However, it can also lead to more drastic proposals.

For instance, one of the architects of the DE translation model, Charles Kraft, is reported to have One participant in a seminar led by Kraft reported that Kraft suggests that, if one wants to communicate the biblical idea of a sheep and shepherd in a place where sheep are unknown, a local equivalent of the sheep must be found. If the cultural equivalent is raising pigs, then, Kraft argued that it would be appropriate to render John the Baptist's reference to Jesus in John 1:36 as, "Behold, the *piglet* of God!"[29] Not all such suggestions are as brazen, but even the less absurd suggestions for substitution can be theologically problematic.

As it plays out in certain MIT volumes, religious language and the names of biblical characters are often substituted for their Qur'anic equivalents. MIT proponent John Travis presents the motivation for this substitution, writing, "It is crucial to have an appropriately contextualized Bible . . . that intentionally uses affectively and cognitively meaningful vocabulary for Muslim readers."[30] Some of this contextualized vocabulary is relegated to using to the Qur'an's preferred names for various biblical figures. While such a choice involves smuggling qur'anic baggage into the biblical character, it may be argued that this is not necessarily an infringement upon the biblical testimony. Lest we think Travis's suggestion is limited to exchanging names, however, in a footnote Travis urges translators to find "culturally appropriate ways to translate 'Holy Spirit,' 'Son of God,' 'Lord,' 'Christian,' and 'church.'"[31]

These suggestions are not new to Travis, but have been prompted by the teachings of earlier missiologists such as Charles Kraft. Already noted as one of the major proponents for the DE translation theory, Kraft argued that media presentations directed at Muslims might find alternative ways of referring to Jesus other than Son, stating,

> The terms for Messiah and prophet serve quite well as substitutes for Son. I personally would not press the deity

---

29   See the account of Kraft's teaching recorded by Georges Houssney, "Watching the Insider Movement Unfold," in *Muslim Conversions to Christ*, eds. Ayman Ibrahim and Ant Greenham, 397–408 (New York: Peter Lang, 2018), 398.

30   John Travis, "Insider Movements among Muslims," in *Understanding Insider Movements*, eds. Harley Talman and Jay Travis (Pasadena, CA: William Carey, 2015), 133–42.

31   Travis, "Insider Movements among Muslims," 137n26.

of Christ either, since it is sure to be misunderstood. . . . [T]he Muslim must be able to feel at home, both in his society and in his religious allegiance.[32]

While Kraft notes that he prays that eventually the Muslim would come to appreciate "the exciting relational aspects of the faith that Jesus characterized by referring to His relationship the God as a Father-Son relationship," he also advocates for a "faith-renewal movement to use all three books (Qur'an, Old and New Testament) as its basis."[33]

The assumed compatibility of the Bible and the Qur'an, then, allows translators and missiologists to interject qur'anic language into biblical translations with the assumption that it will be of no substantial consequence. These assumptions lead to qur'anic deference and alteration of the biblical text at key points. The most egregious has been the controversial attempts to remove references to God as Father or Son—often referred to as Divine Filial Language, or DFL—from the translations intended for Muslim audiences.

Having conducted research into several recent MITs, Adam Simnowitz has provided English translations of key verses to show the damage done to the meaning of the original text.[34] For instance, Simnowitz points to the translation Al-Injil from 2013, providing the translation of Matthew 28:19: "So go and make followers of me [lit. my followers] from all of the nations, immersing them, in the name of the king, the merciful one, and the beloved prince, and the holy spirit of God."[35] In the same translation, he shows Luke 3:18 and the genealogy of Jesus rendered to remove the reference to Jesus as the Son of God: "the son of Enosh, the son of Seth, the son of

---

32 Charles Kraft, "Distinctive Religious Barriers to Outside Penetration," in *Conference on Media in Islamic Culture Report,* ed. C. Richard Shumaker, 65–76 (Clearwater, FL: International Christian Broadcasters, 1974), 76.
33 Kraft, "Distinctive Religious Barriers to Outside Penetration," 76.
34 Adam Simnowitz, "Appendix: Do Muslim Idiom Translations Islamicize the Bible? A Glimpse Behind the Veil," in *Muslim Conversions to Christ,* eds. Ayman Ibrahim and Ant Greenham (New York: Peter Lang, 2018), 501–23.
35 Simnowitz, "Appendix," 504.

Adam, the creation of God."[36] In avoiding the language of Father and Son as it pertains to the first and second persons of the Trinity, Simnowitz concludes,

> By rendering "Father" with non-literal renderings, the Fatherhood of God, one of the most significant and unique doctrines of the Bible, fundamental to the Gospel message, is thus lost. The inevitable consequence of this common feature of MIT is a portrayal of God that is much closer, and perhaps in some instances, identical to the Islamic understanding of God.[37]

In other words, these translation decisions are more than linguistic choices. The consequences of these instances of deference to qur'anic theology undermine the biblical presentation of God in favor of a presentation that is more at home in the Qur'an than the pages of the Bible.

Beyond the exchange of biblical language for qur'anic language, some MITs also include Islamic phrases and theology in places where the biblical text does not call for it. For instance, Simnowitz points to three MITs that insert the first half of the Islamic Shahada into their translations.[38] The first half of the Shehada is the testimony of Islamic faith by which a Muslim confesses that, "There is no god but the God [Allah]." The second half of the Shehada recognizes that, "Muhammad is his messenger." This statement is often repeated in full throughout Islamic life, and it is broadcast five times a day as a part of the call to prayer. Functionally for most Muslims, to hear or to read the first half of the Shahada is to call to mind the statement in its entirety.

Along with several other instances, Simnowitz points out that 1 Corinthians 8:4, 1 Timothy 2:5, and James 2:19 all include this

---

36   Simnowitz, "Appendix," 505.
37   Simnowitz, "Appendix," 509.
38   Simnowitz, "Appendix," 509. Cited MITs are Al-Injil (2013), Al-Sharif (2013), and The Bold Proclamation of the Apostles of Christ (2016).

phrase. Simnowitz correctly chastises this inclusion on theological grounds, stating,

> Regardless of the claim that the first part of the Shahada faithfully expresses biblical monotheism, any MIT that contains it will be understood by most, if not all Muslims as affirming Islam, or as a deceitful means of trying to fool Muslims who are naïve in their understanding of Islam. In common practice, Muslims typically accept the repetition of just the first part of the Shahada as affirmation of its entirety. This implies acknowledging that Muhammad is the final "prophet" superseding all of the preceding "prophets" including Jesus.[39]

In light of the theology of the Qur'an already addressed in this book, Simnowitz is correct in his concern that introducing qur'anic phrasing and theology into biblical translations will result in an undermining of the integrity of the biblical message about God.

While laudable in the desire to gain traction among Muslim readers, MITs present a dangerous trajectory in biblical translation. Not only is there theological reason to protest these MITs, but there is also the practical recognition that producing such obviously new translations of holy books will be perceived by Muslims as confirmation of the qur'anic accusation that Christians are willing to tamper with their texts. This is exactly the conclusion of former Muslim Muhammad Sanavi, who writes,

> If we change or remove titles "Son of God" or "Father" from the text because they are barriers to Muslim readers, we create evidence that the Bible truly has been changed and is now corrupted. For 1,400 years Muslims have known that these phrases are included in the Scriptures, and suddenly in the 21st century they are presented with

---

39   Simnowitz, "Appendix," 510–11.

a "Muslim-friendly" Bible which does not refer to God the
Father or Jesus as the Son of God. Doing this turns the true
Jesus and those who follow him into a laughing stock.[40]

Whatever initial traction might be gained by utilizing more familiar
names and attempting to avoid offensive terminology, the long-term
reward cannot be worth the risk to the integrity of the message. The
Qur'an is not compatible with the Bible, thus inserting its preferred
language cannot be perceived as an innocent translation decision.

ACADEMIC PROPOSALS

Finally, it is important to consider the ways that certain academic
communities are engaging in attempts to reconcile the teaching of
the Bible and the Qur'an. As a note to the reader, the following
section will delve "into the weeds" of contemporary qur'anic scholarship in ways that not every reader will appreciate—feel free to
skim this section if it is less suited to your concerns. Still, I believe
it is important for us to consider these arguments as they will likely
continue to be developed in the future and may eventually spill over
into popular discussions.

Even though these discussions are perhaps less concerned with
Christian evangelism and more interested in ways to engender mutual
appreciation of these sacred texts, it is nonetheless important for our
purposes here to consider the arguments emerging from the academy.
After all, if the Qur'an is compatible with the Bible, we may find it
beneficial to consider how to reinforce our biblical testimony with
the book already embraced by non-Christians.

One author in particular, Abdulla Galadari, has offered a reading
of the Qur'an that he claims can reconcile the Qur'an's teaching on
the doctrine of Christ with the high Christology of John's Gospel.[41]

---

40   Mahammad Sanavi, "The Insider Movement and Iranian Muslims," in *Muslim Con-
      versions to Christ,* eds. Ayman Ibrahim and Ant Greenham, 441–46 (New York: Peter
      Lang, 2018), 442.
41   Abdulla Galadari, *Qur'anic Hermeneutics* (New York: Bloomsbury, 2016), 107. Much
      of the following material is derived from a paper I delivered at the 2020 National

It is worth interacting with his work at length here as he is among the first to engage in what will likely be a growing trajectory of studies that use intertextual polysemy to attempt to reinterpret the Qur'an. His book, *Qur'anic Hermeneutics*, is the primary source of this method, though he has indicated his intention to continue publishing further volumes in the years to come. Before considering the specific proposals he makes, let us briefly unpack what Galadari means by intertextual polysemy, because it is foundational to his project.

METHOD: INTERTEXTUAL POLYSEMY

According to Galadari's proposal, the key to qur'anic hermeneutics is the linguistic category of polysemy, which he says, "exists when a word has multiple meanings related to each other."[42] Especially within Semitic languages—such as Arabic and Hebrew—individual words can often be traced back to common roots which can be used to understand not only the etymology of a given term but also the meaning inherent in a family of words.

As an example drawn from Galadari's proposal, he notes that the word for son (*ibn*) derives from the root *bny* which means "to build." With that in mind, Galadari proposes that the Qur'an may have been misunderstood for the last 1,400 years at the key point of its singular reference to Jesus as *ibn Allah*. According to Galadari's proposal, Qur'an 9:30 might be better understood as a reference to Jesus as "the building of God."[43] If one were to interpret this passage to be a reference to a "building" rather than a "son" it would not take much creativity to reconcile Qur'an 9:30 with Jesus's reference to his body as the temple in John 2:19. We will return to this discussion in a moment.

Not only might a given word exhibit polysemy within the scope of a single language, but Galadari argues that further investigation of Jewish and Christian writings will reveal that intertextual and interlin-

---

Conference of the Evangelical Theological Society as a part of a panel responding to Galadari's book.

42   Abdulla Galadari, *Qur'anic Hermeneutics* (New York: Bloomsbury Academic, 2018), 28.

43   Galadari, *Qur'anic Hermeneutics*, 87–89.

gual polysemy can unlock insight into how to reconcile the seemingly disparate theologies of the Qur'an and the Bible. This methodology is not without its detractors, however, as linguists such as James Barr have long warned against the "root fallacy." Galadari notes this possible criticism of his method, but he dismisses it by stating,

> Barr argues what he considers the root fallacy, which is an extensive reliance of understanding root meanings of the Hebrew language. Since I argue in favor of understanding its roots, polysemous nature, and morphologies, then I must disagree with Barr.[44]

Galadari proceeds to highlight one of Barr's own arguments against the root fallacy using two words formed from a common root: bread (*lahm*) and war (*milhama*).

Where Barr doubts the impact of a shared root on the meaning of these two words, Galadari contends that both words derive from the concept of "joining" together, which is the meaning of the shared root. In order to demonstrate the shared features of the two words, he states, "Bread is the joining of flour together. . . . A battle is when two or more forces collide with each other and therefore joined [sic] together."[45] Despite the etymological possibility of seeing "joining" as the common idea carried through a common root, in order for Galadari's proposal to work, he would need to demonstrate that both words can carry that shared meaning into the context of the sentence and can therefore be interchanged. This is an important aspect of what he proposes in his first argument, where he sees the word for Son as a word that could also mean temple.

JESUS AS THE TEMPLE OF GOD

As briefly noted above, Galadari argues that the Qur'an does not have to be understood according to the historical interpretations that see

---

44   Galadari, *Qur'anic Hermeneutics*, 43.
45   Galadari, *Qur'anic Hermeneutics*, 43.

it clearly rejecting the biblical teaching that Jesus is the Son of God. This argument hinges on his method of polysemy, but it includes some important textual recognitions as well.

First, he notes rightly that the Qur'an uses two different words to convey the idea of "son." The most common word—*ibn*—is only used on one occasion to refer to Jesus. By contrast, the many qur'anic rejections of the idea that God might take a son utilize the word "*walad*" which is more directly connected to the physical process of siring a son. For instance, Qur'an 6:101 says, "Originator of the heavens and the earth—how can He have a son [*walad*] when He has no consort, (and) when He created everything and has knowledge of Everything." In general, then, the Qur'an denies in no uncertain terms that God would ever sire a son.

More specifically, Qur'an 19:34–35 makes a similar comment in conjunction with Jesus, saying, "That was Jesus, son [*ibn*] of Mary—a statement of the truth about which they are in doubt. It is not for God to take any son [*walad*]. Glory to Him! When He decrees something, He simply says to it, 'Be!' and it is." This passage rejects the idea that Jesus is the *walad* of God and, by way of contrast, it refers to Jesus by its preferred title for him: son [*ibn*] of Mary. The Qur'an, then, exhibits a willingness to use both words and appears to intentionally prefer *walad* for its rejection of the idea that God might have a son—likely as a way of emphasizing the preposterous idea that God would consort with Mary and their congress would produce offspring.[46]

Second, then, Galadari rightly notes that the only verse in which the Qur'an uses the phrase *ibn Allah* is found in Qur'an 9:30 where it occurs twice. Curiously, Qur'an 9:30 accuses the Jews of claiming a figure named 'Uzair is *ibn Allah* while also putting the claim that the Messiah is the *ibn Allah* on the lips of the Christians. Given the fact that this is the one place that the Qur'an uses *ibn Allah* and that the Jews use this phrase alongside of Christians, Galadari sees this verse

---

46   See Qur'an 5:116–120 for the Qur'an's clear rejection of the idea that Jesus and Mary should be understood as gods alongside of Allah.

providing a fruitful opportunity to apply his method and identify intertextual polysemy. The result is the claim made above: the Qur'an might intend the reader to see the Jews identifying Ezra (the traditional referent for 'Uzair) as the Temple of God and Jesus likewise. This interpretation would affirm that the Qur'an denies the false idea that Jesus is the son of God by virtue of birth while not anywhere rejecting his ontological and eternal status as the Son who is the second person of the Trinity. However, the context of Qur'an 9:30–31 seems to fight against Galadari's proposal in that the parallel to the phrase *ibn Allah* is to refer to Jesus as *ibn Miriam*. Consider the passage as it stands:

> The Jews say, "Ezra ['Uzair] is the son of God," and the Christians say, "The Messiah is the son of God." That is their saying with their mouths. They imitate the saying of those who disbelieved before (them). (May) God fight them. How are they (so) deluded? They have taken their teachers and their monks as Lords instead of God, and (also) the Messiah, son of Mary, when they were only commanded to serve one God. (There is) no god but Him. Glory to Him above what they associate!

A plain reading of the context seems to indicate that the Qur'an is keen to show the foolishness of Christians who call Jesus the *ibn Allah* in light of the fact that he is merely *ibn Mariam*. Furthermore, while there is perhaps some ambiguity with the conjunction "and," to say that it might be taken to link "God and the Messiah" cuts against the grain of the rest of the passage that chastises Jews and Christians for associating partners with God alone.

Still, even if one were to conclude that it is possible to interpret the Qur'an is such a way as to avoid rejecting Jesus as the true, biblical Son of God, the passages in question do not actively affirm him as such. This brings us to Galadari's second argument: the relationship between John's use of *monogenes* and the Qur'an's phrase "Be! And it is."

JESUS AS THE ETERNAL *MONOGENES*

Galadari's discussion about Qur'an 9:30 is largely aimed at avoiding the interpretation of the Qur'an that would disallow Jesus from being seen as the incarnate Son of God. Beyond this, however, he makes the argument that the Qur'an still be understood to teach that there is an eternal *logos* who is responsible for creation in the same way as John begins his Gospel: "In the beginning was the Word (*logos*) and the Word was with God, and the Word was God."

Galadari's argument requires familiarity with both the Arabic language and the scholarly discussion about the Greek concept of *monogenes* (only begotten) referred to in John 1:14 and other places.[47] Still, his proposal can be summarized as follows. The early creeds of Christianity—notably the Chalcedonian Creed—clarify that the Son is eternally begotten or generated of the Father, not created. Galadari argues that, by utilizing language derived from the idea of "becoming/being" (*takwin*) and rejecting the language of "being born" (*tawlid*), the Qur'an might be engaging with this distinction.[48] He argues that the qur'anic phrase "*kun fa-yakun*" (Be! And it is.) could be an attempt by the Qur'an to view the creative Word—"Be!"—as a corollary to John's *logos*. Thus, Galadari proposes that God's generative word "Be!" could be seen taking on flesh to "become" Jesus the Messiah in verses such as Qur'an 3:59: "Surely the likeness of Jesus is, with God, as the likeness of Adam. He created him from dust, (and) then He said to him, 'Be!' and he was [*kun fa-yakun*]."

The problem with this interpretation, however, is that this creative phrase does not describe a feature of Jesus that is unique to him—something that would be requisite according to John 1:1–2 which

---

47   Cf. John 1:18 and 3:16.

48   Galadari, *Qur'anic Hermeneutics*, 106, writes, "According to the Qur'an, Jesus Christ is not '*walad*' (begotten) of God. On the contrary, God says to Jesus, '*kun fa yakun*' (be and he becomes). If God says to Jesus 'be' (*kn*) and so he becomes (*fa-yakun*), then Jesus is indeed become of God. As such, the Qur'an does not truly deny that Jesus is become of God, but distinguishes begotten from '*tawlid*' and become from '*takwin*' . . . I argue that the Qur'an intends to interpret and identify the Logos with the term "to be" (*kn*), and it is for that reason the Qur'an emphasizes '*takwin*' while denying '*tawlid*.'"

affirms that the *logos* was with God and was God from eternity past. And while Christ's human nature was certainly the same as Adam's, the Qur'an nowhere indicates a distinction that would recognize his divine nature and distinguish the hypostatic union from Adam's mere humanity. Likewise, while the *logos* is involved in creating all things in John 1:3, John 1:14 clearly sets the "creation" of the incarnate *logos* as a distinct act from that which the *logos* created. Furthermore, when one reads the twice-recorded verse found in Qur'an 2:136 and 3:84 we find further evidence that the Jesus of the Qur'an is indistinguishable in nature and purpose from the rest of the prophets:

> Say: "We believe in God, and in that which has been be-stowed from on high upon us, and that which has been bestowed upon Abraham and Ishmael and Isaac and Jacob and their descendants, and that which has been vouchsafed to Moses and Jesus, and that which has been vouchsafed to all the [other] prophets by their Sustainer: we make no distinction between any of them. And it is unto Him that we surrender ourselves."

In other words, the Qur'an compares Adam's nature and Jesus's with no added indication that Jesus is the incarnate *Logos* whatsoever. Likewise, Jesus is viewed in exactly the same manner as all other prophets.

Thus, even if the Qur'an could be made to say that the "Be!" of the phrase "Be! And it is" is the eternal *logos*, it never asserts that the word "Be!" has been with God and is God since the beginning. Again, we find ourselves discussing whether or not the Qur'an denies things required for biblical christology rather than seeing the Qur'an affirm such things. And this recognition delivers us to a final point that bears parallels with the prior discussion about Insider Movement approaches to the Qur'an. Even if a person read the Qur'an to actively affirm the biblical portrait of Christ's ontology—affirming the hypostatic union of the divine Son's incarnation as the last Adam—the qur'anic Jesus cannot be viewed as a savior in any way whatsoever.

JESUS AND SALVATION

Within the academy there will always be a market for creative ways of making new discoveries and offering fresh perspectives on old texts. Galadari's proposal is certainly an impressive one in that it invites a whole new way of reading and interpreting the Qur'an on the basis of a word's semantic range and what it might be made to say. His linguistic savvy and creativity in making connections between possibilities betrays his intelligence. Drawing on his knowledge of the Qur'an and a host of biblical and extrabiblical materials across the spectrum of Semitic languages, Galadari's work will likely lead many within the academy to express an increased interest in the employ of his methodology in the coming years.

For Christians the discussion about what the Qur'an might be made to say or not say about Jesus is sure to be of interest to Christians who are hopeful to see Muslims understand the biblical Jesus. If the Qur'an can be understood in such a way that it does not deny the hypostatic union or the incarnation of the eternal Son, it would seem to go a long way toward mitigating some of the longstanding points of conflict between Muslims and Christians.

However, as noted above, even if one's reading of the Qur'an avoids denying Jesus's biblical ontology, it does not anywhere connect its "christology" to soteriology. For Christians, however, the connection between christology and soteriology is of vital importance both biblically and theologically. For example, one might consider how the Gospel of John—beginning with the high christology of the incarnate *logos*—overtly connects the articulation of who Jesus is with what Jesus accomplishes in John 20:30–31: "Now Jesus did many other signs in the presence of the disciples, which are not writing in this book; but these are written so that you may believe that Jesus is the Christ, the Son of God, and that by believing you may have life in his name."

Likewise, for the early church, discussions about the two natures of Jesus and how to articulate the hypostatic union were intimately and immediately centered around discussions of how this God-man could achieve salvation from sin for Adam's race. Consider the way that Cyril of Alexandria discussed the relationship between Christ's humanity and divinity and its connection with salvation:

> When they say that the Word of God did not become flesh, or rather did not undergo birth from a woman according to the flesh, they bankrupt the economy of salvation, for if he who was rich did not impoverish himself, abasing himself to our condition out of tender love, then we have not gained his riches but are still in our poverty, enslaved by sin and death, because the Word becoming flesh is the undoing and the abolition of all that fell upon human nature as our curse and punishment. If they so pull up the root of our salvation and dislodge the cornerstone of our hope, how will anything else be left standing? As I have said, if the Word has not become flesh then neither has the dominion of death been overthrown, and in no way has sin been abolished, and we are still held captive in the transgressions of the first man, Adam, deprived of any return to a better condition; a return which I would say has been gained by Christ the Savior of us all.[49]

Cyril's understanding is representative of the early councils: Christological precision matters immensely because it is the gateway to soteriology. If Jesus is either not fully divine or if he is not fully human, the result is a bankrupted economy of salvation.

For the Qur'an, Jesus's role is no different than any of the other messengers. He delivers the same call to Islam as did the prophets before

---

49   Cyril of Alexandria, *On the Unity of Christ,* trans. John McGuckin (Crestwood, NY: St. Vladimir's Seminary Press, 1995), 59–60. Cyril also writes of Romans 6:5, "As it is said, 'If we have been conjoined with him in the likeness of his death, so also shall we be in the likeness of his resurrection' (Rom 6:5). It follows therefore, that He Who Is, The One Who Exists, is necessarily born of the flesh, taking all that is ours into himself so that all that is born of the flesh, that is us corruptible and perishing beings, might rest in him. In short, he took what was ours to be his very own so that we might have all that was his." This quote is an extrapolation of the Niceno-Constantinopolitan Creed which connects the nature of the incarnate Son with salvation: "For us men and for our salvation, he came down from heaven, and by the Holy Spirit was incarnate of the Virgin Mary, and became man."

him. Neither is his message fundamentally different than that of Ahmed who will come after him. Even if the Qur'an need not be understood to deny Jesus's death, it certainly does not make his crucifixion and resurrection the central focus of redemptive history in the way that the Bible does. All that to say, then, projects like Galadari's are interesting exercises in linguistics and comparative literature. Yet, if the intent of such readings is to present the Qur'an and Bible as complimentary texts, I believe it is an interpretive road that leads to a theological dead end.

CONCLUSION

While the previous chapter encouraged Christians to read the Qur'an for themselves, this chapter has sought to caution Christians who might be inclined to use Qur'an in dialogue with Muslim friends and neighbors. The three proposals that we considered—the CAMEL method, Insider Movements, and Intertextual Polysemic exegesis—all exhibit a generally positive posture toward the Qur'an as a source of truth. While none of the proposals explicitly teach that the Qur'an contains sufficient data to provide a reader with an understanding of the Gospel, they all include an optimistic view of the Qur'an as a natural tie-in to the biblical testimony.

As the previous chapters have demonstrated, however, the Qur'an's history, internal claims, and traditional interpretations fight against such a positive view of its message. As it has been received throughout the last 1,400 years, most Muslims view the Qur'an as a corrective of the biblical material rather than a supplement to it. Thus, even if a Christian is inclined to propose some of the novel interpretations offered above, it is unlikely that their exegesis will convince a Muslim to overturn centuries of confessional interpretation.

Many of the proposals offered above are likely to be received in the same way as the attempts of Muslim polemicists who argue that John 14:16 should be understood as a reference to Muhammad rather than the Holy Spirit.[50] Since there is no manuscript evidence for a

---

50   See the unsubstantiated and unattested argument that perhaps the original form of *paracletos* (helper) was supposed to read *periclytos* (highly exalted/praised one) as a

textual reason to propose this reading and since there is no historical evidence that this passage had been interpreted in this fashion it is understandable why such an attempted interpretation from Islamic apologists has not gained traction. Likewise, when Christians engage in unattested reinterpretation of another's sacred text, the hoped-for momentum is unlikely to occur.

Still, beyond pragmatic reasons for criticizing the positive proposals for using the Qur'an, there are more troubling issues on a theological level. For instance, if a person goes to the Qur'an in order to prove who Jesus is from its pages, the implicit argument is that the Qur'an is an authority on the person of Jesus. As such, one risks endorsing the Qur'an as a source of revelation, particularly when considering the actions and teachings of Jesus that are not attested in the Bible. If one communicates that the Qur'an is revealing something about Jesus that is true but not attested in the biblical account, the danger is that you have opened the canon of Scripture, suggested that for a Muslim, the Qur'an provides necessary information about Jesus to lead them to a full understanding, and confused the lines of what is Special Revelation and what is not.

With the weight of 1,400 years of anti-Gospel interpretation of the Qur'an, its overt statements that contradict the biblical account, and its silence on the aspects of the Gospel that are biblically essential, a Christian should take a more cautionary approach to how they interact with the Qur'an than the three offerings suggested above. That is not to say that there is no room for a Christian to engage with the Qur'an and its message in the process of attempting to communicate the biblical message. The following chapter will consider how the story of Abraham and his near-sacrifice of his son might be leveraged as a fruitful way of bridging to a Gospel-centered discussion that yet avoids endorsing the Qur'an as a source of revelation.

---

reference to Muhammad, the highly praised one as articulated by Qais Ali, "Muhammad Was Predicted to Come in the Gospel of John," at Answering-Christianity.com, https://www.answering-christianity.com/prediction.htm. This proposal is also recorded in Ali, *The Qur'an*, 144n416.

9

THE GOSPEL AND THE PROBLEM OF THE QUR'AN

And We ransomed him with
a great sacrifice.
Qur'an 37:107

s we have walked through the Qur'an in the preceding pages, we have seen a number of ways that its message is incompatible with the biblical Gospel. While this sentiment might present itself on the surface as an uncontroversial truism, the previous chapter showed that there are some who have attempted to reconcile the two sacred texts. Likewise, as we noted in chapter 4, the Qur'an presents itself as a book that is compatible with the prior scriptures. Thus, it has been helpful to walk through some of the divergent ways that the Qur'an leads its readers away from the Gospel that Paul outlined in 1 Corinthians 15:3–5.

Still, the question that the previous chapter posed about using the Qur'an in conversation with Muslim friends and neighbors should not be taken as a reason to neglect addressing the Qur'an's message at all. In fact, while being wary of accidentally endorsing the Qur'an, there are still ways to engage with its content fruitfully. This final chapter will offer a way to approach the Qur'an that encourages understanding, capitalizes on the opportunity to compare similar content, and also avoids confusing the Qur'an as revelation.

In order to demonstrate this approach, the qur'anic account of Abraham's near sacrifice of his son will be scrutinized and considered for its role in the qur'anic metanarrative. Where the CAMEL method conflates the biblical account and the qur'anic account, however, the following proposal will argue that there is more explanatory traction gained by noting the way that the story functions in Christianity as well as how it features within Islam. That traction comes through a series of questions that revisits the overarching story told by each text in order to ask, "In which metanarrative does this story seem to fit best?"

Prior to getting into the specific details of this proposal, however, it is good to consider the underpinnings of this posture. To do so, we will draw on the helpful work of Daniel Strange as he articulates it in his book *Their Rock Is Not Like Our Rock*.[1] In this book, Strange attempts—from the perspective of a confessional Christian—to answer the basic question, "If there is one God and one way to worship him, why are there so many religions?" Furthermore, Strange proposes that Christians engaged in discussions with people from other religious traditions are in need of an approach to evangelism,

> that both defends and proclaims Christian exclusivity
> with what might be called a "bold humility," a stance that
> seeks first to understand the world of religion and religions
> through a biblical worldview before then applying unique
> and satisfying Gospel truth to a world of pseudo-Gospels
> that promise much but can never ultimately deliver.[2]

His proposal comes from a place of his own conviction of the exclusivity of Christ's Gospel and also a recognition of what this book has been arguing for: the necessity that a Christian understand

---

1   Daniel Strange, *Their Rock Is Not Like Our Rock* (Grand Rapids: Zondervan, 2014).
2   Strange, *Their Rock Is Not Like Our Rock*, 27–28.

his or her non-Christian neighbor and the elements influencing their faith. Prior to considering the Qur'an's account of Abraham's sacrifice, then, it behooves us to take a moment to investigate our convictions regarding what we should do when we discover apparently shared content in non-Christian sources. How do we understand dislocated bits of revelation when their echoes are discovered outside of the biblical context? Strange's contribution provides two key pieces of the approach we will take below. While Strange's book as a whole provides a helpful approach for Christians to develop a biblical theology of religions, the relevant aspects of Strange's contribution for our purposes will be his discussion of what he calls "remnantal revelation" and "subversive fulfillment." Both concepts derive from Strange's conviction that the Bible provides an accurate telling of human history while also offering the most satisfying answers for the questions and desires universally experienced by humanity.

REMNANTAL REVELATION

One of the common protests from skeptics who are looking at the biblical narratives—particularly those of the Old Testament—is that the myths and stories of many other faiths have echoes in the biblical material. The assumption, then, is that the Bible—rather than recording actual history—is drawing on a buffet of ancient mythology and incorporating various aspects of shared stories into its account of history. Many secular religious studies proposals, then, argue that the original form of religion was polytheistic and as the Bible emerged to offer a monotheistic proposal it incorporated existing stories from its polytheistic neighbors and predecessors.

However, having pointed to the landmark work of Wilhelm Schmidt, Strange demonstrates that there is good reason to see that the earliest identifiable human religion appears to be an original monotheism rather than the polytheism that is assumed by much secular scholarship. Strange summarizes Schmidt's findings, writing, "Schmidt's ethnological conclusion was of an original ethical monotheism in the most primitive human societies, which subsequently devolved, but most probably originated from an *Uroffenbarung* (a primeval revelation)."[3] By extension of this argument, then, the Bible teaches a faith that is more reflective of the earliest religion. Therefore, citing Schmidt, Strange contends that it is more likely that the polytheistic use of such narratives provides an example of borrowing and adapting biblical accounts rather than the opposite.

Adding to this extrabiblical corroboration, it is clear from the biblical material that the major world events that are often the subject of non-Christian mythology—such as a worldwide flood, an originally pristine environment, and a common ancestry—occur within the first eleven chapters of Genesis. During this time period there are two occasions where every existing person had immediate interaction with God and a knowledge of his activities: Adam and Eve walked and talked with God in the garden, and Noah and his family heard from God and interacted with him during the judgment and covenant following the flood. In light of this universal exposure to God, Strange contends,

> What is being posited here is a "single source" theory of revelation and knowledge, when the whole of humanity was in proximity of redemptive-historical events, and which therefore defies a simplistic categorization as either natural "general" revelation or supernatural "special revelation."[4]

Therefore, if the sum total of humanity had such immediate interactions with God, it is conceivable that the stories they passed along were carried on a collective memory even after Babel's dispersion of humanity across the face of the earth.

The strength of Strange's proposal is that he recognizes—in fact, he even encourages his readers to expect to find—that there are often points of conceptual overlap with non-Christian religions. In fact,

---

3   See Strange, *Their Rock Is Not Like Our Rock,* 114–15. For a helpful summary of Wilhelm Schmidt's extensive work, see Winfried Corduan, *In the Beginning God: A Fresh Look at the Case for Original Monotheism* (Nashville: B&H, 2013).

4   Strange, *Their Rock Is Not Like Our Rock,* 104.

Strange goes so far as to propose a third category of revelation that stands between general and special revelation to accommodate this realization that bits of redemptive history might be carried on the traditions and memories of non-Christian peoples, writing,

> I wish to label this revelation as "remnantal." While such revelatory material is always sinfully corrupted, distorted, and degenerates to the point of being salvifically useless, it has to be factored into the phenomena of religion in general and therefore of the "religions" in particular.[5]

In other words, Strange uses the phrase "remnantal revelation" to identify those true-but-dislocated accounts of events in redemptive history that are told by non-Christian communities to emphasize that they are more than mere general revelation, though cannot themselves lead to salvation.

Following Strange, then, the "common ground" we have seen throughout this book that is shared between the Bible and the Qur'an might be understood as what Strange identifies as remnantal revelation. As such, we should be encouraged to see the multiple points of contact that are presented to us to use as we seek to communicate the biblical Gospel to our Muslim friends. Likewise, lest we find ourselves overconfident that the overlap indicates similarity, Strange reminds us that these dislocated points of remnantal revelation—removed as they are from the redemptive-historical metanarrative—lead to salvation. This brings us to Strange's second contribution to our discussion.

SUBVERSIVE FULFILLMENT

Upon considering the proposal for remnantal revelation discussed above, some readers might wonder what value there is in distinguishing between general revelation and remnantal revelation. Since neither forms have the capacity to deliver the message of salvation, and since instances of such remnantal revelation may include stories

---

5   Strange, *Their Rock Is Not Like Our Rock*, 104.

and teachings that only bear passing resemblance to their biblical counterparts, it may not be wise to dogmatically insist upon the development of a separate third layer within the traditional systematic discussion on the topic. Still, even if one prefers to reject the formal category of remnantal revelation, the differentiation of this type of data from that which can merely be drawn from observing the created world is yet helpful for a Christian attempting to communicate and share the Gospel with their non-Christian friends. That is because of the proposal that Strange makes later in his book which he refers to as subversive fulfillment.

Subversive fulfillment is not a phrase unique to Strange, but one that he reclaims from within the work of Hendrik Kraemer.[6] Perhaps the best definition of what Strange means by this phrase comes from his quotation of Herman Bavinck:

> All the elements and forms that are essential to religion . . .
> though corrupted, nevertheless do appear in pagan religions.
> Here and there even unconscious predictions and striking
> expectations of a better and purer religion are voiced. Hence
> Christianity is not only positioned antithetically toward
> paganism; it is also paganism's fulfilment. Christianity is the
> true religion, therefore also the highest and purest; it is the
> truth of all religions. What in paganism is the caricature, the
> living original is here. What is appearance there is essence
> here. *What is sought there can be found here.*[7]

This last phrase—*what is sought there is found here*—is perhaps the clearest statement of how such points of remnantal revelation can be

---

6   Hendrik Kraemer, "Continuity or Discontinuity," in *The Authority of Faith: International Missionary Council Meeting at Tambaram, Madras,* ed. G. Paton, 1–21 (London: Oxford University Press, 1939), 5, as cited by Strange, *Their Rock Is Not Like Our Rock,* 267. Strange notes that the phrase has since been used by missiologists such as Lesslie Newbigin and others.

7   Herman Bavinck, *Reformed Dogmatics,* trans. John Vriend (Grand Rapids: Baker, 2004), 1:319–320, as cited in Strange, *Their Rock Is Not Like Our Rock,* 267 (italics added).

leveraged in the process of appealing to a non-Christian on behalf of the Gospel.

The points of overlap between biblical and non-Christian worldviews are often connected to underlying desires and practices that can be traced back to an inherent desire to worship. Biblically speaking, the question for humanity from the garden onward has always been, "What will you worship?" Worship that is directed to anything other than the triune God offered by faith in Christ is simply what the Bible calls idolatry. Non-Christian religions, then, can be understood in their essence to be idolatrous forms of worship. The underlying impulse to worship, however, is one that is good, common, and original to humanity.

As Strange himself writes, "Biblically speaking, the cracked cisterns of idolatry that bring only disillusionment, despair, and unfulfilled desires are wonderfully filled and surpassed in the fount of living water, Jesus Christ the Lord."[8] Therefore, when we discover similarities or remnantal revelation in a non-Christian faith we might be able to affirm the underlying goodness of the desires that brought the particular forms into being. However, by offering to demonstrate how such desires find their satisfaction only when the remnants are relocated into their revelatory setting within the biblical canon, we show how the biblical story subverts all other competing worldviews and metanarratives. Putting these two concepts into practice as we consider the question of how a Christian might share the Gospel with their Muslim neighbor through a personal knowledge of the Qur'an will help to move the discussion thus far from theory into practice.

THE AKEDAH STORY IN THE QUR'AN: WHAT IS SOUGHT THERE

Chapter 8 looked briefly at the story of Abraham's near sacrifice of his son as it appears in the Qur'an. This story is often referred to as "the Akedah" story (from the Hebrew word for "binding") and it appears in both Genesis 22 and Qur'an 37. The story is recounted

---

8   Strange, *Their Rock Is Not Like Our Rock*, 271.

by Jews, Christians, and Muslims as one that plays a formative role in the exercise of each respective faith.

For Jews, this story represents God's clear affirmation of his election and protection of Isaac and Abraham's admirable and exemplary faith. For Christians, Romans 4:9–12 points to Abraham's faith prior to circumcision and the law as a recognition that righteousness has always come by faith. And for Muslims, Abraham serves as an exemplary proto-Muslim who precedes both Jews and Christians. In addition, Muslims also imitate this story as a key aspect of their annual 'Id al-Adha sacrifice, as noted in the previous chapter. With all three faiths laying claim to this narrative as being formative in their self-understanding and contemporary practice, it provides an excellent point of conversation for Christians and Muslims who are attempting to understand one another. Furthermore, in contrast with many other shared narratives, this account bears quite similar features to the biblical story as it appears in the Qur'an.

Since the Qur'anic narrative is relatively concise, it is worth including the full text here for reference. The story occurs in Qur'an 37:99–111:

He said, "Surely I am going to my Lord. He will guide me. My Lord, grant me one of the righteous." So We gave him the good news of a forbearing boy. When he had reached the (age of) running with him, he said, "My son! Surely I saw in a dream that I am going to sacrifice you. So look, what do you think?" He said, "My father! Do what you are commanded. You will find my, if God pleases, one of the patient." When they both had submitted, and he had laid him face down, We called out to him, "Abraham! Now you have confirmed the vision." Surely in this way We repay the doers of good. Surely this—it indeed was the clear test. And we ransomed him with great sacrifice, and left (this blessing) on him and among the later (generations): "Peace (be) upon Abraham!" In this way We repay the doers of good. Surely he was one of Our believing servants.

Though Genesis 22 includes more detail and does not highlight the submission of Abraham's son in the same way as the Qur'an does, the similarities between the two stories stand out.[9]

Among the many parallels with the biblical story, we see that the Qur'an presents Abraham as one who is reliant upon God for the provision of an offspring. It also recounts the vision or dream by which Abraham receives his instructions to sacrifice his son. Likewise, as in the biblical account, God stops Abraham from going through with the slaughter of his son, having been satisfied that Abraham has demonstrated his faithful obedience. Most importantly, God's intervention is followed by what the Qur'an describes as a great, ransoming sacrifice. It is this last aspect of the narrative that allows the Christian to engage in recognizing remnantal revelation and employ it as subversive fulfillment.

AND WE RANSOMED HIM

Before considering how this verse can be used, it is worth unpacking the underlying Arabic in order to understand exactly what is being said in Qur'an 37:107. First of all, the verse consists of a verb, a noun, and an adjective. The verb, utilizing the plural of majesty, includes an attached singular pronoun which refers to Abraham's son.[10] God is the subject of this powerful verb meaning "to ransom" and Abraham's son is the object that is rescued via this ransom. This verb occurs nine times throughout the Qur'an.[11] On six occasions it refers to those who would offer their material wealth or even their children on judgment day in order to pay for their misdeeds.[12] On

---

9   While the current Islamic consensus contends that Ishmael was the son who was commended here, early Islamic commentators were divided over the issue of whether to follow the biblical details which identify Isaac as the son or to identify the unnamed son of the Qur'an's account with Ishmael. See the note on Qur'an 37:101 by Gordon Nickel, *The Qur'an with Christian Commentary* (Grand Rapids: Zondervan, 2020), 450n37.101.

10   Arabic: *fadaynahu.*

11   See Matthew Bennett, *Narratives in Conflict: Atonement in Hebrews and the Qur'an* (Eugene, OR: Pickwick, 2019), 237–39.

12   Qur'an 3:91; 5:36; 10:54; 13:18; 39:47; and 70:11. The first five occurrences explicitly state that God will not accept such a ransom payment. The sixth reference in

two occasions the verb is used to refer to people who would offer money to purchase their freedom, with Qur'an 2:85 referring to the buying back of the enslaved and Qur'an 2:229 indicating that a wife may expedite a divorce by paying a ransom. The ninth occurrence is found here in Qur'an 37:107.

Consulting the four occasions that the word ransom occurs nominally confirms that the underlying concept of ransom as it appears in the Qur'an is connected to a payment offered in an effort to provide liberation.[13] Therefore it is striking when one considers Qur'an 37:107 that God is involved in ransoming Abraham's son. In fact, this is the only positive and affirmative occurrence of ransom language with God as its subject that is found in the Qur'an. We will revisit this after having considered how the Qur'an contends that God ransomed Abraham's son "by a great sacrifice."

BY A GREAT SACRIFICE

As the verse continues, it uses a preposition of instrument (with/by) to show how it is that God's ransoming of Abraham's son was accomplished. Following the preposition, we see that the mechanism of ransom was a sacrifice, and that this sacrifice is further described as being "great." The details here are key to our recognition that this story does not belong to the Qur'an. A series of questions asked of the Qur'an at large can draw attention to this misfit narrative.

First, as we have seen, the Qur'an does not connect sacrifice to ransom in the same way as the Bible does. Instead, sacrifice—connected to Abraham's exemplary submission—is merely one of many meritorious displays of piety within Islamic life. The context of this passage makes the meritorious nature of this test clear, the question that gets at this problem is, "Why did Abraham's son need to be ransomed?"

Second, the idea that God would be offering the ransom implies that God was not simply satisfied by Abraham's faithful submission. It

---

Qur'an 70:11 implies the same, though it does not explicitly state that God will refuse to accept the ransom.

13   Bennett, *Narratives in Conflict*, 240–41. Arabic: *fidya* occurs in Qur'an 2:184, 196; 47:4; and 57:15.

also implies that Abraham's son was in captivity and required a ransom in order to achieve his liberation. As it is stated in Qur'an 37:107, we see God as the one who is paying the ransom for Abraham's son. The question presents itself, "Why did *God* offer a ransom for Abraham's son?"

And third, the question of why any sacrifice was conducted at all looms large in light of broader qur'anic logic. That the vision was completed when Abraham and his son demonstrated their willingness to submit themselves to it is clearly stated in verse 104, "Now you have confirmed the vision" and in verse 106, "Surely this—this was a clear test." If the vision was a clear test, and if Abraham and his son successfully passed this test, what reason remains for a further sacrifice? The Qur'an recognizes that instructions about sacrifices are given as signs from God, but they are simply acts of *taqwa* (piety) received just like any other good works. This explanation of sacrifice is stated clearly in Qur'an 22:36–37, which states,

> The (sacrificial) animals—We have appointed them for you among the symbols of God: there is good for you in them. So mention the name of God over them, (as they stand) in lines. Then when their sides fall (to the ground), eat from them, and feed the needy and the beggar. In this way We have subjected them to you, so that you may be thankful. Its flesh will not reach God, nor its blood, but the guarding (of yourselves) [*at-taqwa*] will reach Him from you. In this way He has subjected them to you, so that you may magnify God because He has guided you. Give good news to the doers of good.

Tradition reports that this verse was revealed in light of a pagan practice of anointing the Ka'ba with sacrificial blood and Seyyed Hossein Nasr comments that this verse was given to illuminate the inner reality of the sacrifice as being an act of piety.[14]

In many ways Qur'an 22:36–37 might be paralleled with David's recognition in Psalm 51:16–17 that God's ultimate desire is

---

14   Seyyed Hossein Nasr, ed., *The Study Qur'an* (New York: HarperOne, 2015), 838n37.

not sacrifice, but a broken and contrite heart. However, since the Qur'an rejects Jesus's sacrificial and substitutionary death, it is left without the culmination of Christ's sacrifice as the *telos*—the goal or aim—of the sacrificial system. Thus, while David—and also the author of Hebrews—is correct that the blood of bulls and goats cannot remove sin, the logic of the biblical sacrifices is such that they serve as a foreshadowing of the once-and-for-all sacrifice of Christ. Christ's sacrifice provides the object of David's faith even before he knows the fulness of God's plans, but it is this very sacrifice that is denied by the Qur'an as we have seen in previous chapters.

Instead of connecting the concept of sacrifice to atonement, the Qur'an instructs Muslims to engage in sacrifice as an affirmation of God's dispensation of divine religion. In the same section cited above, Qur'an 22:34 and 67 both affirm that sacrifices or ritual practices are given as an authenticating sign to every community to whom God provides guidance. Thus, as Muslims perform their annual 'Id al-Adha sacrifice, they are reminded that God has established and perfected Islam as their religion (Qur'an 5:3). Abraham's sacrifice, for Muslims, is a sign that God's final religion is also the primal religion which comes before Judaism and Christianity ever existed.

To summarize, then, the Qur'an expects the idea of sacrifice to serve as a sign that God has provided guidance for a new community. Though the Qur'an's version of the Akedah provides the specific sacrifice that the Islamic community will use to identify and confirm itself, the passage itself leaves the questions above unanswered. Since sacrifice is not connected to atonement, the language that Qur'an 37:107 uses to describe this sacrifice as a ransom paid by God is unfitting to this circumstance according to the Qur'an's logic. These questions can provide a bridge to investigating the biblical version of the story and presenting how the Bible provides the answers that the Qur'an lacks.

THE BIBLE: WHAT IS SOUGHT THERE IS FOUND HERE

As seen above, the Qur'an attempts to use the story of Abraham's sacrifice to affirm the God-given Islamic identity. Still, in light of our discussion of Qur'an 37:107, this story does not appear to belong to the Qur'an. It is doubtless a story that is derived from biblical revelation. In fact, it serves as an instance of Strange's remnantal revelation. The dissonance between this account and the broader qur'anic context, however, also makes it an excellent candidate for Strange's subversive fulfillment. Showing that this story fits better within the biblical metanarrative allows the Christian to challenge the qur'anic use of this story while also providing a more compelling satisfaction for those who would see their identity established not in their own pious actions, but in God's adopting atonement completed in Christ, the source of God's ultimate provision. The following section will briefly provide an outline of one way that a Christian might move from the Qur'an to the Bible without endorsing the Qur'an in the ways that the CAMEL method does.

A BRIDGE: THIS STORY DOESN'T BELONG TO THE QUR'AN

Recognizing that a Muslim may or may not be familiar with this story as it appears in the Qur'an, it can be helpful to read the passage in the Qur'an prior to discussing it in detail. Having read these verses, the three questions posed in the section above can provide helpful traction with a Muslim friend in utilizing a shared passage. First, *Why did Abraham's son need to be ransomed?* Second, *Why did God ransom Abraham's son?* And third, *If Abraham and his son already passed the test, what reason remains for a further sacrifice?* By demonstrating that this account has parallels in the Bible, one is readily able to move from the Qur'an to the Genesis 22 account and its position in the overarching story of the Bible. Following the questions about why God would ask Abraham to sacrifice an animal after God has already commended Abraham's submission, transitioning into the Bible can be accomplished by asking, "This story doesn't quite seem to fit within the Qur'an in the same way as it fits within the Bible. Can I show you how it belongs within the Bible as a part of its bigger story?" Upon consulting Genesis 22, several details will present themselves to your Muslim neighbor that are not featured within the Qur'an.

THE PROVISION OF THE LORD

First, one feature of the biblical story that does not appear in the Qur'an is Abraham's naming of the mountain in Genesis 22:14: "So Abraham called the name of that place, 'The LORD will provide'; as it is said to this day, 'On the mount of the LORD it shall be provided.'" While this may seem like a small detail, the question that can be helpful in transitioning to a broader biblical treatment is, "What was provided for Abraham here and why do people many generations later say that the LORD will provide on his mountain?"

While the Qur'an tells a story in which it appears that God has provided a ransom for Abraham's son through a substitutionary sacrifice, we have seen that the qur'anic logic surrounding sacrifice does not require such a provision. Sacrifice is given to demarcate peoples who have been given revelation, yet this story includes no additional provision of revelation. Indeed, the Qur'an identifies this event as a mere test of the faith of Abraham and his son. Therefore, the question remains, "What provision does Genesis speak of?" The answer is Christological and soteriological.

IN YOUR OFFSPRING SHALL ALL NATIONS OF THE EARTH BE BLESSED

Second, according to the Qur'an, God's blessing is available to all people who do good works like Abraham, as indicated by Qur'an 37:109–10, "Peace (be) upon Abraham! In this way We repay the doers of good." In contrast, the Bible specifies that Abraham's offspring will be the source of blessing to all the nations of the earth. The reader sees this promise in Genesis 22:18 which says, "and in your offspring shall all the nations of the earth be blessed, because you have obeyed my voice."

While the Hebrew word for "offspring" (zera) here is ambiguous as to whether or not it should be understood as a collective singular referring to all of Israel or a true singular pointing to the Messianic figure, the translators of the Septuagint used the unambiguous singular form of the Greek word (spermati) to indicate a single referent. All the more so, the apostle Paul capitalizes on this very promise to show that Abraham's saving faith is focused on God and his coming offspring—the Messiah/Christ—in Galatians 3:16: "Now the promises were made to Abraham and his offspring. It does not say, 'And to offsprings,' referring to many, but referring to one, 'And to your offspring,' which is Christ."[15]

A BURNT OFFERING INSTEAD OF HIS SON

Finally, the third key addition to the narrative that is found in Genesis 22 is the clarity surrounding the sacrifice as a substitution for Isaac. The Qur'an provides no explanation for the ransom that God offers through the great sacrifice or where it comes from. In fact, consulting various early Islamic commentaries, one finds a great deal of diversity of opinion as to what makes this sacrifice great. Some commentators suggest that the object of the sacrifice was great because it was a reincarnated form of the pleasing sacrifice offered by Abel in Genesis 4.[16] Others argue that the sacrifice is great simply by virtue of the future time when it would be rehearsed annually as a part of the Islamic 'Id al-Adha ritual.[17]

Regardless of the specific Islamic interpretation of the Qur'anic paucity of detail, the Bible specifies that the animal is a ram, that the sacrifice is a burnt offering, and that the ram is sacrificed instead of Isaac. The specificity regarding what kind of sacrifice is in view here both distinguishes the biblical sacrifice from Islamic practice and

---

15 A brief treatment of this discussion can be seen in the article by Sam Shamoun, "A Series of Answers to Common Questions," at Answering-Islam.org, https://www.answering-islam.org/Shamoun/q_abrahams_seed.htm.

16 See commentary on Qur'an 37:107 by Al-Jalalayn, *Tafsir al-Jalalayn*, trans. Feras Hamza (Amman, JO: Royal Institute for Islamic Thought, 2020), https://www.al-tafsir.com/Tafasir.asp?tMadhNo=0&tTafsirNo=74&tSoraNo=37&tAyahNo=107&tDisplay=yes&UserProfile=0&LanguageId=2. According to tradition, Ibn Abbas is also said to have claimed that the sacrificial animal was a ram kept in Paradise for forty years, indicating that he may have received a similar tradition regarding Abel's sacrifice ascending to Paradise and then being kept until Abraham's sacrifice. See commentary to this point by Ibn Kathir, "The Story of Ibrahim and His People," *Recite Qur'an: Tafsir Ibn Kathir*, http://www.recitequran.com/en/tafsir/en.ibn-kathir/37:107.

17 Syed Abul A'ala Maududi, *An Introduction to the Understanding of the Qur'an*, trans. Zafar Ishaq Ansari, http://www.islamicstudies.info/tafheem.php?sura=37&verse=99&to=113.

allows for further biblical exploration of how to understand burnt offerings and their relationship to atonement. Utilizing these three key distinctives, then, a Christian can further the conversation by exploring how the Akedah story fits within the rest of the biblical metanarrative.

RELOCATING THE AKEDAH WITHIN THE BIBLICAL HORIZONS

For Christians who are well-versed in the biblical storyline, the connection between Abraham and Isaac's story in Genesis 22 and God's provision of the incarnate Son as the substitutionary atonement for the sins of believers is readily apparent. However, lest we introduce confusion to our Muslim friends, we must not move too quickly to make the parallel between Issac as a son spared through the provision of the divine Son who willingly serves as a sacrifice. Faithfully communicating the biblical concept of sacrifice and its relationship to atonement requires us to explain the biblical development of the idea of burnt offerings and the logic of biblical atonement. This can be naturally accomplished in the process of noting the three biblical details discussed above.

BURNT OFFERING

As we have seen, Muslim sacrificial practice involves the slaughtering of an animal and the dissemination of sacrificial meat as a means of provision, charity, and blessing to the community. However, the concept of a burnt offering remains foreign within Islam. Even as it appears within Genesis 22, the specific reference to a burnt offering requires conceptual development in order to understand the biblical logic of sacrifice. Up to this point, the biblical narrative records various sacrifices (Abel, Noah, and Abraham) that await an explanation.[18]

---

18 One might also interpret God's provision of animal skins as coverings for Adam and Eve upon their eviction from the garden (Gen. 3:21) as a prototype for future sacrifice; however, for the purposes of this discussion, it is probably more helpful to identify places where the biblical story develops sacrifice, using the explicit language of sacrifice and burnt offering.

The reader requires the rest of the biblical narrative to provide an understanding of why sacrifices and burnt offerings are commanded in the first place.

One place that readily lends itself to greater explanation of burnt offerings is the first chapter of Leviticus. In Leviticus 1:3–4 God himself connects the burnt offering with atonement, instructing Moses,

> If his offering is a burnt offering from the herd, he shall offer a male without blemish. He shall bring it to the entrance of the tent of meeting, that he may be accepted before the LORD. He shall lay his hand on the head of the burnt offering and it shall be accepted for him, to make atonement for him.

This passage discusses various animals that might be offered as burnt offerings, but it is worthy of note that male sheep—rams—are acceptable as burnt offerings. Furthermore, this passage connects burnt offerings with the provision of atonement which raises the question, "Why does the Bible connect sacrifice with atonement?"

SACRIFICE AND ATONEMENT

Again, there might be any number of passages that could be helpful for explaining the link between sacrifice and atonement to our Muslim friends. However, perhaps the clearest and most important explanation for this relationship comes in Leviticus 16–17. These two chapters give the detailed instructions for the Day of Atonement sacrifices which would mark ancient Israel's calendar as the holiest day of the year. The meticulous description of the sacrificial rituals provides the reader with the understanding that sin has made ancient Israel—including her priests—guilty before God (e.g., Lev. 16:5 requires a guilt offering) and also impure (e.g., Lev. 16:16). Atonement, if it is to be a remedy for sin, must eradicate both guilt and impurity if a holy and righteous God is to dwell in the midst of a sinful people.

Therefore, not only does this section detail the instructions for the Day of Atonement sacrifices, but Leviticus 17:11 also explains the logical relationship between sacrifice, blood, and atonement. In these verses, God tells Moses, "For the life of the flesh is in the blood, and I have given it for you on the altar to make atonement for your souls, for it is the blood that makes atonement by the life." This same sentiment is reiterated in verse 14 as well. In other words, God explains that animal sacrifices serve as a symbol of ransom for Israel by substituting their death on behalf of sinners whose lives are forfeit. Having died in the stead of the sinful-but-believing community, these animals also provide in their blood a symbol of life to be presented before God. This blood-as-life serves as an agent of cleansing for those whose sins have defiled them by bringing them into contact with death.

Thus, while Abraham's burnt offering of a ram is not immediately connected to atonement in the Genesis 22 narrative, the concept continues to unfold and develop in the Hebrew Bible and leads to a mature understanding of sacrificial logic in Leviticus. Granted, this conceptual connection can—and perhaps should—be unpacked further with more extended study.[19] Yet for the purposes of initially showing a Muslim friend the conceptual development of sacrifice, burnt offering, and even the role of a ram in the Hebrew Bible's presentation of atonement, a brief look at Leviticus is helpful.

HEBREWS AND THE
ONCE-FOR-ALL FULFILLMENT

While Leviticus establishes the connection between sacrifice and atonement along with the logic of substitution, forgiveness, and cleansing, it is important for our Muslim friends to recognize—with David—that the sacrifice of animals is not God's desire, nor does it actually remove sins. Instead, sacrifice in the biblical sense remains a symbolic foreshadowing of what God will do in Christ. To demonstrate this biblically, a Christian can invite their Muslim neighbor to study the book of Hebrews. Perhaps more clearly than any other

---

19   For a detailed and thorough assessment of these issues, I highly recommend the work of Jay Sklar, *Sin, Impurity, Sacrifice, Atonement: The Priestly Conceptions* (Sheffield, UK: Sheffield Phoenix, 2015). Likewise, see Mark Boda, *A Severe Mercy: Sin and Its Remedy in the Old Testament* (Winona Lake, IN: Eisenbrauns, 2009).

biblical book, Hebrews explains the preparatory and incomplete role of animal sacrifices while demonstrating that the Levitical sacrificial system serves as a shadow of its true object: the substitutionary death of Christ. But more than just that, the book of Hebrews explains how Christ's resurrection to eternal life and his ascension to the right hand of God inaugurates his session as an eternal high priest. Having offered himself as a once-for-all sacrifice, the ascended Christ can plead his eternal blood as an offering that accomplishes an eternal atonement for believing sinners.[20]

Genesis 22:14 records Abraham naming Mount Moriah "The LORD will provide." It also notes that the contemporary audience still refers to this event to reinforce their claim that, "On the mount of the LORD it shall be provided." In Exodus 19–31, as Moses has ascended to be with the Lord on Mount Sinai, God provides a covenant for his people and a sacrificial system by which he could secure his presence in the midst of his stiff-necked people. These animal sacrifices were unable to remove sin in and of themselves, and needed to be performed day after day by priests who first needed to atone for their own sins (Heb. 10:1–14). Yet in this sacrificial ritual, God was patiently instructing his people about what he would do once and for all in sending the perfect once-for-all sacrifice in his incarnate Son who would also serve as an eternal high priest whose completed work of forgiveness and purification is extended to all those who by faith would trust in his atoning work.

The story of Abraham and Isaac, then, provides the ever-developing biblical storyline with a story of a man whose willingness to sacrifice was commended, and whose sacrificial substitute was provided by God. As the story of the Bible continues, the role of sacrifice in making a sinful people fit for the presence of a holy and righteous God dwelling

---

20 The whole argument of Hebrews is uniquely helpful for explaining atonement and Old Testament history to Muslims. However, chapters 7–10 are particularly helpful for demonstrating the Levitical sacrificial system was intended as a signpost to the Gospel of Christ's perfect life, substitutionary death, victorious resurrection, and eternal intercession which provide atonement for sinners who place their faith in his completed work.

in their midst explains the role of sacrifice and blood in making atone-ment. And finally, the book of Hebrews explains how the whole idea of sacrifice prepares us for the only sacrifice that can remove sin, cleanse impurity, and invite believers to boldly come into God's presence with the Gospel-emboldened audacity to cry out "Abba, Father!" This is a full and rich story, and Abraham's sacrifice is at home here in a way that it is dislocated within the story told by the Qur'an.

CONCLUSION: THE GOSPEL AND THE PROBLEM OF THE QUR'AN

Returning to the questions regarding the Akedah story in the Qur'an, then, it has become evident that the biblical account moves in a direction that diverges from the Qur'an. Whereas the Qur'an uses Abraham's story as a way of reiterating the singular call to submission before God, the Bible continues to slowly unfold God's remedy for humanity that will address the sin problem and restore the possibility that God might live in the midst of his image-bearers. Sacrifice in the Bible is not merely a symbol of demarcation given to a new people to certify their particular installment of revelation. Instead, sacrifice tutors ancient Israel in the economy of salvation, foreshadows the eternal rescue planned by God, and demonstrates the gravity of sin and its extensive effects.

The Qur'an includes the language of ransom in its account of the Akedah, yet it does not teach the necessity of ransom. The Qur'an commends Abraham's faith but also commands a sacrifice whose te-los is not a substitutionary Messiah. The Qur'an offers guidance and blessing to those who follow Abraham's example, but by divorcing Abraham's faith from God's faithfulness to atone for human sin, the Qur'an presents an optimism in its anthropology that expects hu-mans to be able to satisfactorily follow Abraham's example and divine guidance. And finally, the Qur'an presents an eternal paradise that is accessible to humanity despite their sin and imperfection. Admissions to such a paradise is possible only because an ever-distant God does not present a danger to a sin-stained people in the same way that the God-with-us of the Bible does.

Whatever parallels might be made between the Bible and the Qur'an at various points ultimately fade away in recognizing the irreconcilable visions for God's interaction with his creation presented by both texts. Therefore, when Christians who are eager to establish common ground with their Muslim neighbors encounter similarities in the Qur'an, they must keep in mind that the similarities have been drawn into an orbit controlled by qur'anic concerns and no longer operating according to the order of biblical gravity.

In the end, despite the fact that the Qur'an appeals to biblical characters, repurposes biblical ethics, and refers to biblical history, its message is irreconcilable with and antithetical to the Gospel message. In order to be a good neighbor to the Muslims with whom we are engaged, I believe that a Christian should read and engage the Qur'an. However, having traced the teachings of the Qur'an and mapped them alongside of the biblical telos, the two paths radically diverge at the point of understanding God's purposes in and for creation, the nature of sin, and the means of forgiveness and atonement. With these central teachings diverging radically from one another, one must consider all other common ground to be exhibitions of merely superficial similarity.

A Christian burdened to share the Gospel with a Muslim neighbor cannot look at the Qur'an optimistically as providing any kind of corroborating testimony to the saving message of Jesus. Still, the Christian does well to look at the Qur'an in order to understand how it will influence the understanding of the language and ideas necessary to sharing the Gospel. If the Christian is called to love his or her Muslim neighbor, then learning where their worldview bends away from biblical truth is an essential first step to helping them find Jesus to be the way, the truth, and the life.

CONCLUSION

Having worked through this investigation of the Qur'an from a Christian perspective, we have seen multiple points of departure from the biblical worldview that originate in the Qur'an and permeate the Islamic faith. From the different conceptions of revelation to the effect that the theologies of God have upon understanding his characteristics, this project has attempted to expose the underlying divergences between an Islamic worldview and a worldview shaped by the Bible. In so doing, I trust that it has become apparent that if we are to enjoy meaningful communication with our Muslim neighbors, there are many things that will require more work than it would take to quickly agree on statements that appear to share superficial similarity.

The beauty of this work, however, is that it is best done in conversation and relationship. Having an understanding of how the Qur'an has shaped the language, concepts, and worldview of our Muslim friends will allow us to ask more insightful questions as we exhibit the neighbor love that has driven us to seek true understanding. Likewise, in the context of digging beneath apparent similarities to truly hear and understand our Muslim neighbors, we will discover much more profound opportunities to explain why Jesus is the beautiful centerpiece of the biblical story.

Without having understood the qur'anic influence on some of these categories, Christians might find themselves offended at the out-of-hand rejection of the crucifixion and resurrection of Jesus. However, understanding how the ultimate transcendence of God taught by Islam makes the incarnation and substitutionary atonement both impossible and unnecessary, we find that our point of disagreement begins long before the cross. If we rightly understand where the initial parting of ways occurs between these two worldviews, we can more helpfully explain why this interesting resurrection story from two thousand years ago has anything to do with our lives today.

My prayer is that this book has provided some insight to the way that the Qur'an has likely influenced your neighbors—at least in part. But I would be remiss to fail to remind you that your Muslim friend and neighbor is not merely the manifestation of the Qur'an's teaching. Few Muslims consistently live out a pristine embodiment of Islamic theology. Instead, they will likely exhibit a variety of specific and individual responses to their own unique situations, upbringings, concerns, hopes and dreams.

Hopefully this book has given you insight into some broad ways that the Qur'an may have influenced your friends. But this insight is best employed as we learn to ask questions that will lead to deeper and more profound understanding of your neighbor as an individual. Rather than allowing discussions to remain on an ideological level—asking what the Qur'an teaches about the nature of God, for instance—you might consider asking how your Muslim friend relates to God. You might ask about their understanding of why they hope to obtain paradise and what they are looking for there. Or you might ask, "Did God create humans to dwell with him?" At this point you begin to understand your Muslim neighbors for who they are and what they hope for, rather than inviting them into a competition to prove their system more intellectually satisfying than yours.

All of this is intended to remind us that winning an intellectual or ideological argument is not the same as winning a person to the gospel of Jesus. Ideologies and theological systems need to be investigated, and can be shown to be wanting, but at the end of the day, we do not merely hold out Christianity as an intellectually superior system; we hold out Christ as the Good Shepherd whose love and faithfulness drove him to lay down his life for his sheep. Our desire is to help our Muslim neighbors to recognize the voice of the Shepherd calling their names and speaking a better word of forgiveness, cleansing, and redemption than can be found elsewhere.